ART DIRECTORS CLUB OF LOS ANGELES
7080 Hollywood Blvd., Suite 410
Los Angeles, California 90028
213/465-8707

Executive Director *Barbara Shore*

Distributors to the trade
in the United States
and Canada:
Watson-Guptill
Publications
1515 Broadway
New York, N.Y. 10036

Distributed throughout
the rest of the world by:
Hearst Publications
International
105 Madison Avenue
New York, N.Y. 10016

PUBLISHER:
Madison Square Press
10 East 23rd Street
New York, N.Y. 10010

Printed in Hong Kong

ISBN 0-8230-5829-8

ADLA: 6 CREDITS

COVER AND
BOOK DESIGN . . . . . . *Bill Murphy*
Rod Dyer Group

BOOK
COMMITTEE . . . . *Gary Valenti*
Julie Evidon
Pat Tom

PROJECT
COORDINATION . . . . *Pat Tom*

TYPOGRAPHY . . . . . . *Versa Type, Inc.*

EDITORIAL
ASSISTANT . . . . *Julie Prendiville*

PHOTOGRAPHY . . . . . *Susan Werner*

CONTRIBUTORS . . . . *Versa Type, Inc.*

ADLA SIX

TABLE OF CONTENTS

▲ Library of Congress Selections

ADLA has had an exciting and fulfilling last year. From the tremendously successful Computer Seminar to the great speakers to our very first charitable event where we raised $10,000 for the homeless in Los Angeles.

An important part of our year was the Annual Awards Competition which is highlighted in this book. The work here shows not only the best of a year but since it is the end of the decade, the best of our work is not just reflective of where we have been but where we are headed.

The 90's bring with them great promise and great challenge. The promise to do better work in an ever changing global marketplace. The socio-political guideposts that we have used for our entire lives are changing or being replaced. With the advent of a European "State" as well as the "Democratization" of many communist countries the symbols, images and messages we have created and relied upon will be created anew for the next decade and beyond.

Los Angeles has a very prominent role to play in this new landscape. And within this community, ADLA must meet the challenges ahead. The way to do this is with great people. Over this past year as President, I have worked with a great number of dedicated individuals. The board has been tireless. And the mere fact that you hold a book in your hands means that dozens of people, from the call for entries and judging weekend all the way through to the production of this Annual, donated their talent and their time and for this we are all forever greatful.

In the coming decade of environmental and social concerns, I look forward to working with all of our members to make the ADLA a significant organization not only in our industry but in our community as well. As outgoing President, I thank all of you for making this past year so personally rewarding.

Scott A. Mednick
President

Monthly programs are the backbone of the Art Directors' Club of Los Angeles. While the show competition has always had more of a cache, programs are the raisou d' etre, allowing members and guests to come, listen and learn from our speakers and network with their peers. At our monthly venues we present speakers as diverse as Woody Pirtle, Joel Wayne, April Greiman and Lee Clow.

The ADLA has made a concerted effort over the past few years to mix it up, inviting speakers from the world of design, advertising and entertainment. Programatically the ADLA has tried to reach all segments of our communication industry. I think we are unique in this aspect.

I want to thank all of our speakers who've given so generously of their time to share with us their knowledge, history and stories and I want to thank all the members and guests for making the effort to come out for our programs.

On a hot August weekend last summer, a group of talented art directors, designers and writers from around the country judged nearly 4,000 entries of work. I thank them again.

This annual, ADLA: SIX, represents a search for innovation—a process that, at best, is only a freeze frame in time. My hope is that this showing of work gives us a chance to recognize the accomplishments and the creativity of the people in our industry.

Organizing and documenting the work in this annual was a major undertaking. It was both a privilege and a pleasure to work with the many talented people who contributed their time.

Gary A. Valenti
Vice President

Nan Faessler
Vice President

On the evening of November 10, 1989 over 900 advertising and design professionals gathered at the Pacific Design Center to spotlight the 400 winning entries on exhibition, all included in this ADLA:6 Annual. At the Awards Presentation, awards were given out to the top entries in each category. There were 64 awards plus 'Best of Show' for each of the categories: Advertising, Graphic Design, Editorial and Entertainment.

Nan Faessler and Max Goodrich awarded the Annual George Rice and Sons Scholarship, to senior graphic design students Eric Hirschberg and Anne Kelly attending the University of California, Los Angeles.

Gary Hinsiche took the podium to announce and present this year's ADLA Medal for Lifetime Achievement, honoring Robert Miles Runyan for his creative innovations in the graphic design industry. Gary Hinsiche shared many humorous stories and the history of Robert Miles Runyan Design.

Our thanks to those who attended for their continued support. To the hardworking show committee for their successful efforts, and to the third year design students from the University of California, Long Beach for their enthusiastic help thank you.

AWARDS NIGHT

Dianna Orr
Pat Tom
Gary Valenti

VOLUNTEERS

Maureen Agius
Donna Akahoshi
Angelo Casimiro
Carl Andy Dean
Suchada Dejaarponkun
Wayne Fujita
Matt Gnibus
Sharon Gunderson
David Lomeli
Betsy Molina
Jun Morishita
Doug Mukai
Julee Nishimi
Lisa Steinberg
Frank Vallejo

JUDGING COMMITTEE

Glenda Alcott
Laura Crotty
Mark Harmel
Tamara Keith
Richard Maritzer
Jeff Natkin
Dave O'Connell
Booker Rinder
Judy Seckler
Gary Valenti
Phil Waters

VOLUNTEERS

Glenda Alcott	Kevin Mason
Christopher Angerman	Mary McCormick
Ingrid Avallon	Victoria Miller
Becca Bootes	Caroline Misner
Jim Bracy	Amy Modly
Margo Chase	Natalie Ohanessian
Aram Chobanian	Candice Ota
Mandy Crespin	Candace Pearson
Anne Eichelberger	Noel Petter
Ted Englebart	Julia Precht
Bryan Friel	Lisa Raine
Susanne Haddon	Lori Rand
Dana Herkelrath	Andrea Reibsmen
Leah Hoffmitz	Elise Rosenthal
Rick Jackson	Glenn Sagon
Les Jarrin	David Stern
Jeff Kozminske	Chris Storlie
Wendy Kramer	Ken Thackwell
Sachi Kuwahara	Beth Marie Thomann
Jim Marrin	Linda Warren
Roger Marshutz	Donna Wittlin
Richard Maritzer	Aram Youssefian

BOOK COMMITTEE

Julie Evidon
Bill Murphy
Mercedes Murphy
Julie Prendiville
Pat Tom
Gary Valenti

Robert Miles Runyan
Lifetime Achievement
Award Recipient

Vuarnet

1984 Olympics

Crown Zellerbach

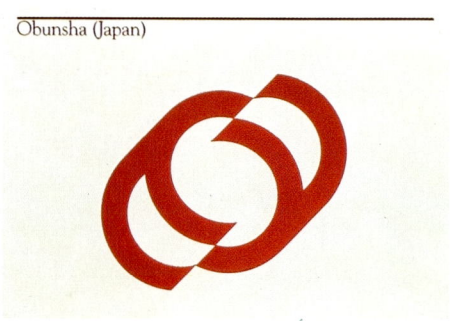
Obunsha (Japan)

As colorful as his sun splash on the S.S. Independence, as distinctive as his mark for Crown Zellerbach, and as internationally known as his 1984 Olympics identity program, the recipient of the 1989 ADLA Lifetime Achievement award is designer Robert Miles Runyan.

At the helm of Robert Miles Runyan and Associates in Playa Del Rey, California, the energetic, flamboyant leader has served as mentor to some of the most dynamic designers in the business. He laughingly refers to his operation, situated in an old Spanish Masonic lodge by the sea, as "Runyan's University."

Credited as "the father of the modern annual report," Runyan began his career almost four decades ago, stamping his unique imprint on the 1959 Litton annual report. His imaginative use of photography, type and design has graced the pages of many books—and countless other projects—since.

In covering an exhibit on annual reports at the Cooper-Hewitt Museum, The New York Times said, "The art of the annual report has drawn some of the best talents in design, including Norman Rockwell, Andrew Wyeth, Robert Miles Runyan and Milton Glaser."

Commenting on the Times' comments, Runyan smiles, "I took that as a super compliment."

ALAN BARZMAN
Partner
Bert, Barz & Company

Alan Barzman is the *Barz* in *Bert, Barz & Company*. He writes, produces and directs humorous radio campaigns, and is an accomplished kazooist. Besides that, he is also a well-known commercial voiceover talent. In addition to countless radio commercials, he has been heard as a voiceover on numerous TV commercials, including Hills Brothers Coffee, Glidden Paints, Surf Detergent and the Charley the Tuna Starkist commercials (he was the voice of the blowfish, the shark, the whale, the squid and the clam). He has been a Keebler Elf and even did a cameo as one of the Chicken Nuggets. Mr. Barzman once auditioned for the voice of an animated fungus, but didn't get it.

He is a graduate of the University of Oregon, and received his Master's degree from Boston University. Upon completion of his formal studies, Mr. Barzman returned to his hometown of Portland, Oregon, where he delivered telephone books before going to work for a radio station. During the Korean Conflict, he was awarded the Occupation Medal of Germany.

Mr. Barzman moved to Los Angeles just prior to the Hippie craze, and began his career in humorous radio by writing for the legendary Stan Freberg.

He has received many IBA, SUNNY, BELDING, ANDY, ONE SHOW, ADDY and CLIO awards, and has lectured on the subject of humorous radio advertising in England, Australia and Wichita. In 1987, he was honored by the Radio Advertising Bureau in New York as a recipient of the Orson Welles Creative Lifetime Achievement Award, and he is listed in "Who's Who in Advertising."

Mr. Barzman does not especially enjoy horseback riding, skiing, or tennis...although he once made sixty-five consecutive free-throws in his backyard when no one was around.

TOM BENTKOWSKI
Design Director
LIFE Magazine

Tom Bentkowski was born and raised in Buffalo, New York, and studied Visual Communication at Pratt Institute in Brooklyn, earning a degree in Fine Arts. After graduation, he went to work at New York Magazine, as Assistant Art Director and, ultimately, as Art Director. He went to Los Angeles to help launch New York's sister publication New West, and was that magazine's Associate Art Director.

He worked subsequently as a design consultant for L'Express, the Saturday Review, the New York Times, Art & Antiques, and for the National Hockey League. He collaborated with Joan Kron on the development of The Home Show, a prototype Sunday supplement magazine for the Washington Star. He worked with Walter Bernard on the redesign of the Atlantic Monthly, was guest Art Director for a Sports Illustrated special issue, and re-designed the World Press Review. He spent four years a Special Projects Art Director of Time Magazine.

Concurrently with the above, for seven years he wrote a monthly record review for New York, and he has taught Graphic Design and Magazine Design at Pratt, The School of Visual Arts, and the Parsons School of Design. In 1987, he redesigned LIFE Magazine, and became its Director of Design. His work has been cited by The American Institute of Graphic Arts, The Art Directors' Club of New York, The Society of Publication Designers, as well as by Graphis, Print, and Art Direction magazines.

In addition, during his tenure at both Time and LIFE, each magazine won the National Magazine Award for Design. He lives in a small house on the Hudson River, hand made in 1860 by a Scottish stonemason.

CRAIG BUTLER
Partner
Butler/Kosh/Brooks

An art Center Graduate, Craig began his career at Doyle Dane Bernbach working under Si Lam on the Volkswagen and Ohrbach's accounts. In 1979, he began Butler, Inc. producing work for the film, music and fashion industries. Besides being a co-founder and the designer of the WORKBOOK, Craig also designs for American Isuzu, Mitsubishi, Vidal Sassoon and Champion International. Craig is the current President of the ADLA.

DIANE COOK TENCH
Senior VP/Creative Supervisor
Martin Agency

Diane Cook Tench is senior vice president/creative supervisor of The Martin Agency. A graduate of Minneapolis College of Art and Design she has worked as an art director for Mobil, FMC, Coty and U.S. West.

Her work for these and other clients has won over 100 national awards, including gold and silver medals in the One Show, Clios and Effies. She has also received five best of show awards from The Richmond Advertising Club.

Most recently, she won both a Bronze Lion from the Cannes Film Festival and a gold medal in the International Film Festival for a campaign she created for FMC Corporation. She also received first place in the 1987 Reader's Digest annual Anti Drunk and Drive Creative Challenge.

JEAN CRAIG
President/Creative Director
Kresser/Craig

Jean was one of only five advertising women from the West included in Advertising Age's "100 Best & Brightest" having won over 200 awards throughout her career, from every major show.

Jean began her career with The Lansdale Company, where she helped create irreverent advertising for Dorman's Men's Clothiers; and Guild, Bascom & Bonfigli, where her work helped launch Suzuki motorcycles in the United States.

From 1965 to 1977, Jean was an Associate Creative Director at Foote, Cone & Belding, working on Hughes Airwest, Mazda, Ore-Ida, and United California Bank. Her work while at FCB, for Sunkist Growers, received national and international recognition. She created the original Sunkist campaign built around the theme, "You have our word on it."

In 1977, Jean became a partner in her own agency, Cunningham, Root & Craig, and over an eight year period built a superb creative reputation for the small Los Angeles shop.

In 1985, a merger created Kresser/Craig. Billing $18 million at the outset, the agency has quadrupled in four years. Kresser/Craig's accounts include ARCO, California's largest corporation; am/pm mini markets, Kenwood Electronics, Daihatsu, Travelodge, Winston Tire Stores, Calavo Foods, Marie Callendar's, Tecmo Video Games, Monroe Auto Equipment and Daniel's Jewelers.

Jean founded the Los Angeles Creative Club and is on the Board of the Art Directors Club of Los Angeles. She has also been on the Board of the Advertising Club of Los Angeles, and the Western States Advertising Agencies Association, as well as the Faculty of UCLA Extension. Jean has four children and lives in Malibu.

BOB DION
Art Director
BBDO

I've been in the business for over 30 years, starting with my first job in Chicago at Needham, Louis and Brorby. In 1966, I moved to LA with Needham to help start the office with the Continental Airlines account. My next move was to New York, still with Needham, where I worked on Xerox, ITT, Triumph Automobiles, Campbell's Foods and a string of other accounts.

I left Needham in 1969 to work for McCann International as creative director in Buenos Aires, Argentina. I traveled throughout South America doing work for General Motors, Exxon, ITT, Nestle, Goodyear, and Coca Cola.

I returned to the U.S. in 1971 because of political unrest in Argentina. I worked at a few places in LA before joining Chiat/Day in 1976. I was one of three creative directors at Chiat. (The others were Mark Doyle and Lee Clow.)

In 1979, when Chiat/Day opened an office in the East, I went to New York as creative director. When I left to take a sabbatical in 1986, the office had grown from practically nothing to billings over $60 million.

After my year off, I returned to Chiat/Day as special projects director, working on Royal Caribbean Cruise Lines and Gaines Pet Foods. I left Chiat in 1987 and moved back to LA as creative director on the Apple Computer account at BBDO.

Throughout my career I taught advanced advertising design at Art Center College in Pasadena.

In November of 1989, I left BBDO to work freelance. I have moved to the wine country in Northern California with my wife Louise, and our two-year-old son, Benjamin. We bought a vineyard and are building a house in St. Helena.

My freelance work takes me all over the country, but with my Macintosh, printer, fax and copier, I can do most of my work in St. Helena. My moving days are over.

KIT HINRICHS
Partner
Pentagram

Kit Hinrichs was born and raised in Los Angeles and studied at the Art Center College of Design. After graduating in 1963, he worked as a designer in several New York design offices before forming the design partnership of Russell & Hinrichs. In 1972 he joined with his wife, Linda, to form Hinrichs Design Associates. In 1976 they joined with Marty Pedersen, Vance Jonson and Neil Shakery to form Jonson, Pedersen, Hinrichs & Shakery. Kit remained a principal of JPH&S until he, Linda and Neil merged with Pentagram in 1986.

Pentagram Design is a multi disciplined partnership of designers founded in London in 1971. The firm consults on a broad range of design projects, including corporate identity programs, trademarks, editorial design, information systems, packaging, posters, books, exhibition design, annual reports, promotionaal material, interior design, architecture, urban planning, as well as product design.

Kit has been an instructor at the School of Visual Arts in New York, at the Academy of Art in San Francisco, and at the California College of Arts and Crafts in San Francisco. He has been a guest lecturer at the Stanford Design Conference and numerous other design associations and universities across the country.

Kit has received several gold and silver awards from the New York Art Directors Club and the Los Angeles Art Directors Club, in addition to honors from the Society of Publications Designers, the Type Directors Club, the American Institute of Graphic Arts, the San Francisco Art Directors Club and Financial World Magazine. Kit most recently received the Margret Larsen Award for excellence in art direction from the San Francisco Show.

DOUG OLIVER
Principal/Design Director
Morava & Oliver Design Office

Douglas Oliver is a principal and design director at Morava & Oliver Design Office located in Santa Monica, California. He earned degrees from the University of Kansas and Art Center College of Design in Graphics/Packaging. Upon graduation in the fall of 1978, he joined Cross Associates in Los Angeles and was soon designing annual reports for St. Regis Paper and Carter Hawley Hale Stores, Inc. In 1981, he joined Robert Miles Runyan and Associates, where he continued his annual report work and broadened his experience with major corporate identity projects and special projects for the 1984 Olympic games.

Since joining Emmett Morava in Founding Morava & Oliver Design Office in 1983, Doug has designed annual reports or corporate collateral for major clients ranging geographically from Hawaii to Georgia, and Beverly Hills to New York.

Doug's work has received numerous major design awards and has been included in graphic design shows including The Mead Annual Report Show (New York), *Communication Arts Design Annual*, the AIGA Show (New York), New York Art Directors' Club, Art Directors' Club of Los Angeles (ADLA), *Print Casebooks*, STA 100 (Chicago), and the AR 100 (Chicago). His work has also been selected for inclusion in the permanent design collection of the Library of Congress.

STEVEN PANAMA
Executive VP
Kaleidoscope Films, Inc.

HOUMAN PIRDAVARI
Art Director
Fallon/McElligott

Born in 1960, Houman Pirdavari grew up in front of a television set. He was observed at the age of five paying much closer attention to commercials than the programs they interrupted. In 1977, he stumbled across a collection of New York Art Director's and Communications Arts Advertising Annuals in his high school library. By then his fate was sealed.

He left home in 1979 with a makeshift portfolio of "concepts." A discouraging two and half months of job hunting would follow, until he was hired by Temme Thurman Advertising in Newport Beach, California. For two years he did paste-up, occasional design work, and frequent stat/doughnut runs.

Houman's big break came in 1981, when Lee Clow took a gamble and hired him as an art director at Chiat/Day, Los Angeles. Surrounded by demigods, he cut his teeth on Yamaha Motorcycles, Apple Computers and Nike.

In 1984 he left Chiat/Day to freelance in Los Angeles for a year. Fed up with not producing anything (and L.A. in general) he moved to Minneapolis to join Fallon McElligott.

Since 1985, Houman Pirdavari has created campaigns for Rolling Stone Magazine, Bloomingdale's, Federal Express, Timex and Penn Tennis Balls. His work has earned Clios, gold medals from The New York One Show, Art Directors' Club of New York and Cannes, and a regular showing in Communication Arts Advertising Annuals since 1982.

NANCY SHALEK
President
The Shalek Agency

In just six years, The Shalek Agency has swelled from a small creative boutique to a large West Coast agency with nearly $30 million in annual billings. Shalek attributes her success to several factors: The Shalek Agency is run by a woman, it has maintained its autonomy and it garners national awards for advertising that produces results.

"The fact that I'm a woman is a curiosity to a lot of people I do business with, which both amuses and annoys me," Shalek explains. "I've learned to use it to my advantage. Sometimes when people see a woman, it throws them off balance and gives me a strong position to deal from."

The unique seat Shalek occupies is one she has earned. After receiving an undergraduate degree in comparative literature from the University of Pennsylvania, she taught high school and college students in Boston how to take standardized tests. Driven by an insatiable appetite for personal and professional growth, Shalek made a deal with her husband, James, who agreed to put her through business school if she supported the couple while he studied law.

"I was a new business developer, so I was always looking to the future," Shalek said. "I do the same thing today in advertising. If you do what has been done before or what's being done now, in the time it takes to complete your project it becomes old news. And an advertising agency's true mission is to help its clients get to the future."

Shalek advertisements have featured controversial characters portrayed by the outspoken comedienne Rosanne Barr and the late female impersonator Divine; songs by the brash musical group, the Surf Punks; and startling television images such as a man's head exploding while using the Epyx 500XJ computer game joystick. Shalek points out that her popular ads raise more than eyebrows; they raise profits.

TOMMY STEELE
Art Director
Capitol Records

With seventeen years of experience in graphic design, Tommy Steele is currently the Art Director of Creative Services at Capitol Records, Inc., managing worldwide record packaging involving LP covers, compact discs, cassettes, singles sleeves, and merchandising and advertising campaigns for such artists as Tina Turner, The Beach Boys and The Doobie Brothers. From 1984-1988 he ran his own Los Angeles-based design studio, SteeleWorks, that specialized in entertainment graphics lettering, illustration and book design. His work there included such top-selling record covers as Tom Petty and the Heartbreakers, Neil Young, Steve Miller Band and Sheena Easton. He is the author/designer/photographer of four best-selling popular culture graphics books for Abbeville Press—"The Hawaiian Shirt", the art and history of this folk art; the award-winning "Bowl-O-Rama", the visual arts of bowling; "Close Cover Before Striking", the graphics of early matchcover art; and finally "Lick'em, Stick'em", the lost art of poster stamps.

Steele has served as art director/designer for CBS, MCA Elektra/Asylum and Warner Bros. Records. and as film graphic designer for Robert Abel & Associates, creating visuals for special effects animation, cable television titles and commercials for the international fashion market.

He attended Art Center College of Design and Loyola University in Los Angeles in fine art.

JOEL WAYNE
Senior VP Worldwide Creative
Warner Brothers

JACK WOODY
Twelvetrees Press

ROLAND YOUNG
Principal
Shiffman/Young Design Group

Joel Wayne, Senior Vice President of Worldwide Creative Advertising for Warner Bros., is responsible for the total creative advertising campaigns in all media for the more than 20 major films the studio releases each year.

Mr. Wayne joined the Burbank-based film company in 1979 as Vice President of Creative Advertising. Prior to his association with Warner Bros., he served as Executive Vice President and Creative Director for Grey Advertising in New York. An award-winning art director with the agency for 17 years, Mr. Wayne is the recipient of nearly 60 Clio Awards as well as some 25 New York Art Director Club Awards.

Among his responsibilities as Senior Vice President of Worldwide Creative Advertising at Warner Bros. is to work with the strategic planning of all worldwide creative advertising campaigns, taking domestic campaigns and translating them into the international marketing area.

Famous for his sometimes outrageous, always innovative album covers, Roland Young is co-principal at Tracey Shiffman/Roland Young Design Group, and an instructor at Art Center.

Born in San Francisco's Chinatown in April, 1938, Roland attended California College of Arts and Crafts, the Chouinard Institute, and was graduated from Art Center in 1961.

Roland served his apprenticeship with internationally renowned designer, Louis Danziger. He then freelanced in Los Angeles and in 1965 joined Capitol Records. In 1971, he moved to A&M Records where he became head of the graphics department.

Roland is the recipient of numerous national and international design awards, and is included in the Who's Who in the West, 1978 edition.

LLOYD ZIFF
Art Director
Ziff Design Group

BERNARD REILLY
Curator
Library of Congress

THIS IS THE SIXTH YEAR THAT THE LIBRARY OF CONGRESS HAS MADE SELECTIONS FOR ITS PERMANENT COLLECTION FROM THE ADLA COMPETITION.

THE ART DIRECTORS CLUB OF LOS ANGELES PROVIDES ONE OF THE TWO SOURCES IN THE COUNTRY UTILIZED BY THE LIBRARY FOR THIS PURPOSE.

THE COLLECTION'S CURATOR, MR. BERNARD REILLY, RETURNED TO LOS ANGELES TO EVALUATE THE ENTRIES BASED ON TYPOGRA-PHY AND THE BOOK ARTS, INCLUDING ILLUS-TRATION, LAYOUT AND OTHER VISUAL ASPECTS OF PRINTING. HE CONSIDERED NOT ONLY DESIGN EXCELLENCE AND ORIGINALITY BUT DOCUMENTARY SIGNIFICANCE, I.E. HOW A PARTICULAR PIECE (OR SERIES) REFLECTS SOCIETAL VALUES, TRENDS AND ATTITUDES.

MR. REILLY NOTED THAT BUILDING THE NA-TIONAL COLLECTIONS ALONG THESE LINES ENABLES THE LIBRARY TO PROVIDE STUDENTS, PUBLISHERS, SCHOLARS, FILMMAKERS AND GENERAL RESEARCHERS WITH A RESOURCE WHICH IS UNMATCHED ANYWHERE ELSE IN THE COUNTRY.

READERS CAN IDENTIFY THE LIBRARY'S SELECTIONS BY THE ▲ SYMBOLS THROUGH-OUT THE BOOK.

Year after year, ADLA is supported by the generousity of many businesses. They contribute money, time, talent, creativity and moral support. Once again we thank all of them for their superb commitment to our organization and to our profession.

CONTRIBUTORS

Agfa Compugraphics
Andresen Typographics
Appleton Papers, Inc.
Champion International Corporation
Donahue Printing Co., Inc.
Encore Video
Filmcore
Jarrin-King
Scott & Daughters Publishing
Simpson Paper Company
VersaType, Inc.

SPEAKERS

Ed Benguiat
Photolettering

Steve Hayden
BBDO/LA

B. Martin Pedersen
Graphics Press, Inc.

Andy Kuehn
Kaleidoscope

Jack Summerford
Summerford Design, Inc.

Wayne Hunt
Wayne Hunt Graphic Design, Inc.

Woody Pirtle
Pentagram, New York

The ADLA George Rice
Student Scholarship Award
Recipients

Eric Hirschberg
University of California, Los Angeles

Anne Kelly
University of California, Los Angeles

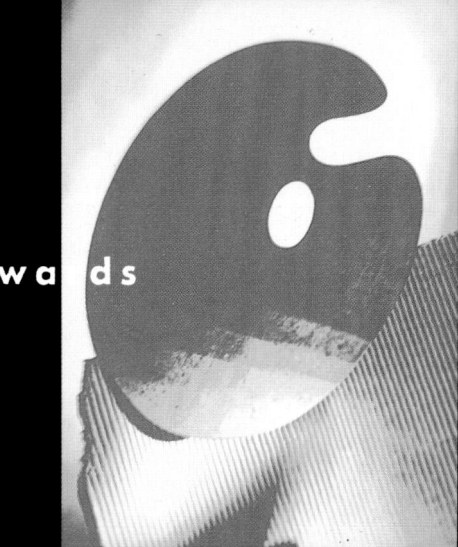

wards

*CREATIVE
DIRECTOR*
Maggie Gross, Sr. Vice
President, Advertising
ART DIRECTOR
Jim Nevins
*EDITORIAL
DIRECTOR*
Timothy Cohrs
*DIRECTOR OF
MEDIA*
Jayne Greenberg
ACCOUNT MANAGER
Richard Crisman
*PRODUCTION
MANAGER*
Laurie Kanes
STUDIO MANAGER
Mike Madrid
PHOTOGRAPHER
Annie Leibovitz
CLIENT
GAP
AGENCY/STUDIO
GAP

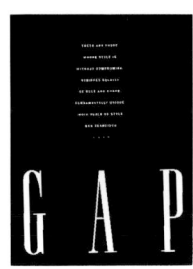

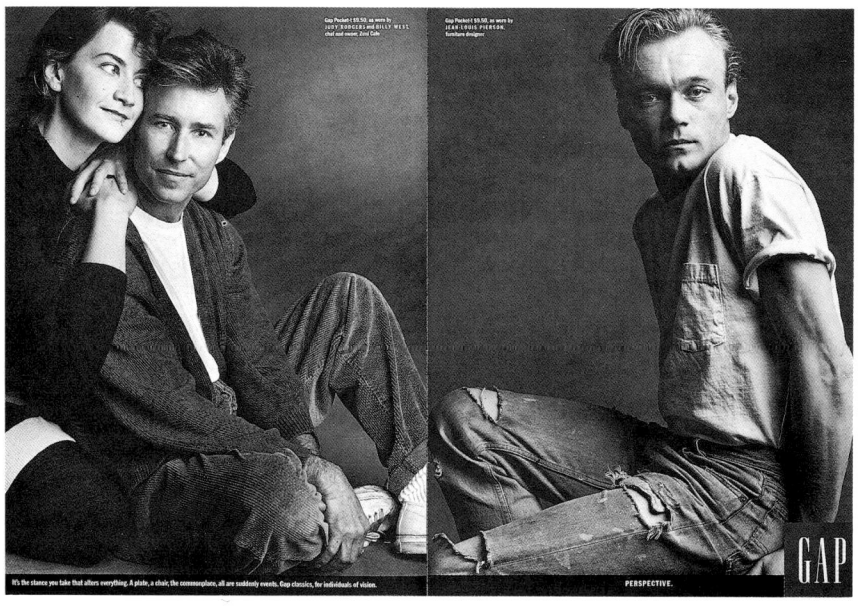

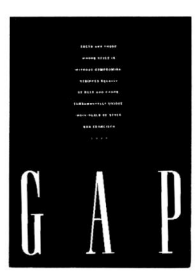

*CREATIVE
DIRECTOR*
Maggie Gross, Sr. Vice
President, Advertising
ART DIRECTOR
Jim Nevins
*EDITORIAL
DIRECTOR*
Timothy Cohrs
*DIRECTOR OF
MEDIA*
Jayne Greenberg
ACCOUNT MANAGER
Richard Crisman
*PRODUCTION
MANAGER*
Laurie Kanes
STUDIO MANAGER
Mike Madrid
PHOTOGRAPHER
Annie Leibovitz
CLIENT
GAP
AGENCY/STUDIO
GAP

ART DIRECTOR
Michael Hall
DESIGNER
Michael Hall
ILLUSTRATOR
Michael Hall
CLIENT
Hall Kelley
AGENCY/STUDIO
Hall Kelley, Inc.

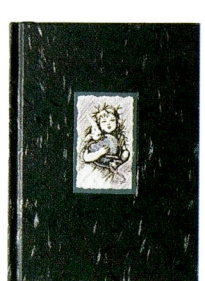

ART DIRECTORS
David Carter/Lori
B.Wilson
DESIGNER
Lori B.Wilson
WRITER
Lori B.Wilson/
Kathy Lane
ILLUSTRATORS
David Carter/Gary
Lobue Jr./Wai-Tak
Lai/Lori B.Wilson/
Cynthia Waldman/
Randall Hill/Allen
Wearer/Dee Thomas
CLIENT
David Carter Design
AGENCY/STUDIO
David Carter Design

ART DIRECTOR
Wai-Tak Lai
DESIGNER
Wai-Tak Lai
ILLUSTRATOR
Jacinda Lai
CLIENT
The Robert D. Zimmer
Group
AGENCY/STUDIO
David Carter Design

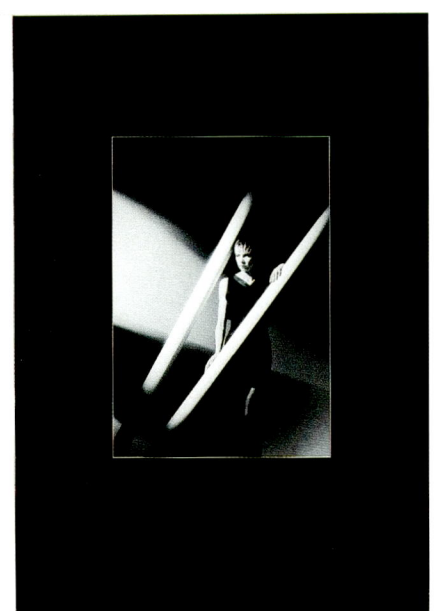

DESIGNER
Tom Bonauro
PHOTOGRAPHER
Michele Clement
CLIENT
Michele Clement Studio
AGENCY/STUDIO
Michele Clement Studio
▲

ART DIRECTOR
Jacqueline Jones
DESIGNER
Jacqueline Jones
PRODUCER
Amy Nathan
WRITER
Jo Mancuso
PHOTOGRAPHER
Kathryn Kleinman
FOOD STYLIST
Amy Nathan
CLIENT
Chronicle Books
AGENCY/STUDIO
Jacqueline Jones
Design

ART DIRECTORS
David Edelstein/
Lanny French/Rick
Jost/Carol Davidson
DESIGNERS
David Edelstein/Lanny
French/Rick Jost/
Carol Davidson
WRITERS
David N. Meyer II/
Kathy Cain
PHOTOGRAPHER
Nick Vaccaro
CLIENT
Generra
AGENCY/STUDIO
Edelstein Associates
Advertising Inc.
▲

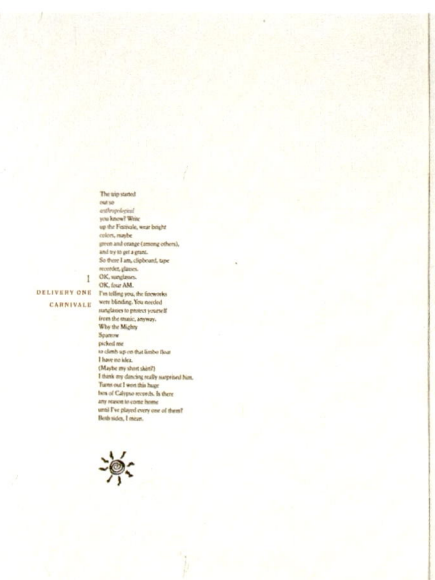

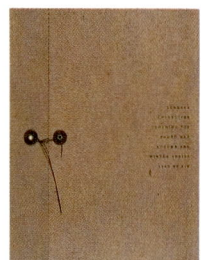

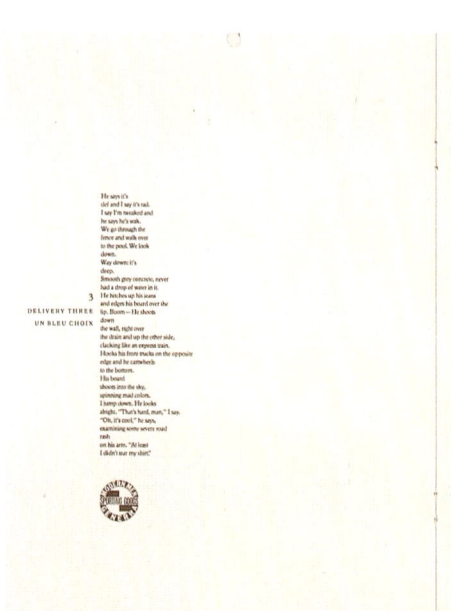

They control the media.

In Fortune 1000 corporations and small, family-run enterprises, in Big Eight accounting firms and Big Ten universities, in fields as diverse as advertising and oil refining, people are more successful and more productive than they've ever been before. And their ideas are being seen, heard, and understood more clearly than ever before.

As a result, their budgets are getting approved, their recommendations are winning support, and their plans are being implemented.

The messages haven't changed, but the means of presenting them have. Apple® Macintosh® computers are making the difference—on Wall Street and on Main Street, in Hollywood studios and in the halls of academia.

Macintosh computers help people get what they want by allowing them to communicate exactly what they want—in the way that's most appropriate for both their message and their audience. Reports, slides, and overheads that impress and persuade an audience. Interactive learning tours that allow students to proceed at their own pace and according to their specific areas of interest. And inspiring presentations complete with sight, sound, and motion.

We call these means of communication Apple Desktop Media.™ "Media" because Macintosh gives you many different ways to express an idea. "Desktop" because that's where it all happens. "Apple" because we—the people who started the desktop publishing revolution—are now taking you even further.

And as you can see, this revolution is making all the media.

Presenting Apple Desktop Media.

ART DIRECTORS
Paul Pruneau/Liz Sutton
PRODUCTION ART
Dorene Meadows
WRITER
Brad Londy
PRODUCTION COORDINATION
Charlie Dana
PHOTOGRAPHER
Paul Matsuda/ Bill Gallery
TYPOGRAPHER
Macintosh
CLIENT
Apple Computer, Inc.
AGENCY/STUDIO
Apple Creative Services

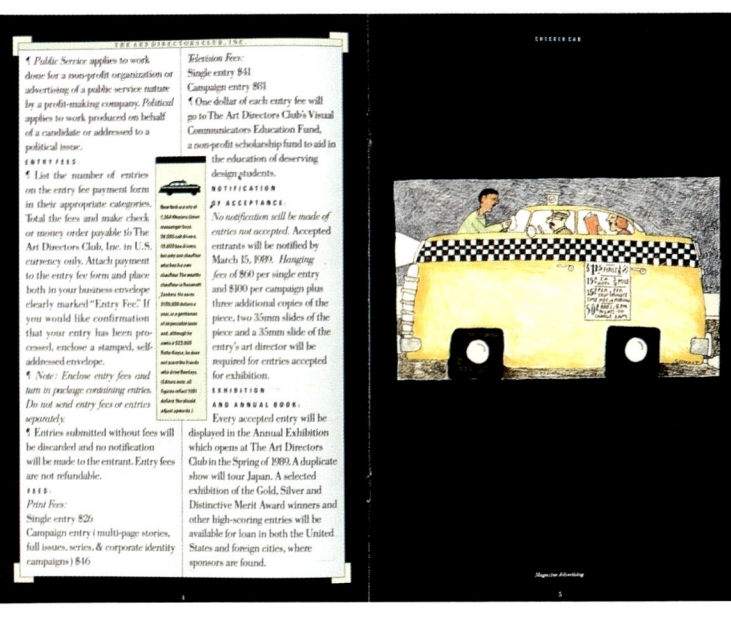

ART DIRECTOR
Kit Hinrichs
DESIGNERS
Kit Hinrichs/Karen Boone
ILLUSTRATORS
Joe Duffy/Seymour Chwast/Carol Wald/ Kit Hinrichs/Jack Unruh/Ivan Chermayeff/ Philippe Weisbecker/ Woody Pirtle/Doug Johnson/James McMullan/John Craig
CLIENT
New York Art Directors Club
AGENCY/STUDIO
Pentagram

ART DIRECTOR
Andy Dijak
WRITER
Dick Sittig
PHOTOGRAPHER
David LeBon
CLIENT
Nissan Motor
Corporation
AGENCY/STUDIO
Chiat/Day/Mojo Inc.
Advertising

Now you
don't have to
give up
your firstborn
to own
a sports car.

As a parent, you expect to make certain sacrifices for your children.

Your Hawaiian vacation for their college education.

Your new set of golf clubs for their new set of braces.

Your really great sports car for a really sedate family sedan.

You gladly do all these things for your kids.

Except give up your sports car.

There are times, after all, when as a parent you just have to put your foot down.

Which is exactly the idea behind the new Nissan® Maxima®.

The 4-Door Sports Car®.

Put your foot down and you'll quickly discover its 3-liter, multi-port, fuel-injected V6. Derived from our powerful Z-Car engine, it churns out 160 horsepower and keeps pace with

some of the world's fastest sports cars.

While on twisting roads, a four-wheel independent suspension with front and rear stabilizer bars ensures cornering that is anything but sedan-like.

And standard on the Maxima 4DSC™ pictured here, is our advanced, second-generation ABS braking system. It electronically modulates each wheel to ensure straighter, shorter stops, even on wet pavement.

Of course, if you had a conventional sports car that performed this well, it would be only natural to want to take your best friends for a ride.

The nice thing about our sports car is, you can take all of them at once.

Maxima. The 4-Door Sports Car.™

Built for the Human Race.

ART DIRECTOR
Mike Mazza/Pam
Cunningham
WRITER
Brian Belefant
PHOTOGRAPHER
Bob Grigg/Doug
Taub/Jay Ahrend
ILLUSTRATOR
Alan Daniels
CLIENT
Nissan Motor
Corporation
AGENCY/STUDIO
Chiat/Day/Mojo Inc.
Advertising

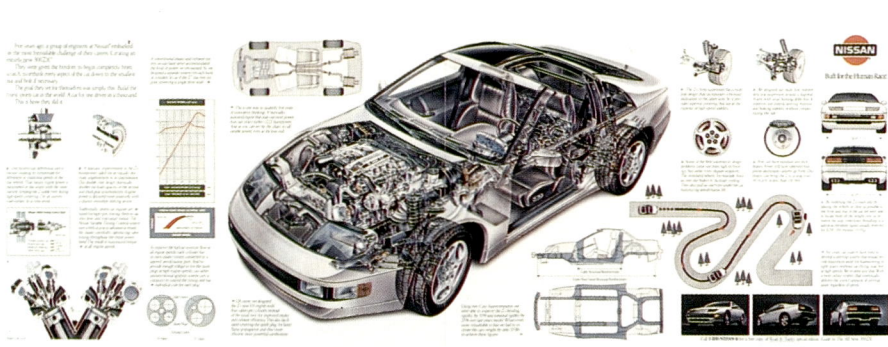

CLIENT
Consolidated Paper
AGENCY/STUDIO
Wardrop Murtaugh
Temple Advertising

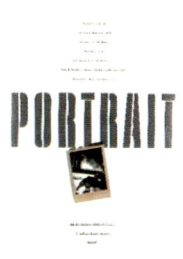

ART DIRECTOR
John Van Dyke
DESIGNER
John Van Dyke
WRITER
Dan Koger
PHOTOGRAPHERS
Still Life-
Terry Heffernan
Portrait B&W-
Jeff Corwin
CLIENT
Weyerhaeuser Paper
Company
AGENCY/STUDIO
Van Dyke Design
Company - Seattle

ART DIRECTOR
James Sebastian
DESIGNERS
James Sebastian/Junko Mayumi
PHOTOGRAPHER
Bruce Wolf
INTERIOR DESIGNER
William Walter
CLIENT
Martex/West Point Pepperell
AGENCY/STUDIO
Designframe Inc. — NYC

ART DIRECTORS
John Doyle/Ann Dakis/
Margaret McGovern/
Amy Watt
DESIGNERS
John Doyle/Ann Dakis/
Margaret McGovern/
Amy Watt
WRITERS
Peter Pappas/Paul
Silverman
PHOTOGRAPHERS
John Holt, Eric Meola
CLIENT
Timberland
AGENCY/STUDIO
Mullen

ART DIRECTOR
Nan Dearborn
DESIGNER
Miho
PROJECT DIRECTOR
Ron Underwood
WRITERS
Brian Horrigan/Ilya
Suslov/Ralph Caplan/
Jeffrey Meikle/Stephan
MacDonald/Ann de
Forest/Philip Meggs/
Robert Campbell/Philip
Langdon/Michael Crosby
PHOTOGRAPHERS
Steven Heller, U.S.I.A./
Ford/ Wurman/April
Greiman/ etc.
CLIENT
U.S.Information Agency,
Washington D.C.
AGENCY/STUDIO
Miho

ART DIRECTORS
Amy Dakos/Craig
Butler
DESIGNER
Craig Butler
WRITERS
Terry Bissel/Dotti
Bradley
PHOTOGRAPHER
Melissa Rodwell
CLIENT
Tom Sewell/Publisher
AGENCY/STUDIO
Butler Kosh Brooks

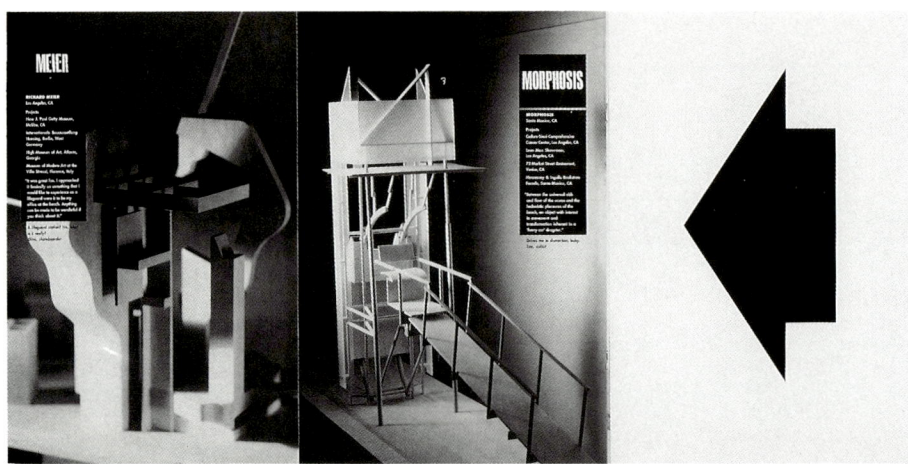

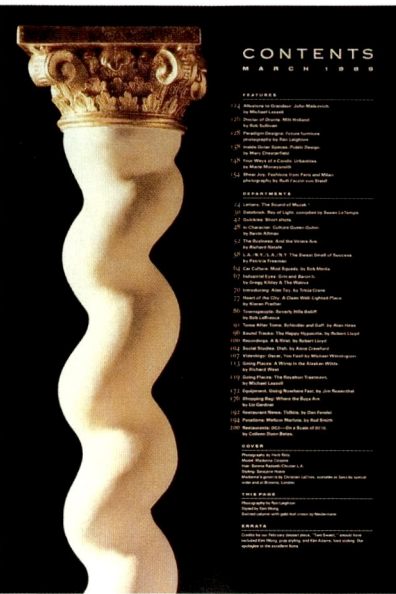

ART DIRECTOR
Marilyn Babcock
DESIGNERS
Michael Brock/
Marilyn Babcock
DESIGN DIRECTOR
Michael Brock
PHOTOGRAPHER
Herb Ritts
CLIENT
L.A. Style
AGENCY/STUDIO
Michael Brock Design

ART DIRECTOR
Michael Brock
DESIGNER
Michael Brock
DESIGN DIRECTOR
Michael Brock
PHOTOGRAPHER
Ron Leighton
CLIENT
L.A. Style
AGENCY/STUDIO
Michael Brock Design

Best of Show Editoral

ART DIRECTOR
Lynn Robb
DESIGNER
Lynn Robb
WRITER
David Keeps
PHOTOGRAPHER
Victoria Pearson-
Cameron/Steven
Meisel/Adrian
Buckmaster
ILLUSTRATOR
Sally Simonetti
CLIENT
Jody Watley
AGENCY/STUDIO
Lynn Robb Design

ART DIRECTOR
Gordon Mortensen
DESIGNER
Gordon Mortensen
WRITER
Barbara Gibson
CLIENT
Radius, Inc.
AGENCY/STUDIO
Mortensen Design

ART DIRECTORS
Andy Dijak/
Corey Stolberg
WRITER
Dick Sittig
PHOTOGRAPHERS
Pete Tangen/Gary
McGuire
HAND-LETTERING
Kelly Hume
CLIENT
Nissan Motor
Corporation
AGENCY/STUDIO
Chiat/Day/Mojo Inc.
Advertising

ART DIRECTOR
Jean Robaire
DESIGNER
Jean Robaire/
 Joann Lobono
WRITER
John Stein
PHOTOGRAPHER
Paul Gersten
CLIENT
Everest & Jennings
AGENCY/STUDIO
Stein Robaire Helm

ART DIRECTOR
Tommy Steele
DESIGNERS
Mark Ryden/Peter
Walberg
ILLUSTRATOR
Mark Ryden
AGENCY/STUDIO
Capitol Records
Art Department

*Best of Show
Entertainment - Print*

ART DIRECTOR
Preuit Holland
DESIGNER
Preuit Holland
WRITER
Marc Deschenes
CLIENT
Marc Deschenes
 Headhunter
AGENCY/STUDIO
Marc Deschenes/
Preuit Holland

If you've got a great book,
call Marc Deschenes.
If you're a miserable hack,
call (212) 246-4200.

ART DIRECTOR
Tracy Wong
WRITER
Tracy Wong
PHOTOGRAPHER
Steve Hellerstein
CLIENT
New York Lung
Association
AGENCY/STUDIO
Goldsmith/Jeffrey

ART DIRECTOR
Craig Frazier
DESIGNER
Craig Frazier
WRITER
Craig Frazier
ILLUSTRATOR
Craig Frazier
CLIENT
Friday Night Live/
Marin Public School
System
AGENCY/STUDIO
Frazier Design

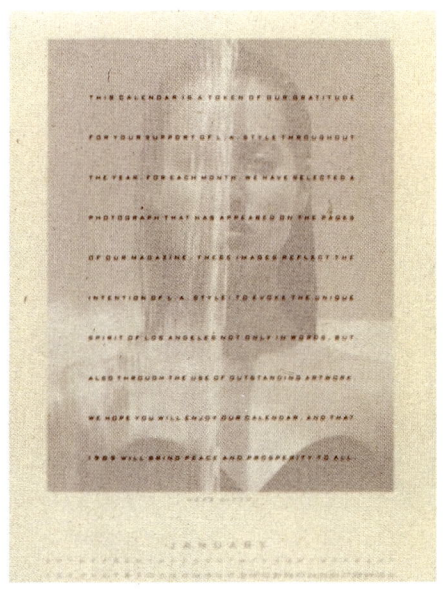

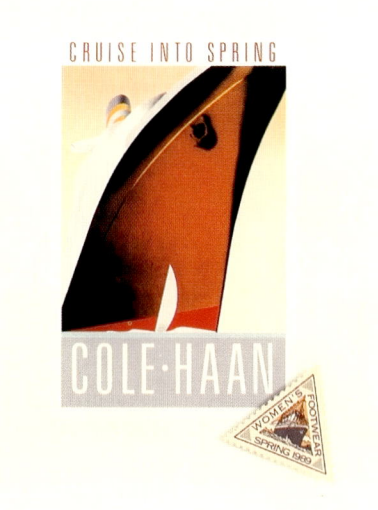

ART DIRECTOR
Michael Brock
DESIGNERS
Michael Brock/
Gaylen Braun
PHOTOGRAPHER
Various
CLIENT
L.A. Style
AGENCY/STUDIO
Michael Brock Design

ART DIRECTOR
Rosemary Conroy
DESIGNER
Rosemary Conroy
WRITER
Brian Flood
PHOTOGRAPHER
Jack Richmond
ILLUSTRATOR
Cheryl Roberts
CLIENT
Cole-Haan
AGENCY/STUDIO
Cipriani Kremer
Design Group
PRODUCTION
COMPANY
Acme Printing
Company

ART DIRECTOR
Tommy Steele
DESIGNER
Andy Engel
CLIENT
Capitol Records/Blue
Note Records
AGENCY/STUDIO
Andy Engel Design, Inc.

ART DIRECTOR
John Coy
DESIGNERS
Sean Alatorre/Tom Bouman
CLIENT
Riordan Foundation
AGENCY/STUDIO
COY, Los Angeles

ART DIRECTOR
John Doyle
DESIGNER
John Doyle
WRITER
Paul Silverman
PHOTOGRAPHER
Eric Meola
CLIENT
Timberland
AGENCY/STUDIO
Mullen

Timberland. Because the earth is two-thirds water.

As the saying goes, water, water everywhere—but where is the good waterproof clothing?

If you think waterproof clothing means sticky rubber boots and unbreathable plastic slickers, we urge you to visit a store that stocks Timberland and examine our richly leathered boots and shoes called Ultralights. As their name suggests, they provide the ultimate in waterproofing at half the weight—the theory being that if your feet are less tired they'll get you out from under the raincloud with greater speed. They are among a select group of casual and dress footwear featuring fully leather-lined Gore-Tex® interiors, available from us only.

But to face wind, water, earth and sky your body needs more than boots and shoes. So Timberland now offers storm coats, field jackets and other rugged wearables for land and sea.

Water is everywhere, and so are we.

Timberland ®
Boots, shoes, clothing, wind, water, earth and sky.

Timberland. Where the elements of design are the elements themselves.

Unlike other footwear makers who slavishly follow the winds of change, we Timberland people take our inspiration from the winds that never change. Be they the mighty gales that hammer the Carolina coast, the sandstorms that parch the Southwestern canyons, or the tropical murmurs that dance across the Pacific, calling you to points unknown.

It has always been our belief that the elements that shape the earth itself, the very ground we walk on, should also shape the shoes in which we walk. Whether our path leads to the highest peak in Colorado or the tallest skyscraper in Chicago.

And whether we are from the West or East. Women or men.

These elements, quite simply, are wind, water, earth and sky. In alliance with the world's most enduring leathers, they are the elements that make up our entire women's collection.

Designed for today. And years from today.

Timberland ®
Boots, shoes, clothing, wind, water, earth and sky.

The elements of Timberland design are solid brass eyelets, oil-impregnated leather, wind, water, earth and sky.

If you're looking for the elements of Timberland design, you won't find them sitting in a shoebox.

We're not saying you won't be impressed when the clerk takes out your brand new handsewns.

In fact, you'll quickly realize these shoes are built like none other you've tried on before. The rich, rugged flanks of leather, the glinting eyelets, the meticulous handstitching will make all that instantly clear.

But like all Timberland gear—be they waterproof boots, boat shoes, storm coats, weather wear – your new handsewns will want a little time in the open environments to hit their stride.

And after a decade has come and gone, after forty seasons of wind, water, earth and sky, you'll look down one day and see your Timberlands at their peak. Weathered, scarred and proud. As enduring as the path you travel.

Timberland ®
Boots, shoes, clothing, wind, water, earth and sky.

ART DIRECTORS
Lynne Court/Paul
Ison/Lisa Langhoff
DESIGNER
Lynne Court
*PRODUCTION
MANAGER*
Christine Ferguson
WRITER
Tony Assenza
PHOTOGRAPHER
Bob Grigg
ILLUSTRATOR
Kevin Hulsey
CLIENT
Nissan Motor
Corporation in U.S.A.
AGENCY/STUDIO
The Designory, Inc.
*PRODUCTION
COMPANY*
Anderson Litho
Company

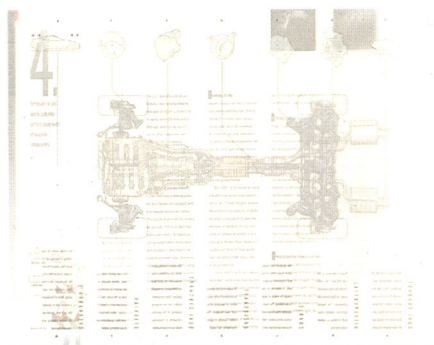

ART DIRECTOR
Bob Wyatt
WRITER
Tom Coleman
PHOTOGRAPHER
Harry DeZitter
CLIENT
Schenley/Dickel
AGENCY/STUDIO
Leo Burnett
Company

IF WE PAY TRIBUTE TO THE 4,200 SOLDIERS WHO DIED AT MANASSAS WITH VIDEOS, FROZEN YOGURT AND PREWASHED JEANS, THEN WE'RE THE ONES WHO ARE DEAD.

SAVE THE BATTLEFIELD COALITION.

MAY THEIR SOULS REST IN PEACE. NOT IN A SHOPPING MALL.

SAVE THE BATTLEFIELD COALITION.

LET US NOT FORGET THAT 4,200 AMERICANS DIED HERE TO BUILD A NATION, NOT A PARKING LOT.

SAVE THE BATTLEFIELD COALITION.

ART DIRECTOR
Wayne Gibson
WRITER
Daniel Russ
PHOTOGRAPHER
Mathew Brady/Stock
CLIENT
Save the Battlefield
Coalition
AGENCY/STUDIO
The Martin Agency

*Best of Show Advertising
- Print*

ART DIRECTOR
Gordon Mortensen
DESIGNER
Gordon Mortensen
CLIENT
Radius, Inc.
AGENCY/STUDIO
Mortensen Design,
Palo Alto, CA

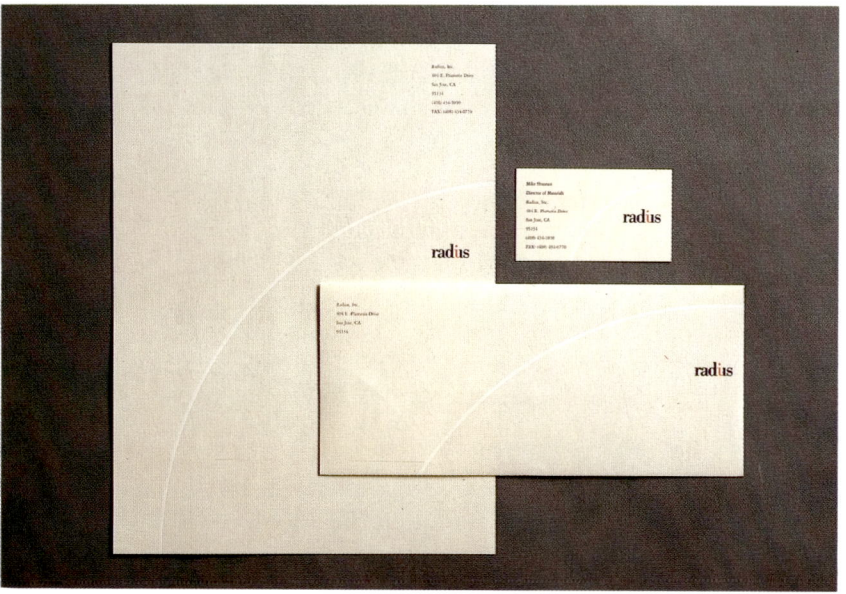

ART DIRECTOR
Henry Vizcarra
DESIGNERS
Henry Vizcarra/
William Heusttis
CLIENT
Gorky's Cafe & Russian
Brewery
AGENCY/STUDIO
30Sixty Advertising &
Design, Los Angeles

ART DIRECTORS
James Sebastian/
John Plunkett
DESIGNERS
James Sebastian/
John Plunkett/
Frank Nichols
AUTHOR
Ralph Stanziola
COPYWRITER
Francis Piderit
CLIENT
Colorcurve Systems, Inc.
AGENCY/STUDIO
Designframe Inc.
– NYC

Best of Show Design

ANYBODY WITH HALF A BRAIN CAN RUN
A NORITSU ONE-HOUR PHOTO SYSTEM.

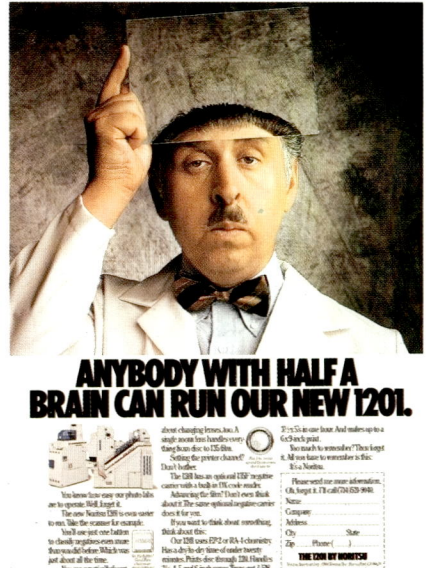

ANYBODY WITH HALF A
BRAIN CAN RUN OUR NEW 1201.

DIRECTIONS TO
THE HEARNS-BARKLEY FIGHT.

Left, Right, Left, Right, Left, Right.

)(LAS VEGAS HILTON

Pathfinder NISSAN

Half man. Half beast.

ART DIRECTOR
David Kaiser
DESIGNERS
David Kaiser/
Peter Wilson
ILLUSTRATOR
H. R. Gieger
CLIENT
American Cinema
Marketing
*PRODUCTION
COMPANY*
Kaiser
Communications, Inc.

ART DIRECTOR
Takenobu Igarashi
DESIGNERS
Takenobu Igarashi/
Kazuhiro Hayase
DIRECTORS
Wolfgang Heuwinkel/
Zanders Feinpapiere AG
PHOTOGRAPHER
Nacasa & Partners
CLIENT
Zanders Feinpapiere AG
AGENCY/STUDIO
Igarashi Studio
*PRODUCTION
COMPANY*
Ad Point, Co. Ltd.

ART DIRECTOR	*ART DIRECTOR*
Anthony Sella	Rudy Hoglund
DESIGNER	*DESIGNER*
Anthony Sella	Tom Bentkowski
CREATIVE	*CLIENT*
DIRECTOR	Time Magazine
Robert Jahn	
WRITER	
Toby Muller	
ILLUSTRATOR	
Nancy Stahl - painter	
CLIENT	
Buena Vista Pictures	
Marketing	
AGENCY/STUDIO	
Touchstone Pictures	
PRODUCTION	
COMPANY	
George Rice &	
Sons Printers	

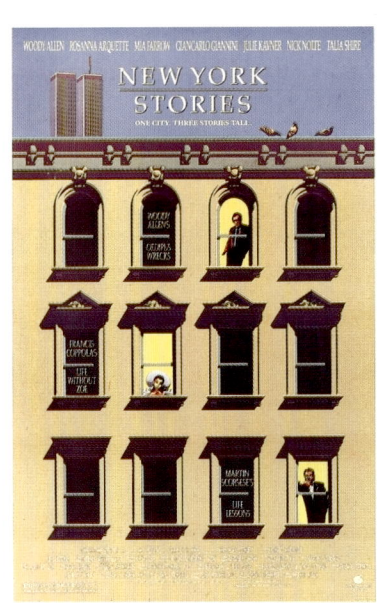

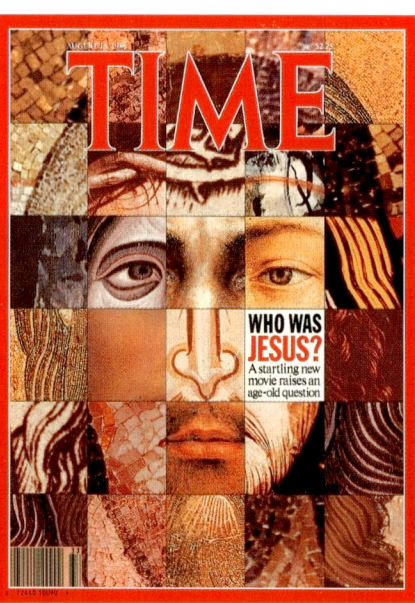

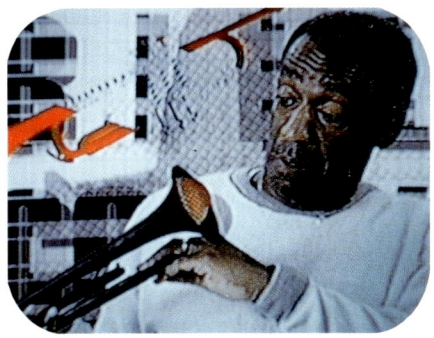  

"NBC FALL CAMPAIGN
THEME PIECE"

SINGERS: Our place is your place
Our house is your house
Come celebrate with us at home
this fall
Feel the excitement
Share in the good times
Home is something you can
believe in
Home is somewhere you can get
it all

CHORUS: Only on *NBC, NBC*
Miles above the rest
Only on *NBC, NBC*
Come home to the best

Only on *NBC, NBC*
Join the family
Come home to the best
only on *NBC*

SINGERS: Join in the party
The Celebration
This is an offer you just can't
refuse
The laughter's flowin'
The stars are glowin'
Home is where the colors are
brighter
Home is number one where you
just can't lose

CHORUS: Only on *NBC, NBC*
Miles above the rest
Only on *NBC, NBC*

Only on *NBC, NBC*
It's where you want to be
Come home to the best
Only on *NBC*

BRIDGE: Home, sweet home
where you can call the tune
Where somethin' good is waitin'
for you
Morning, night and noon.

Home, sweet home
Where all your friends await
Some to greet you early
Some to entertain you late

Home, sweet home
with shows that can't be beat
*THE HUXTABLES, THE HOGANS
HUNTER* and *THE HEAT*

BRIDGE: Home, sweet home
You're in a *DIFFERENT WORLD*
with *ALF* and *MATLOCK, L.A. LAW*
and all those *GOLDEN GIRLS*

*Home, sweet home
You've got the best for company
The nest is never empty when
You're home to NBC*

ART DIRECTOR
Chuck Stepner/
Chris Carlisle
DESIGNERS
Chuck Stepner/
Chris Carlisle/
Steve Lowe/
Martin Brierly
PRODUCERS
Chuck Stepner/
Chris Carlisle
DIRECTORS
Steve Lowe/
Martin Brierly
WRITER
Chuck Stepner/
Chris Carlisle
PHOTOGRAPHER
Marc Reshovsky
CLIENT
NBC Advertising
& Promotion
AGENCY/STUDIO
NBC Advertising
& Promotion
*PRODUCTION
COMPANY*
Propaganda Films

*Best of Show
Entertainment - Video*

ART DIRECTORS
Pam Cunningham/
Mike Mazza
PRODUCER
Richard O'Neill
DIRECTOR
John St. Clair
WRITER
Steve Bassett/
Brian Belefant
CLIENT
Nissan Motor
Corporation
AGENCY/STUDIO
Chiat/Day/Mojo Inc.
Advertising
PRODUCTION
COMPANY
Peterson
Communications

"BANKED TRACK"

SFX: Banging…
SFX: Car's engine.
(Music underneath. Background singer.)
SFX: Banging.
ANNCR VO: Once again, the last letter of the alphabet is the last word in sports cars.

The new Z. From Nissan.

"CLEAN SHEET"

SFX: LOUD BANGING.

ANNCR VO: This is where we started—a clean sheet of paper. No boundaries. No rules.

No preconceived ideas.

Just desire to build the best sports car in the world. A car for one driver in a thousand.

The car destined to leave its mark.

SFX: LOUD BANGING.

ANNCR: The new Z. From Nissan.

ART DIRECTORS
Pam Cunningham/
Mike Mazza
PRODUCER
Richard O'Neill
DIRECTOR
John St. Clair
WRITER
Steve Bassett/
Brian Belefant
CLIENT
Nissan Motor
Corporation
AGENCY/STUDIO
Chiat/Day/Mojo Inc.
Advertising
*PRODUCTION
COMPANY*
Peterson
Communications

ART DIRECTORS
Pam Cunningham/
Mike Mazza
PRODUCER
Richard O'Neill
DIRECTOR
John St. Clair
WRITER
Steve Bassett/
Brian Belefant
CLIENT
Nissan Motor
Corporation
AGENCY/STUDIO
Chiat/Day/Mojo Inc.
Advertising
PRODUCTION
COMPANY
Peterson
Communications

"THE LETTER"

ANNCR VO: Nissan has just delivered the
ultimate proof of how well we understand
cars...and the people who love to drive them.
It arrived in the form of a letter.

SFX: BANG!

ANNCR VO: The new Z. From Nissan.

"MAILROOM"

SCENE: A GROUP OF MAIL BOYS HOLD COURT. IN ONE CORNER JOEY AND BERNIE ARE TALKING.

SUPER: Mail Room

ALEX: You got any inter-office mail for Nine?

BERNIE: Nope.

ALEX: Hey, me neither.

JOEY: Hey, maybe they stopped sending memos.

BERNIE: Oh, get real. Those suits on Nine are always sending stuff to each other.

ALEX: Yeah well, if you didn't pick 'em up, and I didn't deliver 'em, how do they get 'em?

FELIX: Computers.

JOEY: Seven's got computers, they send tons of memos.

FELIX: These kind are different, same ones they got in LA.

ALEX: Well Bernie, you got any overnights from LA?

BERNIE: Nope.

ALEX: Weird...very weird.

SUPER: Macintosh

SENIOR CREATIVE DIRECTOR
Steve Hayden
COPYWRITER
Gary Graf
ART DIRECTOR
Mike Campbell
PRODUCERS
Tony Frere/Trish Reeves
ACCOUNT SUPERVISOR
Jimmy Yaffe
DIRECTOR
Joe Pytka
PRODUCTION COMPANY
Pytka
EDITOR
Dennis Hayes
EDITORIAL COMPANY
Dennis Hayes Film Editing

Best of Show Advertising - Broadcast

ART DIRECTOR
Bob Dion
PRODUCERS
Tony Frere/
Trish Reeves
DIRECTOR
Joe Pytka
WRITER
Ken Segall
CLIENT
Apple Computer, Inc.
AGENCY/STUDIO
BBDO L.A.
PRODUCTION
COMPANY
Pytka

*Best of Show Advertising
- Broadcast*

"THE SLEEPING GIANT"

SUPER: Sleeping Giant

MARTHA: Will they be much longer?

RECEPTIONIST: I don't believe so.

MARTHA: OK thanks. OK Steve, so you're up right after me.

STEVE: Right, and·everybody focus on Gleason, he makes the decisions.

JAMES: Hey, I think this is our lucky day.

STEVE: Campbell & Graf? That's who we're up against?

MARTHA: (LAUGHS.) When was the last time they had an original idea, World War II?

JAMES: Hello, Leonard. Still in the old building?

LEONARD: Just fine, thanks. Good luck now.

STEVE: Oh, that Leonard. He is so glib.

JAMES: All I can say is, if those guys get this business, we didn't want it anyway.

STEVE: We want it, we want it.

MARTHA: Hey, look at this—it's their leave-behind.

STEVE: This should be funny.

MARTHA: This is not funny.

JAMES: Let me see that.

STEVE: (WHISTLES THROUGH HIS TEETH.)

MARTHA: What do you think woke them up?

FADE TO BLACK. SUPER: Macintosh

SUPER: The power to be your best.

"CAREER MOVE"

SCENE: A GROUP OF SECRETARIES ARE GATHERED AROUND A BOOTH IN A COFFEE SHOP.

SUPER: Career Move

CATE: I've gotta go.

NANCY: But we just got here.

CATE: I've got some calls to make. I'm gonna look for another job.

ANNA: What!

CATE: Our group's getting computers.

ANNA: So.

CATE: So, I haven't figured out the new typewriters yet.

NANCY: Look, here's your chance to do a lot more than just typing.

CATE: Yeah, but...

ANNA: Relax. Bob Dion learned how to use one.

CATE: Bob Dion, the guy who still needs help with the copy machine?

NANCY: Yeah, that's the one.

SUPER: Macintosh. The power to be your best.

CATE: ...maybe I will have a little something.

ART DIRECTOR
Mike Cambell
PRODUCERS
Tony Frere/Trish Reeves
DIRECTOR
Joe Pytka
WRITER
Gary Graf
CLIENT
Apple Computer, Inc.
AGENCY/STUDIO
BBDO L.A.
PRODUCTION COMPANY
Pytka

Best of Show Advertising - Broadcast

ART DIRECTOR
Andy Dijak
PRODUCER
Richard O'Neill
DIRECTOR
Eric Saarinen
WRITER
Dick Sittig
CLIENT
Nissan Motor
Corporation
AGENCY/STUDIO
Chiat/Day/Mojo Inc.
Advertising
PRODUCTION
COMPANY
Plum Productions

"ROADS/REV"

MUSIC: UNDER THROUGHOUT.

SFX: UNDER. OUTDOORS, INSECTS, BIRDS, WIND.

KURT VO: You wouldn't believe what the Pathfinder went through on the road to Botatulan. I guess when they ran out of asphalt, they used cobblestones. When they ran out of cobblestones, they used rocks. When they ran out of rocks, they used gravel. When they ran out of gravel they used dirt. ...They never ran out of dirt.

 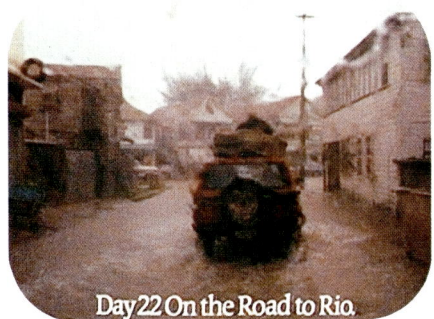 

  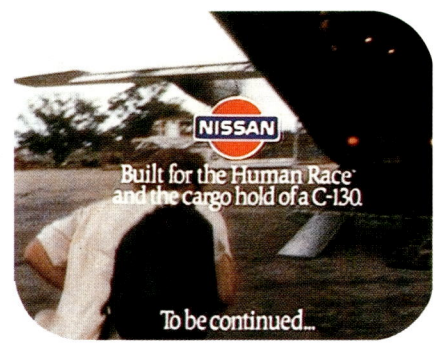

"BELIZE"

MARTY: In Belize, we ran into Hurricane Gilbert...

KURT: ...and an even bigger problem.

TICKET AGENT: No way.

KURT: That's what we gotta do, that's what we gotta do.

ART DIRECTOR
Andy Dijak
PRODUCER
Richard O'Neill
DIRECTOR
Eric Saarinen
WRITER
Dick Sittig
CLIENT
Nissan Motor
Corporation
AGENCY/STUDIO
Chiat/Day/Mojo Inc.
Advertising
*PRODUCTION
COMPANY*
Plum Productions

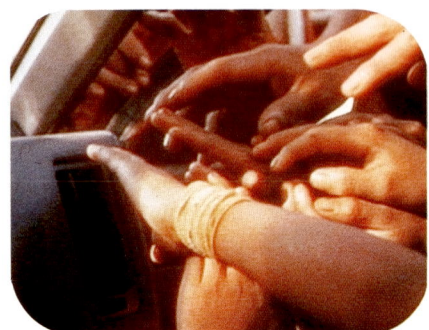  

ART DIRECTOR
Andy Dijak
PRODUCER
Richard O'Neill
DIRECTOR
Eric Saarinen
WRITER
Dick Sittig
CLIENT
Nissan Motor
Corporation
AGENCY/STUDIO
Chiat/Day/Mojo Inc.
Advertising
*PRODUCTION
COMPANY*
Plum Productions

"NATIVES REV. 1"

*SFX: UNDER. PRIMITIVE VILLAGE,
NATIVES, PATHFINDER ENGINE.*

MARTY VO: This is the first time Waeimpie
Indians have ever been filmed. They have
never seen red hair...
...or anything like a Pathfinder. Here on the
equator, the air conditioner was a big hit. And
they seemed to like our music. But we discovered, we like their music...even more.

*MUSIC: UNDER. NATIVE INSTRUMENTS
AND SINGING.*

"MIDNIGHT SNACK"

VIDEO: Open on a darkened garage.

AUDIO:
SFX: (SOFT GROWLING)

VIDEO: Kitchen light comes on as disheveled man pulls curtain aside and peeks into garage.

SFX: (REFRIGERATOR DOOR OPENING. VARIOUS SOUNDS FROM KITCHEN. GROWLING INCREASES)

VIDEO: Man opens door and turns on garage light. Car behaves like a hungry beast, thrashing, opening and closing its hood.

SFX: (SQUEAKY KITCHEN DOOR. FIERCE GROWLING)

VIDEO: Man dangles a large slab of raw meat in front of car. As cars rocking and lurching intensifies, the hood continues to flap.

SFX: (FIERCE, RABID GROWLING)

VO: The Diahatsu Charade from Japan.

VIDEO: Man tosses meat under gaping hood. Car lunges at meat. Hood slams shut.

SFX: (GROWL, HOOD SLAM)

VO: It has a ferocious 16-valve engine.

VIDEO: Car wiggles as if chewing. Man pats car lovingly.

SFX: (MUFFLED GROWL)

VO: So...be nice to it.

VIDEO: Man turns garage light off and shuts door. Car chews contentedly.

SFX: (MUFFLED CHEWING. KITCHEN DOOR SQUEAKS, SLAMS SHUT)

VIDEO: Kitchen light goes out.

SFX: (PAUSE. THEN A LOUD GULP)

SUPER: DIAHATSU. The one small car you'd be proud to own.

ART DIRECTOR
Richard Kyle
PRODUCER
Pam den Hartog
DIRECTOR
Gary Johns
WRITER
Theresa Aycock
CLIENT
Daihatsu America, Inc.
AGENCY/STUDIO
Kresser/Craig
PRODUCTION COMPANY
Johns + Gorman,
Los Angeles

PRODUCTION
DESIGN
Ted Haworth
EXECUTIVE
PRODUCER
Joe Salvaggio
PRODUCER
Paul Fuentes
DIRECTOR
Paul Fuentes
WRITER
Paul Fuentes/Joe
Salvaggio
PHOTOGRAPHER
(D.P.) Timothy Galfas
CLIENT
Home Box Office
AGENCY/STUDIO
Home Box Office
Broadcast Advertising
& Promotion
PRODUCTION
COMPANY
Varitel

"HAWAII '89 OPEN"

MULL: This, class is perhaps the greatest archealogical discovery of our time. A dwelling, known as the split level ranch!…*MARVELOUS!''*

STUDENT 1: What's this, professor?

MULL: CAREFUL! it's very rare! Placed upon the rear end of land vehicles, these indicated one's political preferences, of course, that was before the Quayle dynasty.

STUDENT 2: What is this, professor?

MULL: Fuckin' coke bottle…

STUDENT 3: Who's this, professor?

MULL: Let me see…*Ha!* This was once the husband of Robin Givens!

STUDENT 4: Not the Robin Givens!

MULL: Yes!

MULL: Elvis Presley wore a buckle very similar to that, many think that's what killed him.

STUDENT 4: Professor!

MULL: Yes…

STUDENT 4: What is it?

MULL: That's odd–too big for a bagel, isn't it? Let's check

STUDENT 4: What is it, professor?

MULL: I have no idea.

ANNOUNCER VOICE OVER: HBO. The best time on TV.

"BAR"

SFX: We hear bits of their chatter...he is trying to pick her up. Bar ambience in background.

MAN: Why don't we go up to my place and talk about you starring in this movie I'm producing?

WOMAN: Oh...

SFX: Man making kissing noise.

WOMAN: No.

ANNCR VO: The Eveready Squeezelight, small enough to carry with you, big enough for a real emergency.

ART DIRECTOR
Michael Smith
PRODUCERS
Francesca Cohn/
Kelly Waltos
DIRECTOR
Jeff Gorman
WRITER
Sam Avery
CLIENT
Eveready Battery Co.
AGENCY/STUDIO
Chiat/Day/Mojo Inc.
Advertising
*PRODUCTION
COMPANY*
Johns & Gorman

advertising

NEWSPAPER
ART DIRECTOR
Gary Goldsmith
WRITER
Dean Hacohen
PHOTOGRAPHER
Gilles Larrain
CLIENT
Knoll International
AGENCY/STUDIO
Goldsmith/Jeffrey

ART DIRECTOR
Bill Spewak
DESIGNER
Bill Spewak
WRITER
Bill Spewak
PHOTOGRAPHER
Robert Milazzo
CLIENT
Radio City Music Hall
AGENCY/STUDIO
Grey Entertainment
& Media

ART DIRECTOR
Lloyd Wolfe
WRITER
Rob Rosenthal
PHOTOGRAPHER
Kerry Wetzel
CLIENT
Humane Society
AGENCY/STUDIO
Cole & Weber Advertising

ART DIRECTOR
Susan Westre
WRITER
Chris Wall
PHOTOGRAPHER
Lamb & Hall
ILLUSTRATOR
Trici Venola/
Mark Loncar
CLIENT
Apple Computer, Inc.
AGENCY/STUDIO
BBDO L.A.

ART DIRECTOR
Gary Goldsmith
DESIGNER
Tracy Wong
WRITER
Dean Hacohen
ILLUSTRATOR
Tracy Wong
CLIENT
Voting Bureau
AGENCY/STUDIO
Goldsmith/Jeffrey

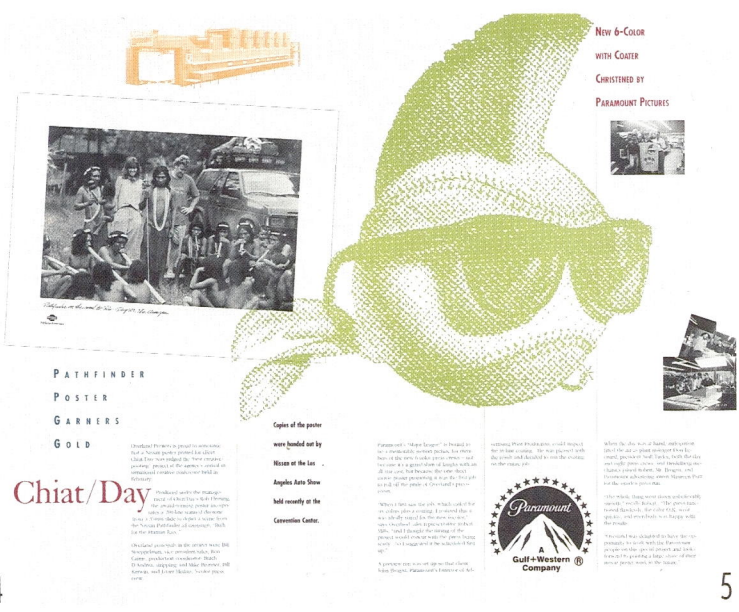

4   5

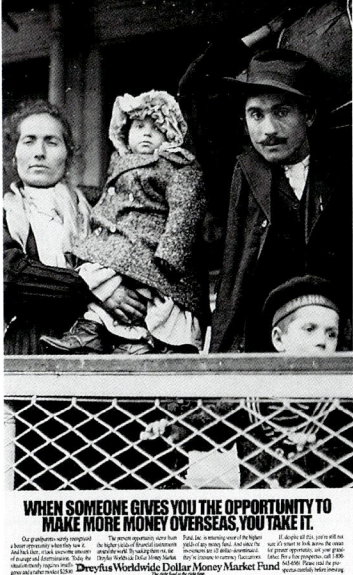

When a politician steps out of line, our man rearranges his face.

How much damage can one man do with his hands? Plenty. If they belong to Jack Ohman, The Oregonian's resident political cartoonist.

Even the slickest political rope-a-dope can't stop his jabs. Then he hits 'em where it hurts: just above that fine line that divides low blow from high comedy.

Be on the lookout for Jack Ohman. And see who gets a facial this week.

Jack Ohman Six Days A Week In Forum. The Oregonian

MEXICAN FOOD SO AUTHENTIC YOU'LL THINK TWICE BEFORE DRINKING THE WATER.

Dos Locos 92 Exchange Street, Portland, ME 04101. Phone 77-LOCOS Open 7 Days a Week.

WHEN YOU'RE TRAVELING 8000 MILES, WHAT'S ANOTHER 6 INCHES?

CHINA AIRLINES

NEWSPAPER CAMPAIGN

ART DIRECTOR
Leslie Sweet
DESIGNER
Leslie Sweet
WRITERS
Pamela Sullivan/Nat Russo
PHOTOGRAPHER
Cailor Resnick - Stock
CLIENT
Dreyfus
AGENCY/STUDIO
Levine, Huntley, Schmidt
and Beaver

PAST PERFORMANCE IS NO GUARANTEE OF FUTURE SUCCESS. BUT WHAT ELSE CAN YOU GO BY?

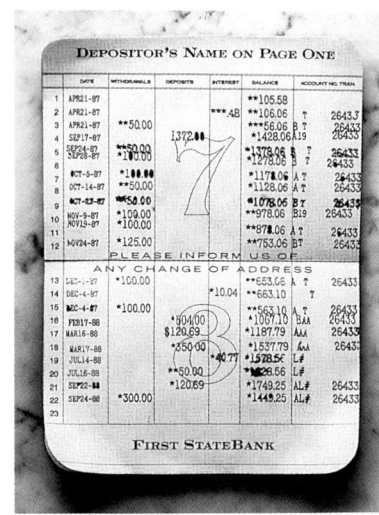

AT THIS RATE, YOU'LL NEVER GET A HOUSE.

WE CREATED TAX-FREE FUNDS.
THEN AGAIN, WE HAD A LOT OF INSPIRATION.

NEWSPAPER CAMPAIGN

ART DIRECTOR
Wayne Gibson
WRITER
Daniel Russ
PHOTOGRAPHER
Mathew Brady/Stock
CLIENT
Save the Battlefield
Coalition
AGENCY/STUDIO
The Martin Agency

IF WE PAY TRIBUTE TO THE 4,200 SOLDIERS WHO DIED AT MANASSAS WITH VIDEOS, FROZEN YOGURT AND PREWASHED JEANS, THEN WE'RE THE ONES WHO ARE DEAD.

SAVE THE BATTLEFIELD COALITION.

MAY THEIR SOULS REST IN PEACE. NOT IN A SHOPPING MALL.

SAVE THE BATTLEFIELD COALITION.

LET US NOT FORGET THAT 4,200 AMERICANS DIED HERE TO BUILD A NATION, NOT A PARKING LOT.

SAVE THE BATTLEFIELD COALITION.

MAGAZINE
ART DIRECTOR
Carl Warner
DESIGNER
Carl Warner
PRODUCER
Karen Garnett
WRITER
Rich Conklin
CLIENT
Team One Advertising
AGENCY/STUDIO
Team One Advertising

ART DIRECTOR
Jan Rudin
DESIGNER
Jan Rudin
WRITER
Andrea May
PHOTOGRAPHER
Jeremiah S. Sullivan
CLIENT
Jeremiah S. Sullivan Studio
AGENCY/STUDIO
Jeremiah S. Sullivan Studio

ART DIRECTOR
Preuit Holland
DESIGNER
Preuit Holland
WRITER
Marc Deschenes
CLIENT
Marc Deschenes
Headhunter
AGENCY/STUDIO
Marc Deschenes/
Preuit Holland

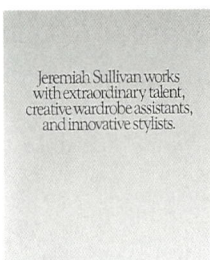
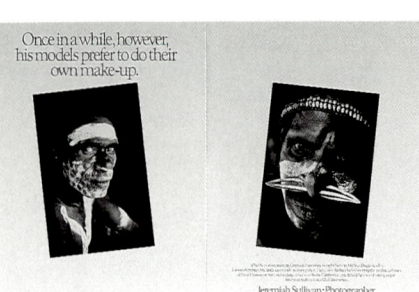

ART DIRECTOR
Richard Crispo
WRITER
Brent Bouchez
PHOTOGRAPHER
Jeff Nadler
ILLUSTRATOR
Joel Spencer
CLIENT
Bear Mountain Ski Resort
AGENCY/STUDIO
Ketchum, L.A.

ART DIRECTOR
Jon Reeder
PRODUCTION MANAGER
Julie Delman
WRITER
Rob Siltanen
PHOTOGRAPHER
Paul Taylor
CLIENT
California Dates Advisory Board
AGENCY/STUDIO
BBDO/L.A.

Finally a healthy bar that tastes like the fruit of the tree instead of the bark.

Imagine the taste of ripe, luscious fruit blended with golden honey and molasses. Baked with 100% whole wheat flour to give it a sweeter, more nut-like flavor.
Imagine it having 33⅓% of the US RDA

of 16 essential vitamins and minerals in every serving. Being high in fiber, low in fat, or with absolutely no cholesterol.
Think of it for break-

fast. Or lunch. Or an any-time snack. With just 160 calories per serving.
Just imagine. Serious nutrition in a great tasting bar. If it all sounds ideal to

you, it is.
IDEAL BARS.™
From Thompson Foods.®
A Division of the
Wm. T. Thompson Co.

The one that coats is the only one you need.

Pepto-Bismol

Eileen Turpin
WRITER
Debbie Schwartz
PHOTOGRAPHER
Patrice Meigneux
CLIENT
Wm. T. Thompson Co.
AGENCY/STUDIO
Schwartz & Rahman
Advertising

MAGAZINE

ART DIRECTOR
Jeff Gregg
WRITER
Donna Speigel
PHOTOGRAPHER
Bruce Gregg
CLIENT
Procter & Gamble/
Pepto-Bismol
AGENCY/STUDIO
Leo Burnett
Company

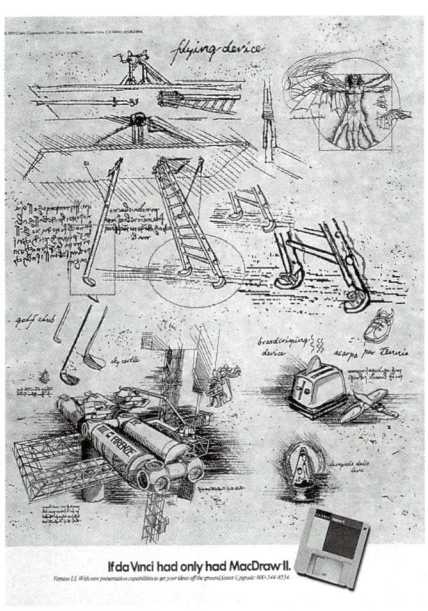

If da Vinci had only had MacDraw II.

If Cheops had only had MacProject II.

Susan Westre
WRITER
Chris Wall
ILLUSTRATOR
Trici Venola
CLIENT
Claris Corporation
AGENCY/STUDIO
BBDO L.A.

ART DIRECTOR
Susan Westre
WRITER
Chris Wall
PHOTOGRAPHER
Stock
ILLUSTRATOR
Electric Paint
CLIENT
Claris Corporation
AGENCY/STUDIO
BBDO L.A.

If Eiffel had only had Claris CAD.

If Shakespeare had only had MacWrite II.

Susan Westre
WRITER
Chris Wall
PHOTOGRAPHER
Stock
ILLUSTRATOR
Electric Paint
CLIENT
Claris Corporation
AGENCY/STUDIO
BBDO L.A.

ART DIRECTOR
Susan Westre
WRITER
Chris Wall
PHOTOGRAPHER
Lamb & Hall
CLIENT
Claris Corporation
AGENCY/STUDIO
BBDO L.A.

MAGAZINE
ART DIRECTOR
Preuit Holland
DESIGNER
Preuit Holland
WRITER
Marc Deschenes
PHOTOGRAPHER
Lamb & Hall
CLIENT
Noritsu America
AGENCY/STUDIO
Marc Deschenes/Preuit
Holland

ART DIRECTOR
Jean Robaire
WRITER
Steve Silver
PHOTOGRAPHER
Terry Heffernan
ILLUSTRATOR
Georgia Deaver
CLIENT
Sunbeam
AGENCY/STUDIO
Chiat/Day/Mojo Inc.
Advertising

ART DIRECTOR
Steven Johnson
WRITER
Rob Ingalls,
V.P./Associate Creative
Director
PHOTOGRAPHER
Rudi Legname
STYLIST
Amy Nathan
CLIENT
Blue Diamond Growers
ACCOUNT
SUPERVISION
Joann Fraser/Mary
Doan/JoAnn O'Brien
PRINT PRODUCTION
MANAGER
Barbara Judson

ART DIRECTOR
Steven Johnson
WRITER
Rob Ingalls,
V. P./Associate Creative
Director
PHOTOGRAPHER
Rudi Legname
STYLIST
Amy Nathan
CLIENT
Blue Diamond Growers
ACCOUNT
SUPERVISION
Joann Fraser/Mary
Doan/JoAnn O'Brien
PRINT PRODUCTION
MANAGER
Barbara Judson

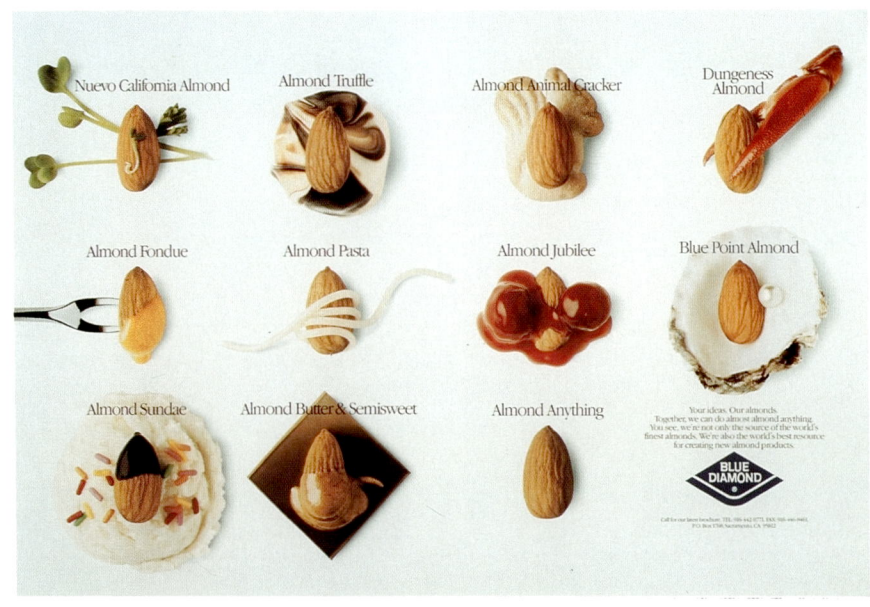

Tossed out of the best bars everywhere.

MAGAZINE

ART DIRECTOR
Frank Grasso
DESIGNER
Frank Grasso
WRITER
Doug Raboy
PHOTOGRAPHER
Harry DeZitter
CLIENT
House of Seagrams
AGENCY/STUDIO
DDB Needham N.Y.

Finally a healthy bar that tastes like the fruit of the tree instead of the bark.

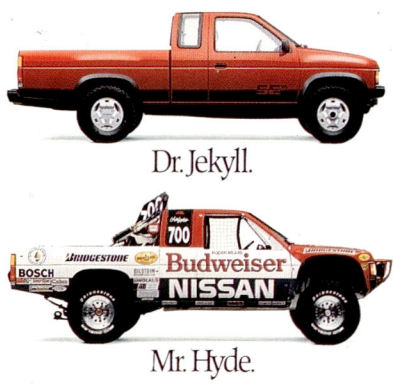

Dr. Jekyll.

Mr. Hyde.

Built for the Human Race.

ART DIRECTOR
Eileen Turpin
WRITER
Debbie Schwartz
PHOTOGRAPHER
Patrice Meigneux
CLIENT
Wm. T. Thompson Co.
AGENCY/STUDIO
Schwartz & Rahman
Advertising

ART DIRECTOR
Mike Mazza
WRITER
Brian Belefant
PHOTOGRAPHER
Lamb & Hall
CLIENT
Nissan Motor Corporation
AGENCY/STUDIO
Chiat/Day/Mojo Inc.
Advertising

   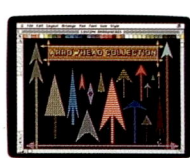

  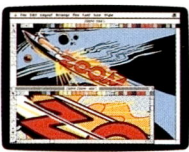 

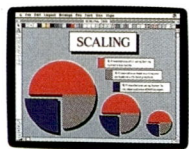 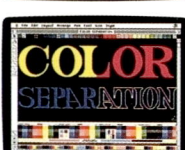  

Nobody reads copy anyway. MacDraw II.

ART DIRECTOR
Susan Westre
WRITER
Chris Wall
ILLUSTRATOR
Trici Venola
CLIENT
Claris Corporation
AGENCY/STUDIO
BBDO L.A.

MAGAZINE
ART DIRECTOR
Michael Arola
WRITER
Carolyn Johnson
PHOTOGRAPHER
David LeBon
CLIENT
Pirelli Armstrong
Tire Corp.
AGENCY/STUDIO
AC&R

ART DIRECTOR
Rick Boyko
WRITER
Steve Rabosky
PHOTOGRAPHER
Dennis Manarchy
ILLUSTRATOR
Dugald Stermer
CLIENT
Foster Farms
AGENCY/STUDIO
Chiat/Day/Mojo Inc.
Advertising

ART DIRECTOR
Paul Boley
WRITER
Richard Rand
PHOTOGRAPHER
Dewitt Jones
CLIENT
Schenley/Dewar's
White Label
AGENCY/STUDIO
Leo Burnett Company

Now you don't have to give up your firstborn to own a sports car.

MAGAZINE

ART DIRECTOR
Andy Dijak
WRITER
Dick Sittig
PHOTOGRAPHER
David LeBon
CLIENT
Nissan Motor Corporation
AGENCY/STUDIO
Chiat/Day/Mojo Inc.
Advertising

As a parent, you expect to make certain sacrifices for your children.

Your Hawaiian vacation for their college education.

Your new set of golf clubs for their new set of braces.

Your really great sports car for a really sedate family sedan.

You gladly do all these things for your kids.

Except give up your sports car.

There are times, after all, when as a parent you just have to put your foot down.

Which is exactly the idea behind the new Nissan® Maxima® The 4-Door Sports Car.™

Put your foot down and you'll quickly discover its 3-liter, multi-port, fuel-injected V6. Derived from our powerful Z-Car engine, it churns out 160 horsepower and keeps pace with

some of the world's fastest sports cars.

While on twisting roads, a four-wheel independent suspension with front and rear stabilizer bars ensures cornering that is anything but sedan-like.

And standard on the Maxima 4DSC™ pictured here, is our advanced, second-generation ABS braking system. It electronically modulates each wheel to ensure straighter, shorter stops, even on wet pavement.

Of course, if you had a conventional sports car that performed this well, it would be only natural to want to take your best friends for a ride.

The nice thing about our sports car is, you can take all of them at once.

Maxima.The 4-Door Sports Car.™

NISSAN
Built for the Human Race™

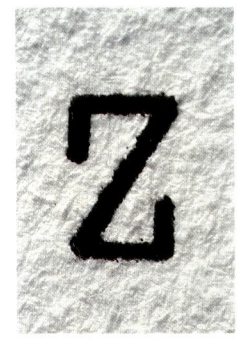

ART DIRECTORS
Mike Mazza/Pam Cunningham
WRITER
Brian Belefant
PHOTOGRAPHER
Bob Grigg/Doug Taub/Jay Ahrend
ILLUSTRATOR
Alan Daniels
CLIENT
Nissan Motor Corporation
AGENCY/STUDIO
Chiat/Day/Mojo Inc.
Advertising

Timberland. Because the earth is two-thirds water.

Timberland. Where the elements of design
are the elements themselves.

The elements of Timberland design
are solid brass eyelets, oil-impregnated leather,
wind, water, earth and sky.

You can always tell a Colombian Coffee party by the way the crowd is dressed.

It was a rather cool affair. The Rockefellers were there. So were the Vanderbanks. So, naturally, was 100% Colombian Coffee, *the richest coffee in the world.*" Not that Colombian Coffee would be appreciated only by the tuxedo set. On the contrary, Most Americans show unflappable loyalty to the coffee they believe is best. In fact, they're willing to pay a premium for it. And more of them flock to supermarkets that display it on their shelves—and restaurants that display it on their menus. Shouldn't you be finding out how offering 100% Colombian Coffee could dress up your bottom line? For more information write to: 100% Colombian Coffee Program, P.O. Box 8545, New York, NY 10150. Or call 1-800-223-3101. Consider this a formal invitation.

MAGAZINE

ART DIRECTOR
Sharon L. Occhipinti
DESIGNER
Sharon L. Occhipinti
WRITER
Lisa Mayer
PHOTOGRAPHER
Art Wolfe
CLIENT
Colombian Coffee
AGENCY/STUDIO
DDB Needham/New York

I see a man and a mule in your future.

"Look into my crystal ball," she whispered. "When the moon is in the seventh house and you sell 100% Colombian Coffee, you'll be rich beyond your wildest dreams." That's no surprise to people who've already seen the future. Even tea leaf readers know over half of America is willing to pay a premium for *the richest coffee in the world.*" What's more, supermarkets and restaurants everywhere have found selling 100% Colombian Coffee leads to some customers than a deluxe divining rod. And profits always seems to be in the cards for retailers who offer our brands. Don't play with fate. If you're not able to contact us telepathically, write for more information to: 100% Colombian Coffee Program, P.O. Box 8545, New York, N.Y. 10150. Or call 1-800-223-3101. It's destiny.

ART DIRECTOR
Sharon L. Occhipinti
DESIGNER
Sharon L. Occhipinti
WRITER
Doug Raboy
PHOTOGRAPHER
Nancy Ney
CLIENT
Colombian Coffee
AGENCY/STUDIO
DDB Needham/New York

The Formula Series. The Science of Action.
Everest & Jennings®

ART DIRECTOR
Jean Robaire
DESIGNER
Jean Robaire/
Joann Lobono
WRITER
John Stein
PHOTOGRAPHER
Paul Gersten
CLIENT
Everest & Jennings
AGENCY/STUDIO
Stein Robaire Helm

MAGAZINE
ART DIRECTORS
Andy Dijak/Corey
Stolberg
WRITER
Dick Sittig
PHOTOGRAPHERS
Pete Tangen/
Gary McGuire
HAND-LETTERING
Kelly Hume
CLIENT
Nissan Motor
Corporation
AGENCY/STUDIO
Chiat/Day/Mojo Inc.
Advertising

ART DIRECTOR
Andy Dijak
WRITER
Dick Sittig
PHOTOGRAPHERS
Pete Tangen/
Gary McGuire
HAND-LETTERING
Kelly Hume
CLIENT
Nissan Motor
Corporation
AGENCY/STUDIO
Chiat/Day/Mojo Inc
Advertising

ART DIRECTOR
Andy Dijak
WRITER
Dick Sittig
PHOTOGRAPHERS
Pete Tangen/
Gary McGuire
HAND-LETTERING
Kelly Hume
CLIENT
Nissan Motor
Corporation
AGENCY/STUDIO
Chiat/Day/Mojo Inc.
Advertising

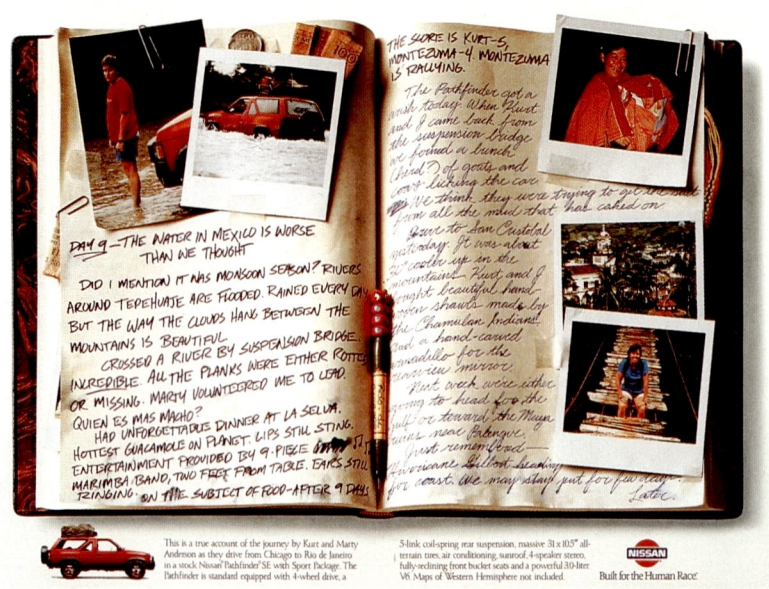

In The Best Theaters, The Sound Is As Big As The Picture.

MITSUBISHI

MAGAZINE

ART DIRECTOR
Rick Boyko
WRITER
Steve Rabosky
PHOTOGRAPHER
Dennis Manarchy
CLIENT
Mitsubishi Electronics
AGENCY/STUDIO
Chiat/Day/Mojo Inc.
Advertising

One Measure Of A Great Theater Is The Size Of Its Screen.

MITSUBISHI

ART DIRECTOR
Rick Boyko
WRITER
Steve Rabosky
PHOTOGRAPHER
Dennis Manarchy
CLIENT
Mitsubishi Electronics
AGENCY/STUDIO
Chiat/Day/Mojo Inc.
Advertising

The Best Way To Watch A Movie Has Always Been On The Big Screen.

MITSUBISHI

ART DIRECTOR
Rick Boyko
WRITER
Steve Rabosky
PHOTOGRAPHER
Dennis Manarchy
CLIENT
Mitsubishi Electronics
AGENCY/STUDIO
Chiat/Day/Mojo Inc.
Advertising

MAGAZINE CAMPAIGN

CREATIVE DIRECTOR
Maggie Gross, Sr. Vice President, Advertising
ART DIRECTOR
Jim Nevins
EDITORIAL DIRECTOR
Timothy Cohrs
DIRECTOR OF MEDIA
Jayne Greenberg
ACCOUNT MANAGER
Richard Crisman
PRODUCTION MANAGER
Laurie Kanes
STUDIO MANAGER
Mike Madrid
PHOTOGRAPHER
Annie Leibovitz
CLIENT
GAP
AGENCY/STUDIO
GAP

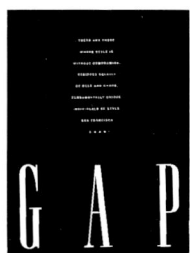

MAGAZINE CAMPAIGN

CREATIVE DIRECTOR
Maggie Gross, Sr. Vice
President, Advertising
ART DIRECTOR
Jim Nevins
EDITORIAL
DIRECTOR
Timothy Cohrs
DIRECTOR OF
MEDIA
Jayne Greenberg
ACCOUNT MANAGER
Richard Crisman
PRODUCTION
MANAGER
Laurie Kanes
STUDIO MANAGER
Mike Madrid
PHOTOGRAPHER
Annie Leibovitz
CLIENT
GAP
AGENCY/STUDIO
GAP

MAGAZINE CAMPAIGN
ART DIRECTOR
John Doyle
DESIGNER
John Doyle
WRITER
Paul Silverman
PHOTOGRAPHER
Eric Meola
CLIENT
Timberland
AGENCY/STUDIO
Mullen

Timberland. Because the earth is two-thirds water.

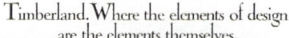
Timberland. Where the elements of design
are the elements themselves.

The elements of Timberland design
are solid brass eyelets, oil-impregnated leather,
wind, water, earth and sky.

MAGAZINE CAMPAIGN

ART DIRECTOR
David Jordan Williams
DESIGNER
Joe Molloy
PHOTOGRAPHER
David Jordan Williams
CLIENT
Ron Rezek Lighting and
Furniture

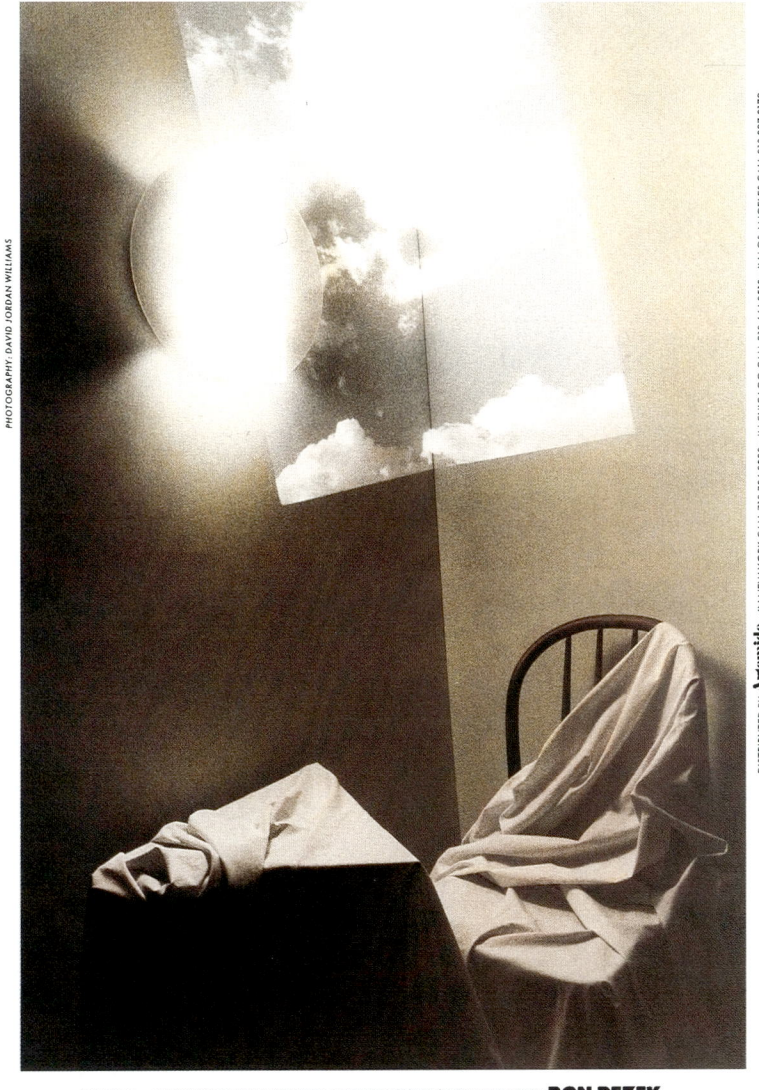

MAGAZINE CAMPAIGN

ART DIRECTOR
Rick Boyko
PRODUCER
Francesca Cohn/Kelly
Waltos
DIRECTOR
Dennis Manarchy
WRITER
Steve Rabosky
CLIENT
Mitsubishi Electronics
AGENCY/STUDIO
Chiat/Day/Mojo Inc.
Advertising
PRODUCTION
COMPANY
Dennis Manarchy
Studios

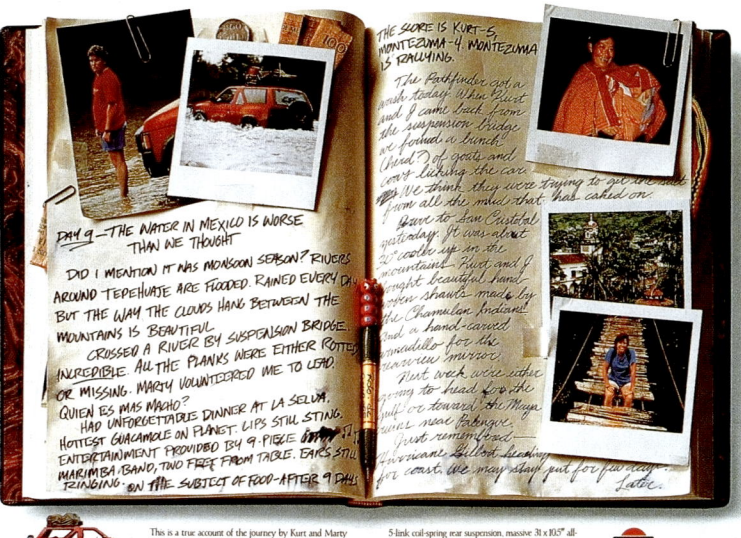

MAGAZINE CAMPAIGN
ART DIRECTOR
Andy Dijak/Corey
Stolberg
WRITER
Dick Sittig
PHOTOGRAPHERS
Pete Tangen/
Gary McGuire
HAND-LETTERING
Kelly Hume
CLIENT
Nissan Motor
Corporation
AGENCY/STUDIO
Chiat/Day/Mojo Inc.
Advertising

MAGAZINE CAMPAIGN
ART DIRECTOR
Bob Wyatt
WRITER
Tom Coleman
PHOTOGRAPHER
Harry DeZitter
CLIENT
Schenley/Dickel
AGENCY/STUDIO
Leo Burnett Company

PUBLIC SERVICE

ART DIRECTOR
Uri Kelman
DESIGNER
Uri Kelman
WRITER
Baylor College of
Medicine/Health
Promotion Office
of Public Affairs
ILLUSTRATOR
Lee Lee Brazeal
CLIENT
Baylor College of
Medicine
AGENCY/STUDIO
Kelman Design
Studio
PRODUCTION
COMPANY
AW Printing

DIRECT MAIL
ART DIRECTOR
Stavros Cosmopulos
WRITER
Stavros Cosmopulos
CLIENT
O'Neill's Auto Body
Works
AGENCY/STUDIO
Cosmopulos, Crowley
& Daly, Inc.

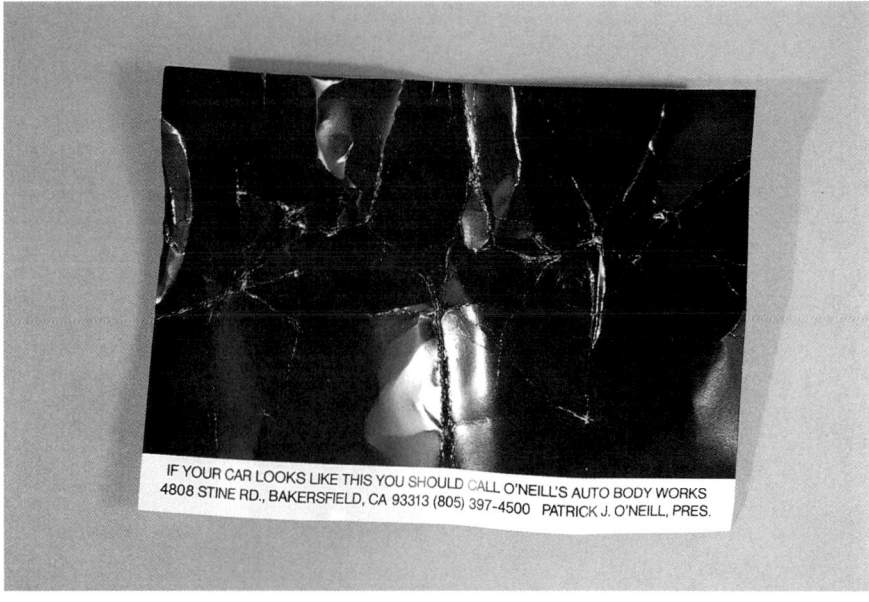

ART DIRECTOR
Steve Rutter
WRITER
David Baldwin
PHOTOGRAPHER
Bart Gorin
ILLUSTRATOR
Leonardo Da Vinci/
Authenticolor
AGENCY/STUDIO
Rutter/Baldwin, NYC

ART DIRECTOR
Jan Rudin
DESIGNER
Jan Rudin
WRITER
Andrea May
PHOTOGRAPHER
Jeremiah S. Sullivan
CLIENT
Jeremiah S. Sullivan
Studio
AGENCY/STUDIO
Jeremiah S. Sullivan
Studio

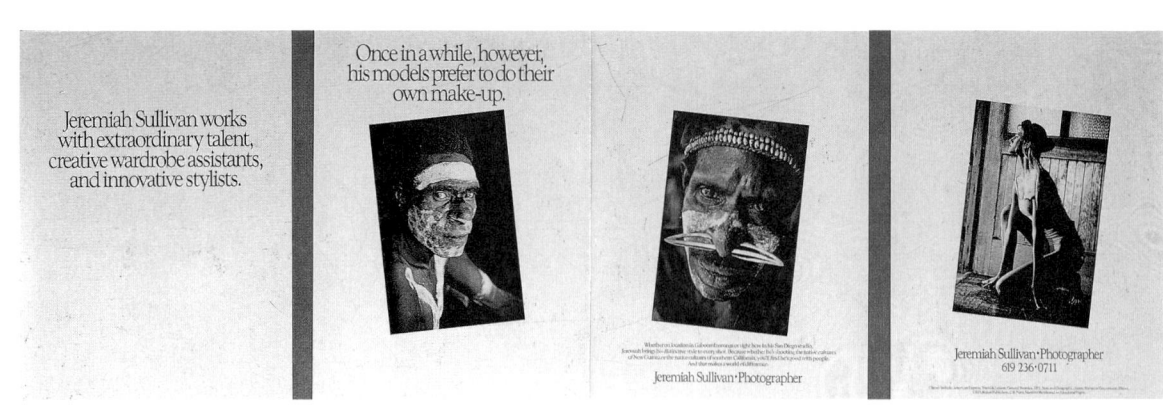

ADVERTISING

DIRECT MAIL
ART DIRECTORS
Tom Lewis/Joel
Cleveland
DESIGNER
Tom Lewis
WRITER
Mark Johnson
PHOTOGRAPHER
Charlie Lathem
Photography
CLIENT
Charlie Lathem
Photography
AGENCY/STUDIO
Lewis Clark &
Graham

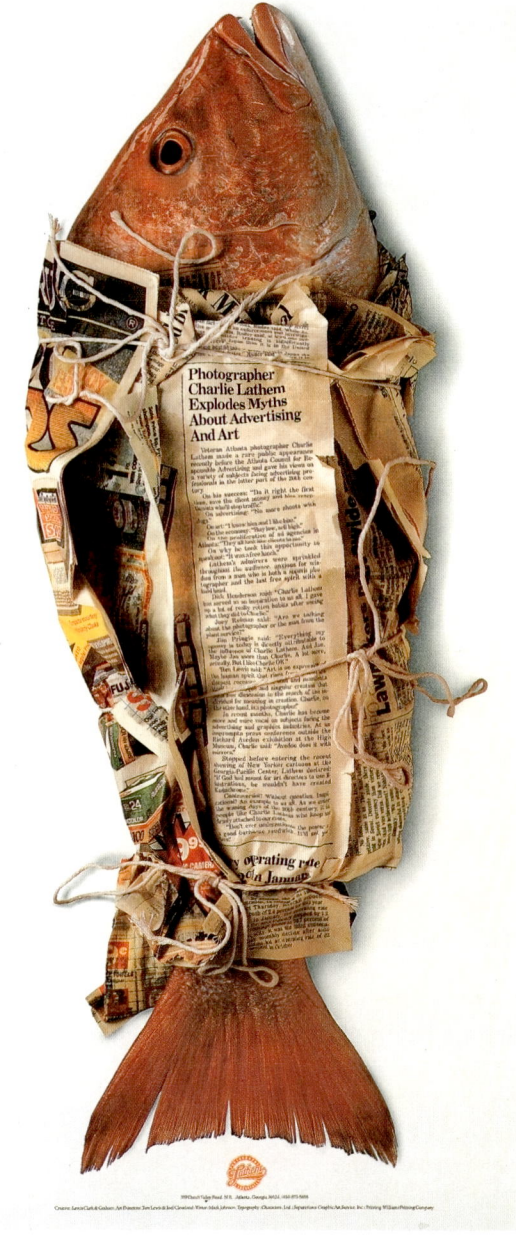

ART DIRECTOR
Chuck Bennett
WRITER
Paul Wilcox
PHOTOGRAPHER
Glen Wexler
CLIENT
Daniel Freeman Hospital
AGENCY/STUDIO
NW Ayer, Inc.

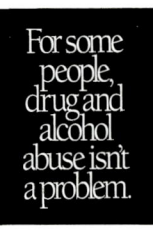

ART DIRECTOR
Gordon Hochhalter
DESIGNER
Bob Meyer
WRITER
Gordon Hochhalter
PHOTOGRAPHERS
Deborah Turbeville/
Pete Turner
CLIENT
Lancaster Web Offset
Printing
AGENCY/STUDIO
R. R. Donnelley &
Sons Company

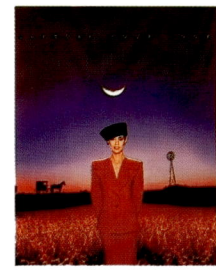

DON'T BE A PEABRAIN. GET A NORITSU ENLARGER.

With our new 611 and 633 enlargers you can make huge 12x18-inch prints. And absolutely whopping profits.

ANYBODY WITH HALF A BRAIN CAN RUN
A NORITSU ONE-HOUR PHOTO SYSTEM.

POINT OF PURCHASE,
DISPLAY

ART DIRECTOR
Preuit Holland
DESIGNER
Preuit Holland
WRITER
Marc Deschenes
PHOTOGRAPHER
Gary McGuire
CLIENT
Noritsu America
AGENCY/STUDIO
Marc Deschenes/
Preuit Holland

ART DIRECTOR
Preuit Holland
DESIGNER
Preuit Holland
WRITER
Marc Deschenes
PHOTOGRAPHER
Lamb & Hall
CLIENT
Noritsu America
AGENCY/STUDIO
Marc Deschenes/
Preuit Holland

BROCHURE, FOLDER

ART DIRECTOR
Frank Lacey
DESIGNER
Frank Lacey
WRITER
Ronald J. Levin &
Gasper Patrico
PHOTOGRAPHER
Philip Dixon
CLIENT
Cal Fed Enterprises
AGENCY/STUDIO
Horlick Levin
Advertising Inc.

BROCHURE, FOLDER
ART DIRECTOR
Bob Nenninger
DESIGNER
Bob Nenninger
CREATIVE DIRECTOR
Alix Riley
WRITER
Alix Riley
CLIENT
Orange County Performing Arts Center
AGENCY/STUDIO
Hunter/Korobkin Inc.

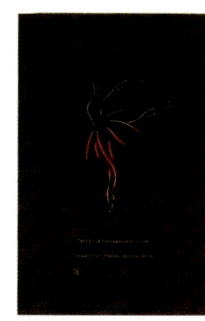

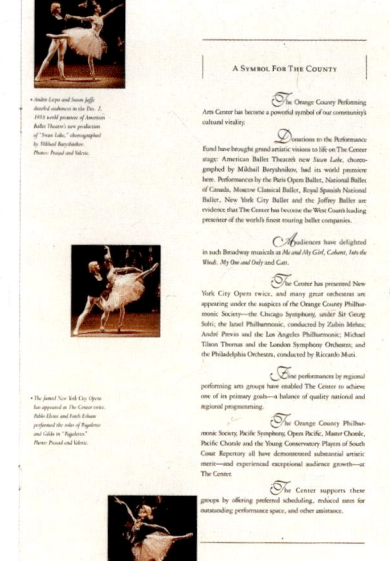

ART DIRECTORS
Paul Pruneau/Liz Sutton
PRODUCTION ART
Dorene Meadows
WRITER
Brad Londy
PRODUCTION COORDINATION
Charlie Dana
PHOTOGRAPHER
Paul Matsuda / Bill Gallery
TYPOGRAPHER
Macintosh
CLIENT
Apple Computer, Inc.
AGENCY/STUDIO
Apple Creative Services

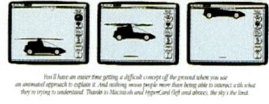

ART DIRECTOR
Andrea Kelley
DESIGNER
Andrea Kelley
PRODUCTION COORDINATOR
Charlie Dana
PRODUCTION ART
Tracy Birney
WRITER
Brad Londy
PHOTOGRAPHERS
Bill Gallery/Bruce Ashley/Mark Tuschman
CLIENT
Apple Computer, Inc.
AGENCY/STUDIO
Apple Creative Services

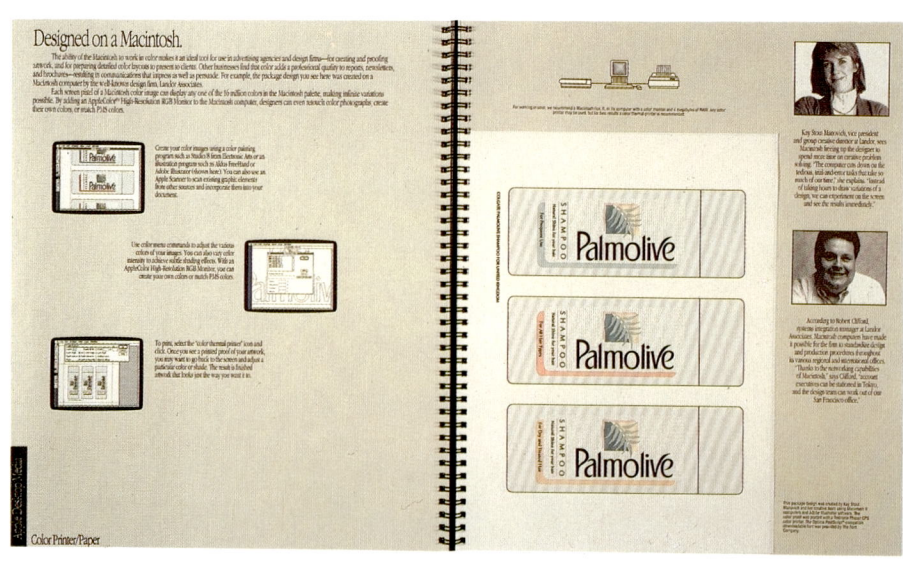

BROCHURE, FOLDER

ART DIRECTORS
Lynne Court/Paul Ison/
Lisa Langhoff
DESIGNER
Lynne Court
PRODUCTION MANAGER
Christine Ferguson
WRITER
Tony Assenza
PHOTOGRAPHER
Bob Grigg
ILLUSTRATOR
Kevin Hulsey
CLIENT
Nissan Motor Corporation
AGENCY/STUDIO
The Designory, Inc.
PRODUCTION COMPANY
Anderson Litho Company

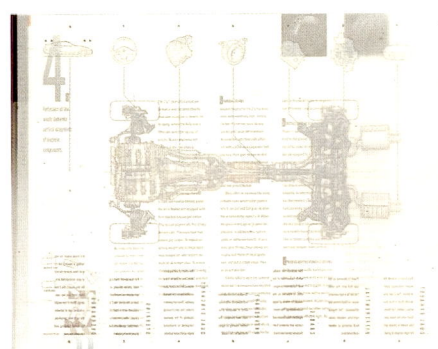

POSTER
ART DIRECTOR
William Wondriska
DESIGNER
William Wondriska
ILLUSTRATOR
William Wondriska
CLIENT
Boston Symphony
Orchestra
AGENCY/STUDIO
Wondriska Associates,
Inc.

ART DIRECTOR
Tom Lewis/Joel
Cleveland
DESIGNER
Tom Lewis
WRITER
Mark Johnson
PHOTOGRAPHER
Charlie Lathem
CLIENT
Charlie Lathem
Photography
AGENCY/STUDIO
Lewis Clark &
Graham

ART DIRECTOR
Angela Dunkle
WRITER
John Stein
PHOTOGRAPHER
Terry Heffernan
CLIENT
Pizza Inn
AGENCY/STUDIO
Chiat/Day/Mojo Inc.
Advertising

IT'S A SHAME TO THINK HE'LL GET MORE BLOOD FROM YOU THIS SUMMER THAN WE WILL.

With less than 10% of Americans donating blood each year, it's become very difficult to keep our blood supply strong. As well as our patients. So please give at Richmond Metropolitan Blood Service. We need you more than he does.

POSTER

ART DIRECTOR
Cliff Sorah
WRITER
Liz Paradise
PHOTOGRAPHER
Stock
CLIENT
Richmond Metro
Blood Service
AGENCY/STUDIO
The Martin Agency

JULY 12, 1913: A DATE THAT LITTLE OLD LADIES WHO CROSS STREETS WILL CHERISH FOREVER.

Here's to all the boys who became men in the 75 years of the Robert E. Lee Council of the Boy Scouts of America.

ART DIRECTOR
Jerry Torchia
WRITER
John Mahoney
PHOTOGRAPHER
Stock
CLIENT
Robert E. Lee Council
AGENCY/STUDIO
The Martin Agency

ANYBODY WITH HALF A BRAIN CAN RUN A NORITSU ONE-HOUR PHOTO SYSTEM.

ART DIRECTOR
Preuit Holland
DESIGNER
Preuit Holland
WRITER
Marc Deschenes
PHOTOGRAPHER
Lamb & Hall
CLIENT
Noritsu America
AGENCY/STUDIO
Marc Deschenes/
Preuit Holland

OUTDOOR
ART DIRECTORS
David Ayriss/
Wally Runnells
WRITER
David Ayriss
PHOTOGRAPHER
Carl Furuta
CLIENT
Nissan Motor
Corporation
AGENCY/STUDIO
Chiat/Day/Mojo
Inc. Advertising

ART DIRECTOR
Corey Stolberg
WRITER
Sam Kaumeyer
CLIENT
Nissan Motor Corporation
AGENCY/STUDIO
Chiat/Day/Mojo Inc.
Advertising

ART DIRECTORS
Mike Mazza/Pam
Cunningham
WRITER
Brian Belefant
PHOTOGRAPHERS
Bob Grigg/Jay Ahrend
CLIENT
Nissan Motor Corporation
AGENCY/STUDIO
Chiat/Day/Mojo Inc.
Advertising

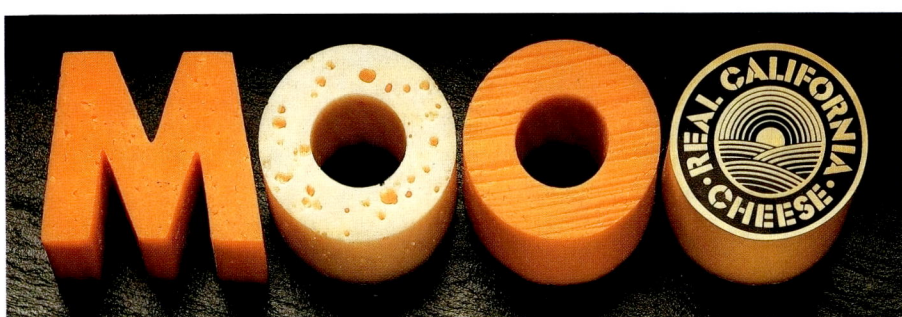

OUTDOOR

ART DIRECTOR
Dennis Lim
WRITER
Brent Bouchez
PHOTOGRAPHER
Mountain Stock
ILLUSTRATOR
Adrem (David Larks/
Ramiro Fauve)
CLIENT
Bear Mountain Ski Resort
AGENCY/STUDIO
Ketchum, L.A.

ART DIRECTOR
Dennis Lim
WRITER
Scott Aal
ILLUSTRATORS
Howard Lim/Dennis Lim
CLIENT
Bear Mountain Ski Resort
AGENCY/STUDIO
Ketchum, L.A

ART DIRECTOR
Mel Sant
DESIGNER
Mel Sant
WRITER
Hal Kaufman
PHOTOGRAPHER
Henry Bjoin
CLIENT
California Milk Advisory
Board
AGENCY/STUDIO
Foote, Cone & Belding/
Los Angeles
PRODUCTION COMPANY
Laura Hanssen

OUTDOOR
ART DIRECTOR
Tracy Wong
WRITER
Tracy Wong
PHOTOGRAPHER
Steve Hellerstein
CLIENT
New York Lung
Association
AGENCY/STUDIO
Goldsmith/Jeffrey

ART DIRECTOR
Tracy Wong
WRITER
Tracy Wong
PHOTOGRAPHER
Steve Hellerstein
CLIENT
New York Lung
Association
AGENCY/STUDIO
Goldsmith/Jeffrey

CREATIVE
DIRECTORS
Joan McArthur/
Ivan Horvath
ART DIRECTOR
Damian Fulton
WRITER
Jim Hayden
CLIENT
Las Vegas Hilton
AGENCY/STUDIO
Ogilvy & Mather

DIRECTIONS TO
THE HEARNS-BARKLEY FIGHT.
Left, Right, Left, Right, Left, Right.

)|(LAS VEGAS HILTON

"PABLO"

SFX: SCREAM/HELICOPTER

PRISONER: Ey, is this stuff any good man?

SFX: JAIL DOORS CLOSING

SFX: POLICE SIRENS

SFX: SCREAM/YELLS FROM PRISONERS

GUARD: Man walking!

PRISONER: Man walking! Here comes a little white boy, man take care of my man.

DRUG DEALER: I want you man, I want my money!

POLICE MAN: Up against the wall.

PABLO: You got nothing on me pig.

SFX: HANDCUFF SOUND

PRISONER: Ey, you fine ass sucker, give some of that. Little boy.

This stuff is good man.

PABLO: Look man you don't know me, give me another line.

SFX: POLICE HELICOPTER CHASING PABLO

POLICE: Tell me who you are son?

SFX: PEOPLE MURMURING

ANNCR: DRUGS ARE REALLY FUN, AREN'T THEY?

SUPER: THINK ABOUT IT

ART DIRECTORS
Andres Sullivan/Jorge Cantu/Roberto Bojorges
PRODUCER
Doug Magallon
DIRECTOR
Brian Lai
WRITERS
Pedro Silva/Jorge Cantu/Roberto Bojorges
CLIENT
Drug Enforcement Agency
AGENCY/STUDIO
Mendoza Dillon & Asociados
PRODUCTION COMPANY
Dexter, Dryer & Lai

 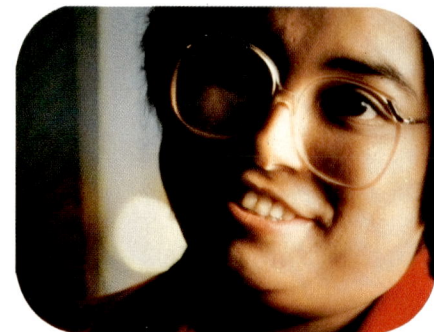 

VONS.
The More Store

ART DIRECTOR
Chip Kettering
CREATIVE DIRECTOR
Dennis Kuhr
PRODUCER
Kaylyn Kramer
DIRECTOR
Danny Levinson
WRITER
Tessa Super
CLIENT
VONS
AGENCY/STUDIO
J. Walter Thompson
PRODUCTION COMPANY
Dan Corps

"BUTCHER"

BUTCHER: When I heard Vons was taking over Safeway, I got a little nervous. A little shaky. But Bill Davila said we were some of the best meat cutters in the business and he didn't want to lose us. Smart guy. And now I'm cutting a higher grade of beef. U.S.D.A. Choice. Doesn't get much better than that. You know, a little change every so often keeps you young.

DAVILA. Try a higher grade of beef at your new Vons. And say hello—to some old friends.

SINGERS: NOBODY ELSE BUT VONS.

"PRODUCT IMAGE"

PRODUCE PERSON: You know, I've been working in the produce department at Safeway for seven years and I thought I'd seen everything. But have you ever seen a kiwano? A tamarillo? Me neither. Listen, we've got all kinds of new things in the produce department since we became Vons. And all the familiar things, like me.

DAVILA: Try something different at your new Vons. And say hello—to some old friends.

SINGERS: NOBODY ELSE BUT VONS.

"CHECKER"

CHECKER: After 11 years as a Safeway checker, I know what things cost. So when other markets tell you they've got the lowest this or that, I know when it's a lot of baloney. But now that Safeway is Vons, they've lowered thousands of prices throughout the store. And with the Unlimited Double Coupons, I think that they do—I mean we really-do have the lowest tape total in town.

DAVILA: Check out the low prices at your new Vons. And say hello—to some old friends.

SINGERS: NOBODY ELSE BUT VONS.

"I HAD ONE OF THOSE"

MUSIC: "HEART AND SOUL" PLAYED ON PIANO BY KIDS.

AVO: Remember how determined your parents were to give you the gift of knowledge, no matter how many gifts it took? Today, you have a big advantage with the Apple IIGS. Apple II computers are found in more schools than any other computer. Your parents gave you the world. You can give your kids the universe.

SUPER: Apple IIGS

SUPER: The power to be your best.

ART DIRECTOR
Bob Cockrell
PRODUCER
Jean Kelly
DIRECTOR
Steve Horn
WRITER
Bob Gerke
CLIENT
Apple Computer, Inc.
AGENCY/STUDIO
BBDO L.A.
PRODUCTION COMPANY
Steve Horn, Inc.

TELEVISION-PRODUCT

 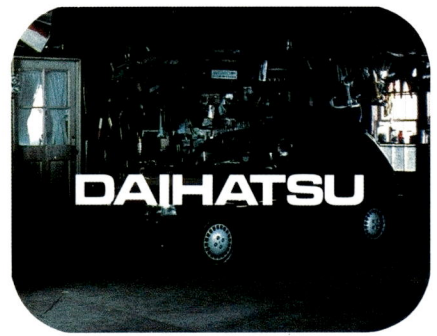

ART DIRECTOR
Richard Kyle
PRODUCER
Pam den Hartog
DIRECTOR
Gary Johns
WRITER
Theresa Aycock
CLIENT
Daihatsu America, Inc.
AGENCY/STUDIO
Kresser/Craig
PRODUCTION COMPANY
Johns + Gorman,
Los Angeles

"MIDNIGHT SNACK"

VIDEO: Open on a darkened garage.
AUDIO:
SFX: (SOFT GROWLING)

VIDEO: Kitchen light comes on as disheveled man pulls curtain aside and peeks into garage.
SFX: (REFRIGERATOR DOOR OPENING. VARIOUS SOUNDS FROM KITCHEN. GROWLING INCREASES)

VIDEO: Man opens door and turns on garage light. Car behaves like a hungry beast, thrashing, opening and closing its hood.
SFX: (SQUEAKY KITCHEN DOOR. FIERCE GROWLING)

VIDEO: Man dangles a large slab of raw meat in front of car. As cars rocking and lurching intensifies, the hood continues to flap.
SFX: (FIERCE, RABID GROWLING)

VO: The Diahatsu Charade from Japan.

VIDEO: Man tosses meat under gaping hood. Car lunges at meat. Hood slams shut.
SFX: (GROWL, HOOD SLAM)

VO: It has a ferocious 16-valve engine.

VIDEO: Car wiggles as if chewing. Man pats car lovingly.
SFX: (MUFFLED GROWL)

VO: So…be nice to it.

VIDEO: Man turns garage light off and shuts door. Car chews contentedly.
SFX: (MUFFLED CHEWING. KITCHEN DOOR SQUEAKS, SLAMS SHUT)

VIDEO: Kitchen light goes out.
SFX: (PAUSE. THEN A LOUD GULP)

SUPER: DIAHATSU. The one small car you'd be proud to own.

  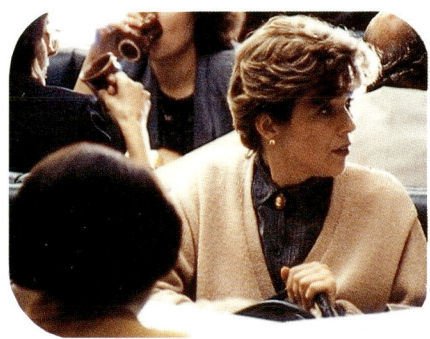

"CAREER MOVE"

SCENE: A GROUP OF SECRETARIES ARE GATHERED AROUND A BOOTH IN A COFFEE SHOP.

SUPER: Career Move

CATE: I've gotta go.

NANCY: But we just got here.

CATE: I've got some calls to make. I'm gonna look for another job.

ANNA: What!

CATE: Our group's getting computers.

ANNA: So.

CATE: So, I haven't figured out the new typewriters yet.

NANCY: Look, here's your chance to do a lot more than just typing.

CATE: Yeah, but...

ANNA: Relax. Bob Dion learned how to use one.

CATE: Bob Dion, the guy who still needs help with the copy machine?

NANCY: Yeah, that's the one.

SUPER: Macintosh. The power to be your best.

CATE: ...maybe I will have a little something.

ART DIRECTOR
Mike Cambell
PRODUCERS
Tony Frere/Trish Reeves
DIRECTOR
Joe Pytka
WRITER
Gary Graf
CLIENT
Apple Computer, Inc.
AGENCY/STUDIO
BBDO L.A.
PRODUCTION COMPANY
Pytka

TELEVISION-PRODUCT

ART DIRECTOR
Bob Dion
PRODUCERS
Tony Frere/Trish Reeves
DIRECTOR
Joe Pytka
WRITER
Ken Segall
CLIENT
Apple Computer, Inc.
AGENCY/STUDIO
BBDO L.A.
PRODUCTION COMPANY
Pytka

"THE SLEEPING GIANT"

SUPER: Sleeping Giant

MARTHA: Will they be much longer?

RECEPTIONIST: I don't believe so.

MARTHA: OK thanks. OK Steve, so you're up right after me.

STEVE: Right, and everybody focus on Gleason, he makes the decisions.

JAMES: Hey, I think this is our lucky day.

STEVE: Campbell & Graf? That's who we're up against?

MARTHA: (LAUGHS.) When was the last time they had an original idea, World War II?

JAMES: Hello, Leonard. Still in the old building?

LEONARD: Just fine, thanks. Good luck now.

STEVE: Oh, that Leonard. He is so glib.

JAMES: All I can say is, if those guys get this business, we didn't want it anyway.

STEVE: We want it, we want it.

MARTHA: Hey, look at this—it's their leave-behind.

STEVE: This should be funny.

MARTHA: This is not funny.

JAMES: Let me see that.

STEVE: (WHISTLES THROUGH HIS TEETH.)

MARTHA: What do you think woke them up?

FADE TO BLACK. SUPER: Macintosh

SUPER: The power to be your best.

"MAILROOM"

SCENE: A GROUP OF MAIL BOYS HOLD COURT. IN ONE CORNER JOEY AND BERNIE ARE TALKING.

SUPER: Mail Room

ALEX: You got any inter-office mail for Nine?

BERNIE: Nope.

ALEX: Hey, me neither.

JOEY: Hey, maybe they stopped sending memos.

BERNIE: Oh, get real. Those suits on Nine are always sending stuff to each other.

ALEX: Yeah well, if you didn't pick 'em up, and I didn't deliver 'em, how do they get 'em?

FELIX: Computers.

JOEY: Seven's got computers, they send tons of memos.

FELIX: These kind are different, same ones they got in LA.

ALEX: Well Bernie, you got any overnights from LA?

BERNIE: Nope.

ALEX: Weird…very weird.

SUPER: Macintosh

SENIOR CREATIVE DIRECTOR
Steve Hayden
COPYWRITER
Gary Graf
ART DIRECTOR
Mike Campbell
PRODUCERS
Tony Frere/Trish Reeves
ACCOUNT SUPERVISOR
Jimmy Yaffe
DIRECTOR
Joe Pytka
PRODUCTION COMPANY
Pytka
EDITOR
Dennis Hayes
EDITORIAL COMPANY
Dennis Hayes Film Editing

TELEVISION-PRODUCT

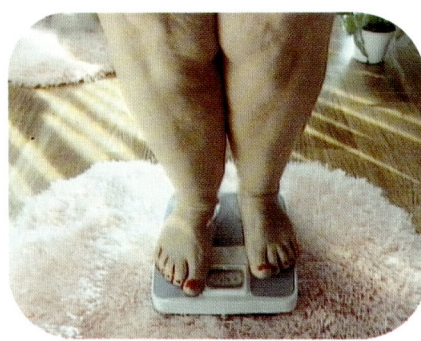 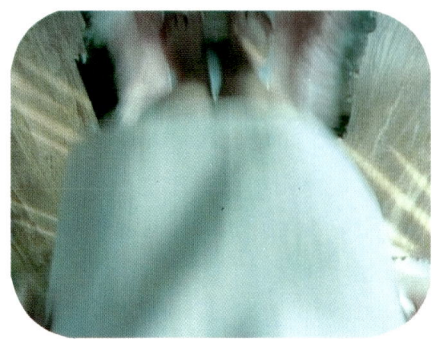 

ART DIRECTOR
Lyle Metzdorf
DIRECTOR
Jerry Cotts
WRITER
Lyle Metzdorf
CLIENT
Blue Bell Creameries, Inc.
AGENCY/STUDIO
Blue Bell Advertising
Associates
PRODUCTION COMPANY
Cotts Films

"FEET"

AUDIO: Music
VIDEO: Large woman in fuzzy slippers steps on bathroom scale
AUDIO:
WOMAN: "Oh no"
VIDEO: Woman moves slippers over scale dial
VIDEO: A large man standing on scale; woman walks up
AUDIO:
WOMAN: Laughing
MAN: "It's not funny"
VIDEO: Extremely heavy woman steps on bathroom scale
AUDIO:
WOMAN: "Oh-aagh"
VIDEO: Woman and scale crash through floor
AUDIO: Heavenly choir singing—"New Diet Blue Bell"
VIDEO: Ice cream carton floats off of scale

 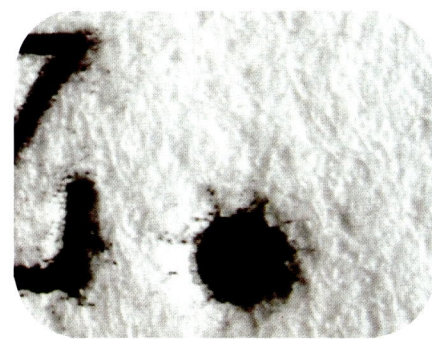 

"THE LETTER"

ANNCR VO: Nissan has just delivered the ultimate proof of how well we understand cars...and the people who love to drive them. It arrived in the form of a letter.

SFX: BANG!

ANNCR VO: The new Z. From Nissan.

ART DIRECTOR
Pam Cunningham
PRODUCER
Richard O'Neill
DIRECTOR
John St. Clair
WRITER
Steve Bassett
CLIENT
Nissan Motor Corportation
AGENCY/STUDIO
Chiat/Day/Mojo Inc.
Advertising
PRODUCTION COMPANY
Peterson Communications

TELEVISION-PRODUCT

ART DIRECTOR
Pam Cunningham
PRODUCER
Richard O'Neill
DIRECTOR
John St. Clair
WRITER
Steve Bassett
CLIENT
Nissan Motor Corporation
AGENCY/STUDIO
Chiat/Day/Mojo Inc.
Advertising
PRODUCTION COMPANY
Peterson Communications

"CLEAN SHEET"

SFX: LOUD BANGING.

ANNCR VO: This is where we started—a clean sheet of paper. No boundaries. No rules.

No preconceived ideas.

Just desire to build the best sports car in the world. A car for one driver in a thousand.

The car destined to leave its mark.

SFX: LOUD BANGING.

ANNCR: The new Z. From Nissan.

 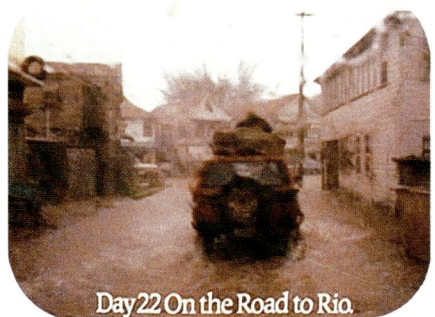 

"BELIZE"

MARTY: In Belize, we ran into Hurricane Gilbert...

KURT: ...and an even bigger problem.

TICKET AGENT: No way.

KURT: That's what we gotta do, that's what we gotta do.

ART DIRECTOR
Andy Dijak
PRODUCER
Richard O'Neill
DIRECTOR
Eric Saarinen
WRITER
Dick Sittig
CLIENT
Nissan Motor Corporation
AGENCY/STUDIO
Chiat/Day/Mojo Inc.
Advertising
PRODUCTION COMPANY
Plum Productions

TELEVISION-PRODUCT

ART DIRECTOR
Michael Smith
PRODUCERS
Francesca Cohn/Kelly Waltos
DIRECTOR
Jeff Gorman
WRITER
Sam Avery
CLIENT
Eveready Battery Co.
AGENCY/STUDIO
Chiat/Day/Mojo Inc.
Advertising
PRODUCTION COMPANY
Johns & Gorman

"BAR"

SFX: We hear bits of their chatter…he is trying to pick her up. Bar ambience in background.

MAN: Why don't we go up to my place and talk about you starring in this movie I'm producing?

WOMAN: Oh…

SFX: Man making kissing noise.

WOMAN: No.

ANNCR VO: The Eveready Squeezelight, small enough to carry with you, big enough for a real emergency.

"HUMAN NEEDS"

SFX: Appropriate throughout.

MUSIC: Up-tempo, classical throughout.

ANNCR VO: Have you ever noticed how cars mean a little more…
…to some people than they do to others?

ANNCR VO: Nissan has.

That's why we build ours the way we do.

We understand that a car fulfills a number of human needs.

And transportation…
…is only one of them.

Nissan. Built for the Human Race.

ART DIRECTOR
Mas Yamashita
PRODUCERS
Michael Paradise/
Richard O'Neill
DIRECTOR
Leslie Dektor
WRITER
Dave Butler
CLIENT
Nissan Motor Corporation
AGENCY/STUDIO
Chiat/Day/Mojo Inc.
Advertising
PRODUCTION COMPANY
Peterman/Dektor

ART DIRECTOR
Andy Dijak
PRODUCER
Richard O'Neill
DIRECTOR
Eric Saarinen
WRITER
Dick Sittig
CLIENT
Nissan Motor Corporation
AGENCY/STUDIO
Chiat/Day/Mojo Inc.
Advertising
PRODUCTION COMPANY
Plum Productions

"ROADS/REV"

MUSIC: UNDER THROUGHOUT.

*SFX: UNDER. OUTDOORS, INSECTS,
BIRDS, WIND.*

KURT VO: You wouldn't believe what the
Pathfinder went through on the road to
Botatulan. I guess when they ran out of
asphalt, they used cobblestones. When they
ran out of cobblestones, they used rocks.
When they ran out of rocks, they used gravel.
When they ran out of gravel they used dirt.
...They never ran out of dirt.

"NATIVES REV. 1"

SFX: UNDER. PRIMITIVE VILLAGE, NATIVES, PATHFINDER ENGINE.

MARTY VO: This is the first time Waeimpie Indians have ever been filmed. They have never seen red hair...
...or anything like a Pathfinder. Here on the equator, the air conditioner was a big hit. And they seemed to like our music. But we discovered, we like their music...even more.

MUSIC: UNDER. NATIVE INSTRUMENTS AND SINGING.

ART DIRECTOR
Andy Dijak
PRODUCER
Richard O'Neill
DIRECTOR
Eric Saarinen
WRITER
Dick Sittig
CLIENT
Nissan Motor Corporation
AGENCY/STUDIO
Chiat/Day/Mojo Inc.
Advertising
PRODUCTION COMPANY
Plum Productions

TELEVISION-PRODUCT
CAMPAIGN

 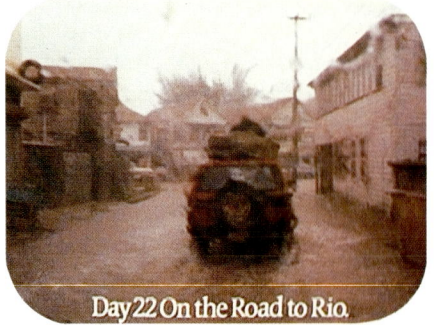 

ART DIRECTOR
Andy Dijak
PRODUCER
Richard O'Neill
DIRECTOR
Eric Saarinen
WRITER
Dick Sittig
CLIENT
Nissan Motor Corporation
AGENCY/STUDIO
Chiat/Day/Mojo Inc.
Advertising
PRODUCTION COMPANY
Plum Productions

"BELIZE"

MARTY: In Belize, we ran into Hurricane
Gilbert...
KURT: ...and an even bigger problem.
TICKET AGENT: No way.
KURT: That's what we gotta do, that's what
we gotta do.

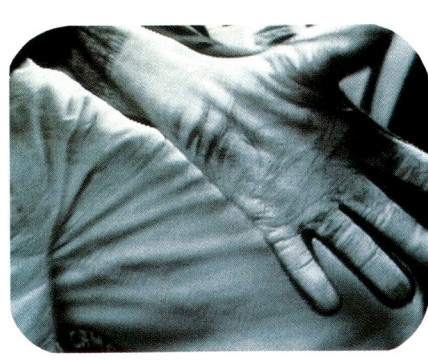  

"MORE DEMANDING"

SFX: APPROPRIATE THROUGHOUT

MUSIC: SUGGESTIVE OF SOMETHING TO COME.

ANNCR VO: Nissan builds cars for people who have a certain...
...enthusiasm for the cars they drive.

MUSIC: EXCITING, SFX START.

ANNCR VO: Of course...
...some drivers...
...are a little more enthusiastic...
...than others.

ANNCR VO: Nissan. Built for the most demanding race of all...the Human Race.

ART DIRECTOR
Mas Yamashita
PRODUCERS
Marty Friedman/Richard O'Neill/Michael Paradise
*DIRECTOR*S
Eric Saarinen/Leslie Dektor
WRITER
Dave Butler
CLIENT
Nissan Motor Corporation
AGENCY/STUDIO
Chiat/Day/Mojo Inc.
Advertising
PRODUCTION COMPANY
Plum Productions/
Peterman/Dektor

ART DIRECTOR
Mas Yamashita
PRODUCERS
Marty Friedman/Richard
O'Neill/Michael Paradise
DIRECTORS
Eric Saarinen/Leslie Dektor
WRITER
Dave Butler
CLIENT
Nissan Motor Corporation
AGENCY/STUDIO
Chiat/Day/Mojo Inc.
Advertising
PRODUCTION COMPANY
Plum Productions/
Peterman/Dektor

"HUMAN NEEDS"

SFX: Appropriate throughout.

MUSIC: Up-tempo, classical throughout.

ANNCR VO: Have you ever noticed how cars mean a little more…
…to some people than they do to others?

ANNCR VO: Nissan has.

That's why we build ours the way we do.

We understand that a car fulfills a number of human needs.

And transportation…
…is only one of them.

Nissan. Built for the Human Race.

"POV"

ANNCR VO: At Nissan, our cars are designed with a unique understanding of the how and why and where of driving…but, more importantly, of the who, sitting behind the wheel.

ANNCR VO: An understanding that there are still a whole lot of you out there who drive not because you have to, but because you like to.

Nissan. Built for the Human Race.

ART DIRECTOR
Mas Yamashita
PRODUCERS
Marty Friedman/Richard O'Neill/Michael Paradise
DIRECTORS
Eric Saarinen/Leslie Dektor
WRITER
Dave Butler
CLIENT
Nissan Motor Corporation
AGENCY/STUDIO
Chiat/Day/Mojo Inc. Advertising
PRODUCTION COMPANY
Plum Productions/ Peterman/Dektor

ART DIRECTORS
Pam Cunningham/
Mike Mazza
PRODUCER
Richard O'Neill
DIRECTOR
John St. Clair
WRITER
Steve Bassett/
Brian Belefant
CLIENT
Nissan Motor
Corporation
AGENCY/STUDIO
Chiat/Day/Mojo Inc.
Advertising
*PRODUCTION
COMPANY*
Peterson
Communications

"BANKED TRACK"

SFX: Banging…
SFX: Car's engine.
(Music underneath. Background singer.)
SFX: Banging.
ANNCR VO: Once again, the last letter of the alphabet is the last word in sports cars.
The new Z. From Nissan.

"CLEAN SHEET"

SFX: LOUD BANGING.

ANNCR VO: This is where we started—a clean sheet of paper. No boundaries. No rules.

No preconceived ideas.

Just desire to build the best sports car in the world. A car for one driver in a thousand.

The car destined to leave its mark.

SFX: LOUD BANGING.

ANNCR: The new Z. From Nissan.

ART DIRECTORS
Pam Cunningham/
Mike Mazza
PRODUCER
Richard O'Neill
DIRECTOR
John St. Clair
WRITER
Steve Bassett/
Brian Belefant
CLIENT
Nissan Motor
Corporation
AGENCY/STUDIO
Chiat/Day/Mojo Inc.
Advertising
*PRODUCTION
COMPANY*
Peterson
Communications

*TELEVISION-PRODUCT
CAMPAIGN*

ART DIRECTOR
Pam Cunningham
PRODUCER
Richard O'Neill
DIRECTOR
John St. Clair
WRITER
Steve Bassett
CLIENT
Nissan Motor
Corporation
AGENCY/STUDIO
Chiat/Day/Mojo Inc.
Advertising
*PRODUCTION
COMPANY*
Peterson
Communications

"THE LETTER"

ANNCR VO: Nissan has just delivered the
ultimate proof of how well we understand
cars...and the people who love to drive them.
It arrived in the form of a letter.
SFX: BANG!
ANNCR VO: The new Z. From Nissan.

"MAILROOM"

*SCENE: A GROUP OF MAIL BOYS HOLD
COURT. IN ONE CORNER JOEY AND
BERNIE ARE TALKING.*

SUPER: Mail Room

ALEX: You got any inter-office mail for Nine?

BERNIE: Nope.

ALEX: Hey, me neither.

JOEY: Hey, maybe they stopped sending
memos.

BERNIE: Oh, get real. Those suits on Nine
are always sending stuff to each other.

ALEX: Yeah well, if you didn't pick 'em up,
and I didn't deliver 'em, how do they get 'em?

FELIX: Computers.

JOEY: Seven's got computers, they send tons
of memos.

FELIX: These kind are different, same ones
they got in LA.

ALEX: Well Bernie, you got any overnights
from LA?

BERNIE: Nope.

ALEX: Weird…very weird.

SUPER: Macintosh

*SENIOR CREATIVE
DIRECTOR*
Steve Hayden
COPYWRITER
Gary Graf
ART DIRECTOR
Mike Campbell
PRODUCERS
Tony Frere/Trish Reeves
*ACCOUNT
SUPERVISOR*
Jimmy Yaffe
DIRECTOR
Joe Pytka
*PRODUCTION
COMPANY*
Pytka
EDITOR
Dennis Hayes
EDITORIAL COMPANY
Dennis Hayes Film
Editing

ART DIRECTOR
Bob Dion
PRODUCERS
Tony Frere/Trish Reeves
DIRECTOR
Joe Pytka
WRITER
Ken Segall
CLIENT
Apple Computer, Inc.
AGENCY/STUDIO
BBDO L.A.
PRODUCTION COMPANY
Pytka

"THE SLEEPING GIANT"

SUPER: Sleeping Giant

MARTHA: Will they be much longer?

RECEPTIONIST: I don't believe so.

MARTHA: OK thanks. OK Steve, so you're up right after me.

STEVE: Right, and everybody focus on Gleason, he makes the decisions.

JAMES: Hey, I think this is our lucky day.

STEVE: Campbell & Graf? That's who we're up against?

MARTHA: (LAUGHS.) When was the last time they had an original idea, World War II?

JAMES: Hello, Leonard. Still in the old building?

LEONARD: Just fine, thanks. Good luck now.

STEVE: Oh, that Leonard. He is so glib.

JAMES: All I can say is, if those guys get this business, we didn't want it anyway.

STEVE: We want it, we want it.

MARTHA: Hey, look at this—it's their leave-behind.

STEVE: This should be funny.

MARTHA: This is not funny.

JAMES: Let me see that.

STEVE: (WHISTLES THROUGH HIS TEETH.)

MARTHA: What do you think woke them up?

FADE TO BLACK. SUPER: Macintosh

SUPER: The power to be your best.

"CAREER MOVE"

*SCENE: A GROUP OF SECRETARIES ARE
GATHERED AROUND A BOOTH IN A
COFFEE SHOP.*

SUPER: Career Move

CATE: I've gotta go.

NANCY: But we just got here.

CATE: I've got some calls to make. I'm gonna
look for another job.

ANNA: What!

CATE: Our group's getting computers.

ANNA: So.

CATE: So, I haven't figured out the new
typewriters yet.

NANCY: Look, here's your chance to do a lot
more than just typing.

CATE: Yeah, but...

ANNA: Relax. Bob Dion learned how to use
one.

CATE: Bob Dion, the guy who still needs
help with the copy machine?

NANCY: Yeah, that's the one.

SUPER: Macintosh. The power to be your
best.

CATE: ...maybe I will have a little
something.

ART DIRECTOR
Mike Cambell
PRODUCERS
Tony Frere/Trish Reeves
DIRECTOR
Joe Pytka
WRITER
Gary Graf
CLIENT
Apple Computer, Inc.
AGENCY/STUDIO
BBDO L.A.
PRODUCTION COMPANY
Pytka

IT'S A GIRL.

**BORN
SEPTEMBER 23, 1988
AT 5:21 P.M.**

**WEIGHT:
250 LBS.**

**LENGTH:
77 IN.**

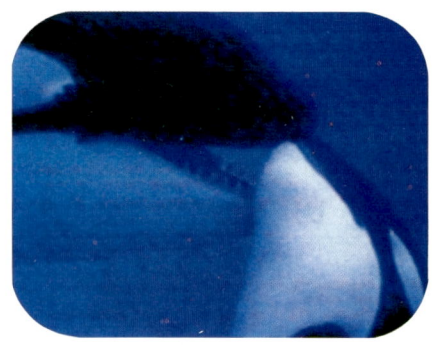

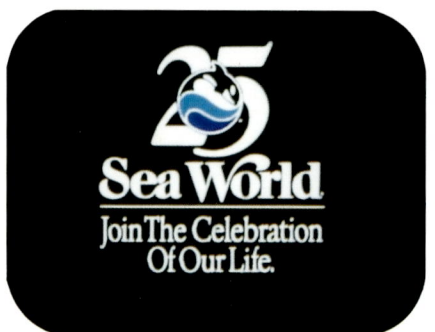

**25
Sea World
Join The Celebration
Of Our Life.**

ART DIRECTOR
Jeff Weekley
PRODUCER
Connie Myck
DIRECTORS
Connie Myck/Jeff Weekley
WRITER
Pieter Dreiband
CLIENT
Sea World of California
AGENCY/STUDIO
DMB&B/DMB&B
PRODUCTION COMPANY
DMB&B

"IT'S A GIRL"

V/O: Mother and Baby Shamu are now
receiving visitors. At Sea World.

"DISCREPANCY"

TELLER: I'm sorry, Mr. Park, we show a different balance on your account.

MAN: I knew it!

TELLER: Mr. Park. You don't understand...

MAN: I trusted you.

TELLER: You see, what I'm trying to tell you...

MAN: But you said, 'we are concerned.'

TELLER: (UNDER) I am.

MAN: And then you said, 'we understand.'

TELLER: I do.

MAN: And now this.

TELLER: Mr. Park...

MAN: Well, I kept some records, too.

TELLER: You have an interest-earning checking account. You have more money than you think.

MAN: (EMBARRASSED) Let's not let this happen again, okay?

ANNCR: At First Federal, we treat you with respect, concern and understanding. But don't worry, you'll get used to it.

ART DIRECTOR
Jerry Gentile
PRODUCER
Shannon Silverman
DIRECTOR
Mark Story
WRITER
Mark Monteiro
CLIENT
First Nation Wide
AGENCY/STUDIO
DDB Needham Worldwide
PRODUCTION COMPANY
Story-Piccolo-Guliner

TELEVISION-BRAND

 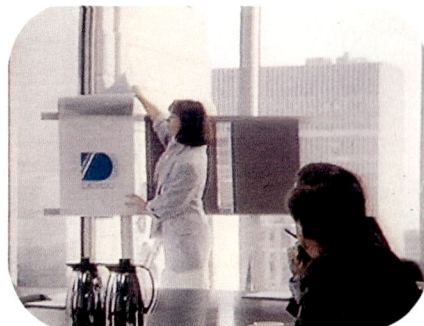 

ART DIRECTOR
Peter Hoppock
PRODUCER
Steve Citrin
DIRECTOR
Michael Grasso
WRITER
Jim Glover
CLIENT
United Airlines
AGENCY/STUDIO
Leo Burnett Company

"HER DAY"

(MUSIC UP. RHAPSODY THEME CONTINUES THROUGHOUT.)

(MUSIC DIPS.)

ANNCR VO: For half a century and more...

business travelers have depended on United Airlines...

to get them to their most important meetings.

United. Rededicated to giving you the service you deserve.

Come fly the friendly skies.

(MUSIC UP, ROUSING FINISH.)

"LOYAL FOLLOWING 1989"

...and their authorized Honda dealers than any other leading import.

Your...Honda Dealers. As dependable as the cars they sell.

ANNC (V.O.): Maybe the reason why so many people are loyal to their Hondas...

...is because their Hondas are so loyal to them.

That's why for 12 years, more people have gone back to Honda...

ART DIRECTOR
Kyle Lewis
PRODUCER
Carole Lockwood
DIRECTOR
Lee Livingston
WRITER
Felipe Bascope
PHOTOGRAPHER
Ernest Holzman
CLIENT
Southern California Honda Dealers Association
AGENCY/STUDIO
Robert Elen & Associates
PRODUCTION COMPANY
Livingston 5

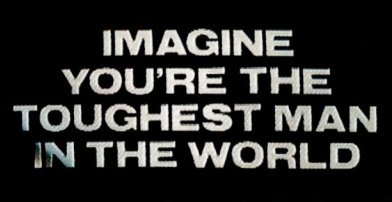

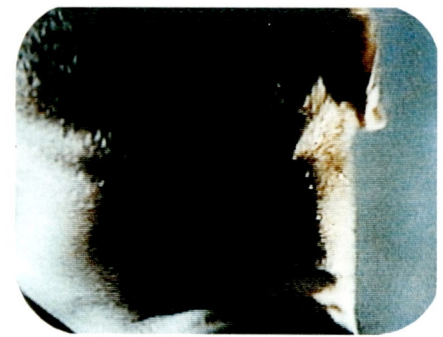

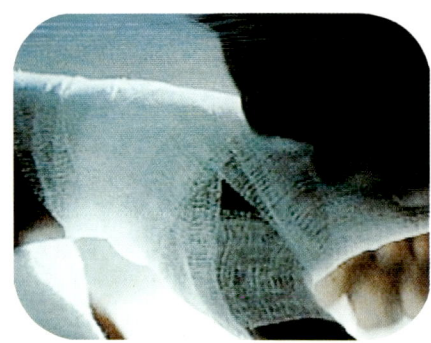

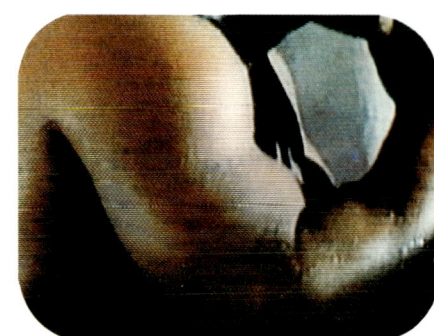

PRODUCER
Paul Fuentes
DIRECTOR
Paul Fuentes
WRITER
Paul Fuentes
PHOTOGRAPHER
(D.P.) Frost Wilkinson
MUSIC/EFX
Susan Israel/John
Wiggins
CLIENT
Home Box Office
AGENCY/STUDIO
Home Box Office On-Air
Promotion
*PRODUCTION
COMPANY*
HBO Studios: Peter
Consiglio, Editor

"MIKE TYSON BEST TIME ON TV

IMAGE SPOT #1"

ANNOUNCER VOICE OVER: "Imagine
you're the toughest man in the world"

"Your body the perfect machine"

"Your 20″ neck would shock absorb punches
from the 2nd toughest man in the world."

"Your legs could sustain the punishment of
going 12 heavyweight rounds."

"Your hands would be your instruments of
destruction."

"And your heart would be what drove you to
win 37 fights and lose none."

"None."

"Now imagine meeting the toughest man
in the world…"

(CHEERING) "And we have a new era in
boxing!"

'In the ring."

"HBO. The undisputed best time on TV."

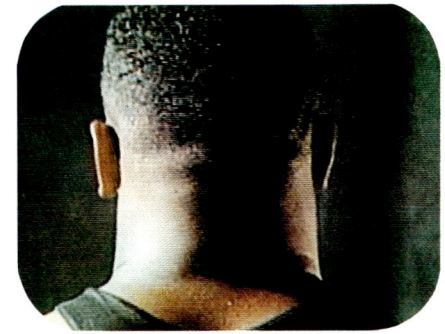
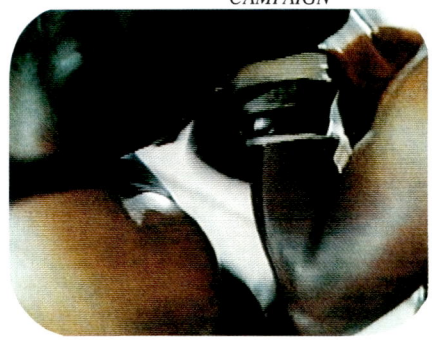
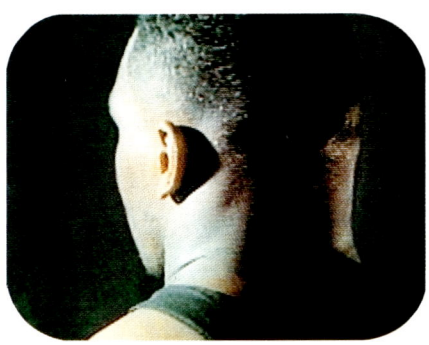

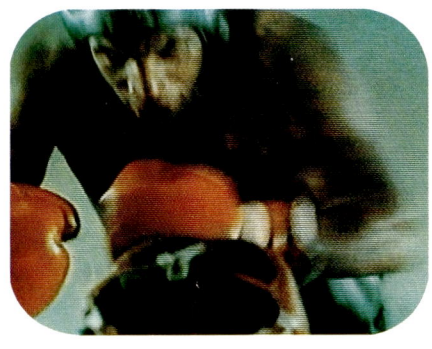

"MIKE TYSON BEST TIME ON TV

IMAGE SPOT #2"

ANNOUNCER: "Everyone has a talent."
"Some people can paint."
"Some people can sing."
"Some people can write short stories."
"Mike Tyson makes short stories out of some people."
"HBO. The undisputed best time on TV."

PRODUCER
Paul Fuentes
DIRECTOR
Paul Fuentes
WRITER
Paul Fuentes
PHOTOGRAPHER
(D.P.) Frost Wilkinson
MUSIC/EFX
Susan Israel/John Wiggins
CLIENT
Home Box Office
AGENCY/STUDIO
Home Box Office On-Air Promotion
PRODUCTION COMPANY
HBO Studios: Peter Consiglio, Editor

 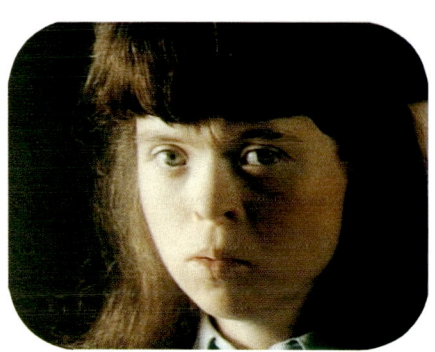

ART DIRECTOR
Herman Davis
DESIGNER
Herman Davis
PRODUCER
Ron Weber
DIRECTOR
Phil Marco
WRITER
Frankie Cadwell
PHOTOGRAPHER
Phil Marco
CLIENT
ARC
AGENCY/STUDIO
Cadwell Davis Partners (USA)
PRODUCTION COMPANY
Phil Marco

"CITIZEN"

If I move next door don't move away. I am
just like you, only slower.

She'd like a place of her own, where she
could cook, where she could invite friends
over.

ARC

The Association for Retarded Citizens. Don't
throw me away.

arc

Association for Retarded Citizens.

"GLASS SORTER"

SFX: Clear glass here. Green glass there. Brown glass there.

I sort glass. That's my job. I learned the job slow, and now I know it by heart.

He earns money. He pays taxes. He's just like you.

ARC

The Association for Retarded Citizens. Don't throw us away.

ART DIRECTOR
Herman Davis
DESIGNER
Herman Davis
PRODUCER
Ron Weber
DIRECTOR
Phil Marco
WRITER
Frankie Cadwell
PHOTOGRAPHER
Phil Marco
CLIENT
ARC
AGENCY/STUDIO
Cadwell Davis Partners (USA)
PRODUCTION COMPANY
Phil Marco

RADIO

PRODUCERS
Mike Bednarski/
Pat Pritchard
WRITERS
Mike Bednarski/
Pat Pritchard
CLIENT
WIS-PAK, INC.
AGENCY/STUDIO
Cramer-Krasselt/
Milwaukee
*PRODUCTION
COMPANY*
Outlaw Sound

PRODUCER
Shannon Silverman
WRITER
Doug Schumacher
CLIENT
GTE
AGENCY/STUDIO
DDB Needham Worldwide

"CAMPING"

SFX: (OUTDOOR SOUNDS)

WOMAN: Out here, roughing it in the wild… You can really get back to nature…

MAN: Honey, where's the remote?

WOMAN: Huh?

MAN: The remote.

WOMAN: Under the electric blanket…really!

MAN: I'm sorry, what were you saying?

WOMAN: I don't think you're getting into the spirit of this whole camping thing at all.

MAN: Nonsense. Just pass the cable listings.

WOMAN: There, do you see what I mean? You're impossible.

MAN: Look, I like nature as much as the next person. I just like mine in very small doses…so I can savor it.

WOMAN: Right, right, right.

MAN (DEFENDING HIMSELF) Hey, I'm the one who brought the Klarbrunn Sparkling Mineral Water. The Klarbrunn with no artificial ingredients, no calories, no caffeine? The Klarbrunn that's all natural, like the great outdoors?

WOMAN: You brought Klarbrunn? I didn't see it.

MAN: Sure it's in the portafridge, top shelf, behind the microwave popcorn.

WOMAN: Oh…

ANNCR: Discover the naturally refreshing taste of Klarbrunn Sparkling Mineral water. Also in natural orange, lemon or lime. In bottles or cans, look for Klarbrunn wherever fine sparkling mineral water is sold.

MAN: You know honey, I've decided I ought to give this camping a fair shot.

WOMAN: Finally.

MAN: What the heck, turn the dehumidifier down a notch, we'll rough it.

WOMAN: You're brave.

MAN: Did you unplug the campfire?

WOMAN: You're hopeless.

ANNCR: Discover Klarbrunn. The sparkling mineral water so pure and refreshing, it's a natural wonder.

"LAST NUMBER REDIAL" BLUES

LYRICS: There's this girl I was so sweet on Jolene,
every boy in town would chase her down know what I mean.

So when I called
just couldn't get through,

I'd dial and dial
didn't know what to do;
so, so much for my dream.

Then I got Last Number Redial
from GTE
that little busy signal no longer troubled me.

I hear that buzz
I wait a while
when I call back
don't have to redial;
and life, life is wonderful
to me.

"CAROL OF THE BELLS"

SFX: OPEN WITH MUSIC "CAROL OF THE BELLS" WITH PHONE SOUNDS DUBBED IN SOUNDTRACK INCLUDING PHONE RINGS AND TONES.

ANNCR: Where are the merriest bells coming from? Your GTE Phone Mart. Where they're ringing out a message of savings on phones and answer machines for everyone on your gift list. Like these wonderful, wacky, even quacky character phones. And advanced cordless models. You'll find other gifts. Like clock radios and desk organizers, at prices that won't take a toll on your budget. Trust your important gifts to your GTE Phone Mart. Where the best phones and answer machines are ringing up for less than you ever imagined.

TAG: Save up to $54 off gifts any executive would love now at your GTE Phone Mart. Offer valid while quantities last.

:10 TAG: From talking bears to boats, save up to $60 on phones kids six to sixty will cherish now at your GTE Phone Mart. Offer valid while quantities last.

:10 TAG: Save up to 35% off Holiday gifts for everyone in the family at your GTE Phone Mart. Offer valid while quantities last.

:10 TAG: Help friends and family stay close with answer machines and cordless phones now up to $40 off at your GTE Phone Mart. Offer valid while quantities last.

"SIDE BY SIDE TEST"

MUSIC UP AND UNDER

WOMAN: This is the first on-the-air, side-by-side test of delivered pizzas. It takes one husband...

MAN: That's me.

WOMAN: And one Domino's Pizza...

SFX: DOORBELL

MAN: Oh, hey...that's it.

WOMAN: And one competitor's delivered pizza.

MAN: That's not here yet.

WOMAN: Ok...well, what you do is you open the Domino's Pizza box and you see...

MAN: Ooh, I see steam.

WOMAN: Right, and when you look at the competitor's pizza you see...

MAN: I see that it's not here yet.

WOMAN: Right. Now the next part of this test is taking a piece of the Domino's Pizza...

MAN: (REACTING): That's hot!

WOMAN: And then a piece of the competitor's pizza.

MAN: You mean the one that's not here yet.

WOMAN: Yeah. Well, there you have it. See, you can have Domino's hot, fresh pizza delivered in 30 minutes or less guaranteed...

MAN: Yeah.

WOMAN: Or you can have some other pizza.

MAN: Ah, that's not here yet...

WOMAN: That's not here yet...

SINGERS AND MUSIC UP AND OUT

Limited Delivery Area

PRODUCER
Diane Hill
WRITER
Tom Rector
CLIENT
GTE Phone Mart
AGENCY/STUDIO
DDB Needham
Worldwide

RADIO

PRODUCER
Greg Bashaw
WRITER
Greg Bashaw
CLIENT
Domino's Pizza
AGENCY/STUDIO
Group 243
Incorporated
*PRODUCTION
COMPANY*
Outlaw Sound

RADIO

PRODUCER	*PRODUCER*
David Prince	Morty Baran
DIRECTORS	*WRITER*
Steve Kessler/Stewart	Luke Sullivan
Sloke	*CLIENT*
WRITERS	U S West
Steve Rabosky/Steve	*AGENCY/STUDIO*
Kessler	The Martin Agency
CLIENT	*PRODUCTION*
Mitsubishi Electronics	*COMPANY*
AGENCY/STUDIO	The Martin Agency
Chiat/Day/Mojo Inc.	
Advertising	
PRODUCTION	
COMPANY	
Steve Kessler Radio	
Productions	

"FOOLS/BIG SCREEN/Rev. 1"

SFX: INSIDE A MEETING HALL, CROWD MUMBLE AND MILLING. SOUND OF GAVEL POUNDING AS THE MEETING COMES TO ORDER.

WOMAN: Don't sit there. Don't sit there.

HEAD FOOL: This meeting of the Loyal Order of Fools will now come to order. First business, new members. State your name and why you qualify to be a fool.

BOB: Hi, I'm Bob, I lost money on an insider trading tip.

CROWD: Eh! Big deal. Who hasn't.

BOB: Yeah, but then I turned myself in.

HEAD FOOL: Next.

LOUISE: I'm Louise, I'm 27 and I went on a cruise to meet people my own age.

CROWD: So what.

HEAD FOOL: You're not a fool...you're just stupid! Next.

DAVE: Yeah, I'm Dave and I bought a big screen television and, uh, well, it wasn't a Mitsubishi.

HEAD FOOL: What a fool.

CROWD: (CHANTING) Fool, fool, fool, fool, fool...

HEAD FOOL: Accepted.

DAVE: Thank you, really.

HEAD FOOL: Unanimous!

DAVE: Oh, wow.

MUSIC: UNDER ANNOUNCER.

ANNCR: Mitsubishi big screen televisions have the clearest, brightest pictures of any big screen you can buy. We invented the world's first 35-inch direct-view TV, and our 60-inch model will turn your living room into a screening room. Mitsubishi big screen TV's. To buy anything else would be, well, foolish.

HEAD FOOL: Welcome to the Loyal Order of Fools. The dues are 10 million bucks.

DAVE: Uh, will you take a check?

HEAD FOOL: Sure.

MUSIC: BUTTON.

"PREFERRED CUSTOMER"

(OPEN ON SFX OF LARGE CROWD IN A STORE AMBIENCE. WE HEAR THE STORE ADDRESSING HIS CUSTOMERS OVER A MEGAPHONE.)

MANAGER: OK. Would all you customers please leave. Put your money away, thank you, and shop somewhere else. Frankly, we're very busy, so please, take your money and leave. Get those checkbooks, wallets and purses out of our store. Thank you. (FADES UNDER)

VO: With some slight exaggeration, this is basically what a busy signal sounds like to your best, most loyal customers.

MANAGER: We're very busy with other customers, so please shop at our competitors store. They're in the phone book. Just take your money over there please. (FADES UNDER)

VO: That's why U S WEST Communications urges small business owners to add an extra phone line dedicated only to your best customers. Big customers that have to get through.

MANAGER: Please go away, and thanks for trying to shop here. (FADES UNDER AND OUT)

VO: So if you own a small business, call U S WEST Communications and see how an extra phone line could improve your bottom line.

MUSICAL STING (:03 Version) & VO: U S WEST Communications.

"BUSY SIGNAL"

(TOUCHTONE DIALING SFX)
(BUSY SIGNAL SFX, WHICH CONTINUE THROUGHOUT SPOT)

MAN; Oh, hello. Is this Midwestern Computer Wholesalers? Yes? Well, I-I'd like to buy as many of your products as I could. Money is no object. I have oodles. Tons and tons of money actually. In fact, I'm standing on a brick-sized bundle of thousand-dollar bills right now. Yes, well anyway, I'd like to give you all this money. Ah-would-would it be convenient if I just ran by now and dropped off a million in cash. I'll just-you know, swing by…drop it off…won't take…

VO; U S WEST Communications would like to remind small business owners that no customer ever bought anything from a busy signal. And that maybe it's time you added that extra phone line to your business.

MAN: Well, would two million be of any bother? I realize it will take up quite a bit of space. Good, two million it is. Nice doing business with you. Goodbye. (BUSY SIGNAL SFX STOPS.)

VO: So if you own a small business, call U S WEST Communications and see how an extra phone line could improve your bottom line.

MUSICAL STING (:03 Version) & VO: U S WEST Communications.

"IRVING'S EARTHWORMS"

SFX: (PHONE RING/PICK UP.)

ESTELLE: Irving's Earthworms.

EDGAR: Estelle…Edgar. I need six gross for Betty's Bait Shack.

ESTELLS: You got it.

SFX: (PHONE CLICK/RING/PICK UP.)

ESTELLE: Iving's Earthworms.

EDGAR: Estelle…Edgar. I need four gross for Fred's Fish Farm.

ESTELLE: No sweat.

SFX: (PHONE CLICK/RING/PICK UP.)

ESTELLE: Irving's Earthworms.

EDGAR: Estelle…Edgar. I need eight gross for Tackle Town.

ESTELLE: Edgar…why don't you call these orders in all at once?

EDGAR: I'm afraid I'll get cut off.

ESTELLE: Are you calling on a GTE public phone?

EDGAR: Yeah.

ESTELLE: On a local call, you can talk as long as you want.

EDGAR: For 20 cents?!

ESTELLE: For 20 cents. You can even get free operator assistance, access to any long distance carrier, use a calling card and get refunds if you goof up.

EDGAR: All on a GTE phone?

ESTELLE: You got it.

EDGAR: Just think…I can travel all over, calling in orders from the really big bait shops…

ESTELLE: Edgar…

EDGAR: Carp 'N' Carry, Halibut Heaven…

ESTELLE: Edgar…

EDGAR: I could even call my mother… collect…

ANNCR: On the road and need to make a call? Look for a GTE public phone. We're keeping calling…simple.

EDGAR: There's only one problem in the meantime…

ESTELLE: What's that?

EDGAR: What am I gonna do with 600 dimes?

RADIO

PRODUCER
Morty Baran
WRITER
Luke Sullivan
CLIENT
U S West
AGENCY/STUDIO
The Martin Agency
PRODUCTION COMPANY
The Martin Agency

PRODUCER
Diane Hill
WRITER
Bert/Barz/Kirby
CLIENT
GTE
AGENCY/STUDIO
DDB Needham
Worldwide Inc.

RADIO

PRODUCER
Diane Hill
WRITER
Bert/Barz/Kirby
CLIENT
GTE
AGENCY/STUDIO
DDB Needham
Worldwide Inc.

"SPY BUSINESS"

SFX: (FOGHORNS, WATER LAPPING, ETC.)

AGENT: (WHISPERS) Psst, hey buddy.

GUY: Yeah?

AGENT: Is there a pay phone around here ?

GUY: You in the spy business?

AGENT: Shh! Yes! How'd you know?

GUY: The raincoat, floppy hat and the fogbank over your head.

AGENT: Oh…the phone?

GUY: Yeah, most of the spies do their business on that GTE public phone on the pier.

AGENT: (WALKING) I didn't know there was a pier in Pomona…

SFX: (PICKS UP PHONE.)

AGENT: Oh darn, I don't have change. (CALLING OFF TO GUY) Pardon me…?

GUY: (OFF) Don't need it, pal. Just press zero.

SFX: (DIALS ZERO)

OPERATOR: Operator. May I help you?

AGENT: I need to make a top secret call…

OPERATOR: Are you in the spy business?

AGENT: Sssh! Yes. I want to call another agent, I mean business associate, in Casablanca…

OPERATOR: You mean agent Double seven-oh, I have his number right here.

AGENT: What?

OPERATOR: Shall I put this on your Spy Calling Card?

ANNCR: When you need to make a business call, look for a GTE public phone. Use your calling card, or, on local calls, talk for as long as you want for just 20 cents. And best of all, with GTE, there's always free operator assistance.

SFX: (PHONE RINGING)

AGENT: (TO HIMSELF) Darn, I forgot the password.

OPERATOR: Higgledy-Piggledy.

AGENT: What?

OPERATOR: That's the password. Higgledy-Piggledy.

AGENT: Thanks, operator. Would you stay on the line? I may have to decipher a secret message.

OPERATOR: Anything for world peace, sir.

ANNCR: On the road and need to make a call? Look for a GTE public phone. We're keeping calling…simple.

"PFC PIZZA"

SFX: (STREET AMBIENCE)
GUY: 'Scuse me, about to use this phone?

MAN: Well, yes, but you first, soldier.

GUY: Soldier?

MAN: The fatigues, the helmet…

GUY: Oh. No, see I just started this company called "PFC Pizza."

MAN: PFC?

GUY: Pizza First Class. This is my very first pizza delivery and I can't find the address, so I have to make a call on this public phone.

MAN: what kind is it?

GUY: It's a GTE.

MAN: No, the pizza.

GUY: Pepperoni.

MAN: Pepperoni?

GUY: See, with the GTE public phone, local calls are only 20 cents and I can talk as long as I want.

MAN: I love pepperoni pizza.

GUY: And I get my money back if I get a wrong number or there's no answer.

MAN: Yes, well I'm with Amalgamated Corporate Acquisitions…

GUY: Oh, "A.C.A."!

MAN: And I have to call long distance to Rhode Island regarding an unfriendly takeover.

GUY: Who are you unfriendly guys taking over now?

MAN: Rhode Island. See, I use a GTE public pizza, uh, phone 'cause I get free operator services, directory assistance, access to any long distance carrier…

GUY: Well, you go first, your unfriendly call seems more important.

MAN: But your delicious-smelling pizza's getting cold.

GUY: I know.

MAN: I'll tell you what—I'll buy it! Here's a hundred dollars.

GUY: Wow! For a pizza?

MAN: And your company.

GUY: Boy, you're unfriendly.

ANNCR: On the road and need to make a call? Look for a GTE public phone. We're keeping calling…simple.

ERRATA

From ADLA 5

ART DIRECTOR
Robert Prins
DESIGNER
Robert Prins
WRITER
Peggy Boltz
PHOTOGRAPHER
Anne Mitchell
ILLUSTRATOR
Gary Baseman
PRODUCTION
Frank Nestler
CLIENT
Lucky Supermarkets/
Advantage Stores
AGENCY/STUDIO
Grey Advertising

design

ANNUAL REPORT
ART DIRECTOR
Kit Hinrichs
DESIGNERS
Kit Hinrichs/Terri Driscoll
WRITER
Delphine Hirasuna
PHOTOGRAPHER
Tom Tracy
ILLUSTRATOR
Will Nelson
CLIENT
Potlatch Corporation
AGENCY/STUDIO
Pentagram

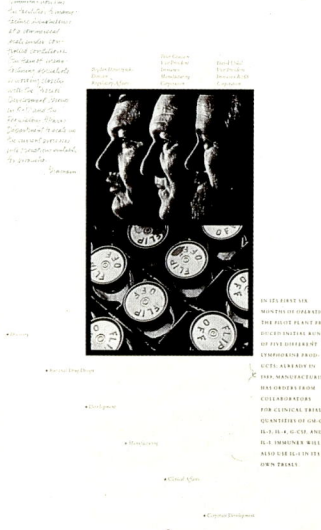

ART DIRECTOR
Kit Hinrichs
DESIGNERS
Kit Hinrichs/
Belle How
WRITER
Valoree Dowell
PHOTOGRAPHER
Steve Firebaugh
ILLUSTRATORS
Wilson McLean/
Jack Unruh/Ed
Lindlof/Doug Craig/
Dave Stevenson/
Doug Fraser
CLIENT
Immunex Corporation
AGENCY/STUDIO
Pentagram

ART DIRECTOR
Petrula Vrontikis
DESIGNERS
Petrula Vrontikis/Vivian
Cordova
WRITERS
Aileen Farnan Antonier/
Perry Grant
PHOTOGRAPHER
Jeff Corwin
CLIENT
The MacNeal-Schwendler
Corporation
AGENCY/STUDIO
Vrontikis/Cordova

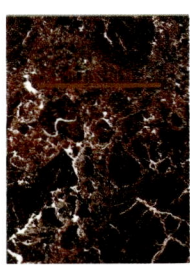

ANNUAL REPORT

ART DIRECTOR
Steve Ferrari
DESIGNER
Steve Ferrari
PHOTOGRAPHER
Terry Heffernan
CLIENT
Dillon Read & Co., Inc.
AGENCY/STUDIO
The Graphic Expression
New York

THE DAI-ICHI MUTUAL LIFE INSURANCE COMPANY

The Dai-Ichi Mutual Life Insurance Company, Japan's second largest insurance company, and LaSalle Partners, a privately held and widely respected national real estate service company, formed an equity relationship intermediated by Dillon Read. The affiliation of Dai-Ichi Mutual Life with a full-service real estate firm will provide better management of the existing portfolio and increased access to future investment opportunities.

In this assignment, we brought to bear our skills in corporate acquisitions and real estate. Dillon Read analyzed and valued LaSalle's three operating divisions: Asset Management, Services, and Development. We determined that the quality of LaSalle's management, its competitive position, and its earnings potential made it a very attractive investment.

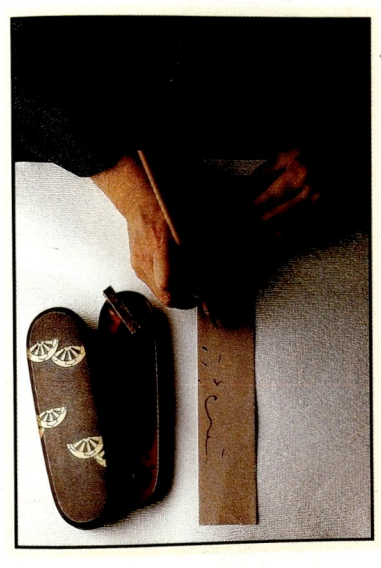

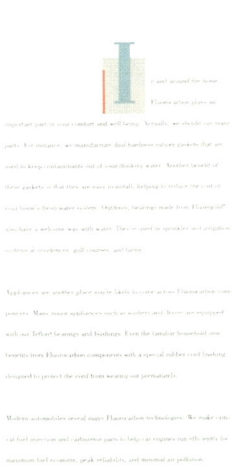

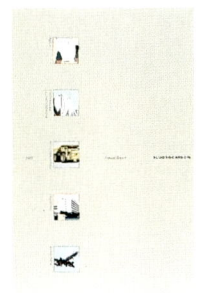

ART DIRECTOR
Ron Jefferies
DESIGNER
Susan Garland
PRODUCER
The Jefferies Association
DIRECTOR
Ron Jefferies
WRITER
Ron Bissell
ILLUSTRATOR
Dennis Mukai
CLIENT
Fluorocarbon Company
AGENCY/STUDIO
The Jefferies Associaion
PRODUCTION COMPANY
The Jefferies Association

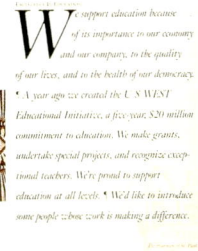

ART DIRECTOR
Kit Hinrichs
DESIGNERS
Kit Hinrichs/Sandra McHenry
WRITER
Theodore Couch
PHOTOGRAPHERS
John Blaustein/Jock McDonald
ILLUSTRATOR
Dave Stevenson
CLIENT
U S West
AGENCY/STUDIO
Pentagram

ANNUAL REPORT

ART DIRECTOR
Greg Samata
DESIGNER
Greg Samata
WRITER
Anne Sharp
PHOTOGRAPHER
Bob Tolchin
CLIENT
Kemper Reinsurance
AGENCY/STUDIO
Samata Associates

ART DIRECTOR
Pat Samata
DESIGNER
Pat and Greg Samata
WRITER
Kate Leatham
PHOTOGRAPHER
Bob Tolchin
ILLUSTRATOR
Cathie Bleck
CLIENT
Carson Pirie Scott
AGENCY/STUDIO
Samata Associates

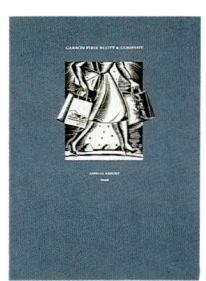

ART DIRECTOR
Jim Berté
DESIGNER
Jim Berté
PHOTOGRAPHER
Norman Mauskopf
CLIENT
Carter Hawley Hale
Stores, Inc.
AGENCY/STUDIO
Robert Miles Runyan &
Associates

ANNUAL REPORT
ART DIRECTOR
Greg Samata
DESIGNER
Greg Samata
WRITER
Lesnik
PHOTOGRAPHER
Jean Moss
CLIENT
Helene Curtis
AGENCY/STUDIO
Samata Associates

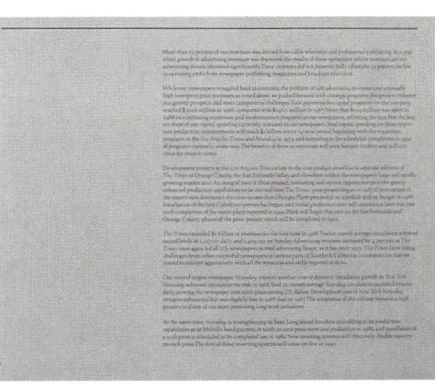

ART DIRECTOR
Jim Berté
DESIGNER
Jim Berté
WRITER
Bonnie Chaikind
ILLUSTRATOR
Paul Bice
CLIENT
The Times Mirror
Company
AGENCY/STUDIO
Robert Miles Runyan &
Associates

ART DIRECTOR
Jennifer Morla
DESIGNER
Jennifer Morla/Marianne
Mitten
WRITER
Leo Furman
PHOTOGRAPHER
Paul Franz-Moore
STYLIST
Sara Slavin
CLIENT
San Francisco Airports
Commission
AGENCY/STUDIO
Morla Design

ANNUAL REPORT

ART DIRECTOR
John Clark
DESIGNER
John Clark
WRITER
Vic Coccimiglio
PHOTOGRAPHER
William Coupon
CLIENT
McDonnell Douglas Finance
Corporation
AGENCY/STUDIO
Cross Associates

ART DIRECTOR
Barbara Vick
DESIGNER
Barbara Vick
WRITER
Linda Peterson
ILLUSTRATOR
Miro Salazar
CLIENT
Capital Guaranty
AGENCY/STUDIO
SBG Partners

ART DIRECTOR
Kit Hinrichs
DESIGNER
Kit Hinrichs
WRITER
Tiiu Lukk
PHOTOGRAPHERS
Michele Clement/
Terry Heffernan,
Jeff Corwin
ILLUSTRATORS
Vincent Perez/Justin
Carroll/Tim Lewis
CLIENT
National Medical
Enterprises
AGENCY/STUDIO
Pentagram

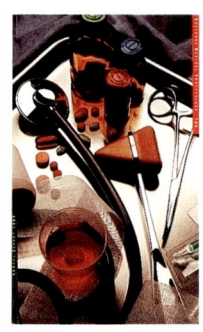

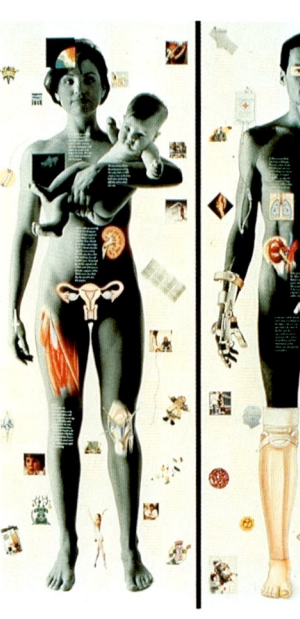

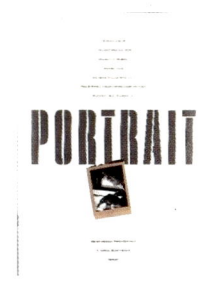

ANNUAL REPORT

ART DIRECTOR
John Van Dyke
DESIGNER
John Van Dyke
WRITER
Dan Koger
PHOTOGRAPHERS
Terry Heffernan - Still Life
Jeff Corwin - Portrait B&W
CLIENT
Weyerhaeuser Paper Company
AGENCY/STUDIO
Van Dyke Design Company
Seattle

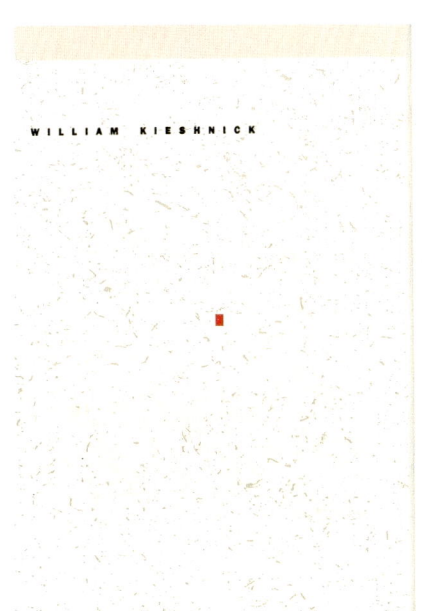

WILLIAM KIESHNICK

BROCHURE, FOLDER

ART DIRECTORS
Butler Kosh Brooks
DESIGNER
Carlos Chávez Córdova
PHOTOGRAPHER
Tom Zimberoff
CLIENT
Champion Papers
AGENCY/STUDIO
Butler Kosh Brooks

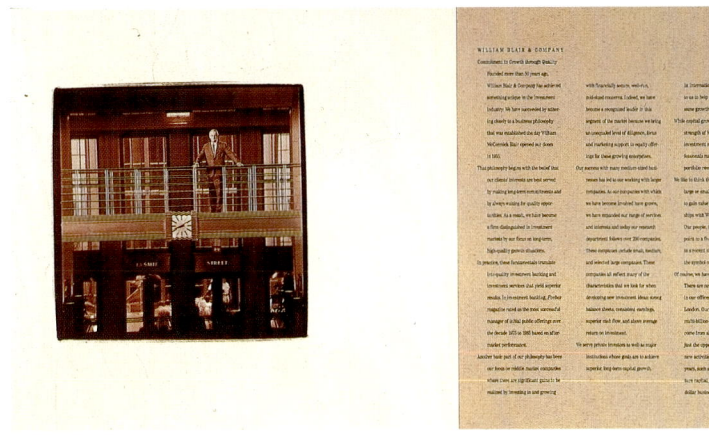

ART DIRECTOR
Andrew Brown
DESIGNERS
Andrew Brown/Kathy Keen
WRITERS
Hill and Knowlton, Inc.
PHOTOGRAPHER
Paul Elledge
CLIENT
William Blair & Company
AGENCY/STUDIO
Hill and Knowlton, Inc.

BROCHURE, FOLDER

ART DIRECTOR
Craig Frazier
DESIGNERS
Craig Frazier/Grant
Peterson
WRITER
Michael Wright
PHOTOGRAPHER
Jock McDonald
CLIENT
Agnes Bourne
AGENCY/STUDIO
Frazier Design

ART DIRECTOR
Linda Hinrichs
DESIGNERS
Linda Hinrichs/
Natalie Kitamura
PHOTOGRAPHERS
Cover:
Will Mosgrove/
Barry Robinson
Major:
George Hall/Don
Fukuda/Shmuel Thaler/
Nikolay Zurek
CLIENT
University of California,
Santa Cruz
AGENCY/STUDIO
Pentagram

DESIGNER
Gail Wiggin
WRITER
Charles Culp
PHOTOGRAPHER
Amos Chan
CLIENT
The Lexington
Corporation
AGENCY/STUDIO
Gail Wiggin Design

BROCHURE, FOLDER

DESIGNER
Rick Landesberg
WRITERS
Susan Russell/James C. Butler/
Henry Romney/Frank Wolling
PHOTOGRAPHER
Various
CLIENT
The Rockfeller Foundation
AGENCY/STUDIO
Landesberg Design Associates

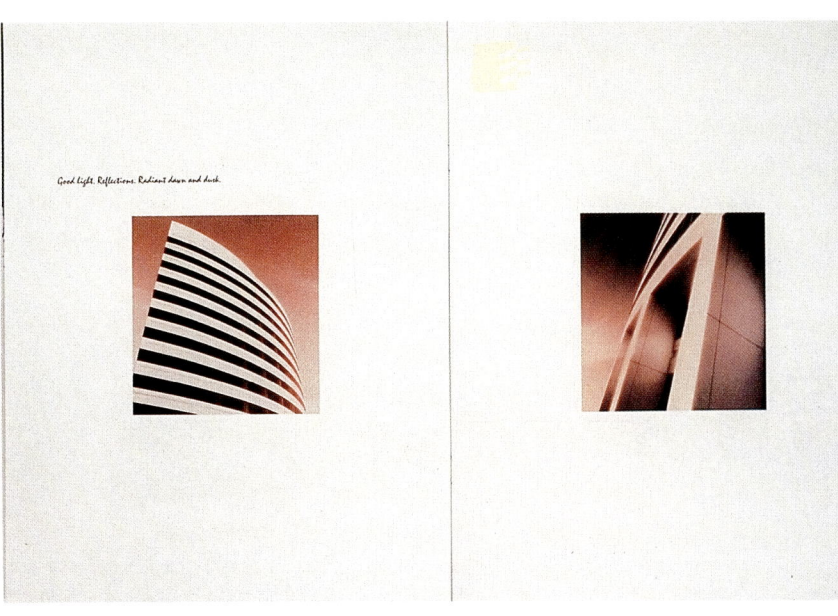

Good light. Reflections. Radiant dawn and dusk.

ART DIRECTOR
Bill Cahan
DESIGNER
Erik Adigard
WRITER
Bob Johnson
PHOTOGRAPHER
Jeffrey Newbury
ILLUSTRATOR
Erik Adigard
CLIENT
The Koll Company
AGENCY/STUDIO
Cahan & Associates

ART DIRECTOR
John Van Dyke
DESIGNER
John Van Dyke
CALLIGRAPHY
Georgia Deaver
WRITER
Jon Bell
PHOTOGRAPHER
Terry Heffernan
CLIENT
Mead
AGENCY/STUDIO
Van Dyke Design
Company, Seattle

BROCHURE, FOLDER

ART DIRECTOR
Butler Kosh Brooks
DESIGNER
Craig Butler
PHOTOGRAPHER
Tom Zimberoff
CLIENT
Champion Papers
AGENCY/STUDIO
Butler Kosh Brooks

GENE AUTRY
HOLLYWOOD, CALIFORNIA

ART DIRECTOR
James A. Stygar
DESIGNER
James A. Stygar
WRITER
Tina Laver
PHOTOGRAPHER
Various
CLIENT
American Wood Council
AGENCY/STUDIO
Stygar Group, Inc.

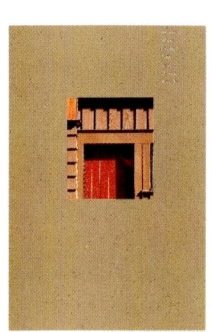

ART DIRECTOR
John Coy
DESIGNERS
John Coy/Sean Alatorre/
Richard Atkins
PHOTOGRAPHER
Bo Hylan
CLIENT
Lightolier
AGENCY/STUDIO
COY, Los Angeles

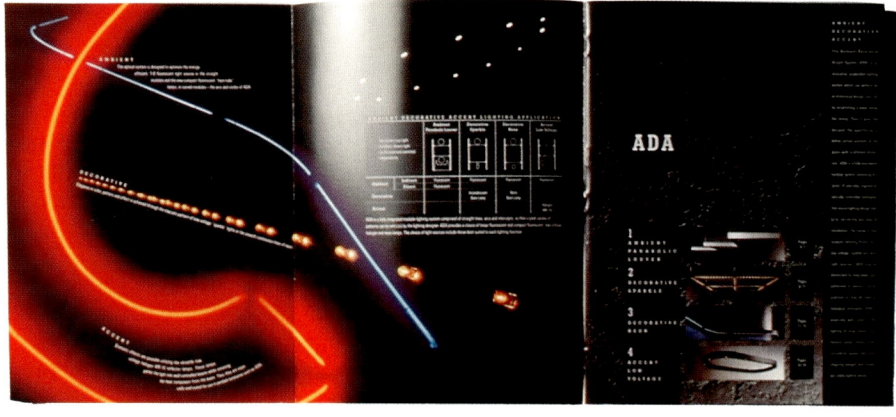

BROCHURE, FOLDER

ART DIRECTOR
James A. Stygar
DESIGNER
James A. Stygar
WRITER
Penelope H. Stygar
PHOTOGRAPHER
James A. Stygar
ILLUSTRATOR
Kristen Funkhouser
CLIENT
Parker Lancaster
Corporation
AGENCY/STUDIO
Stygar Group, Inc.

Walton Lake

ART DIRECTOR
James Sebastian
DESIGNERS
James Sebastian/
Junko Mayumi
PHOTOGRAPHER
Bruce Wolf
INTERIOR DESIGNER
William Walter
CLIENT
Martex/West Point
Pepperell
AGENCY/STUDIO
Designframe Inc.
— NYC

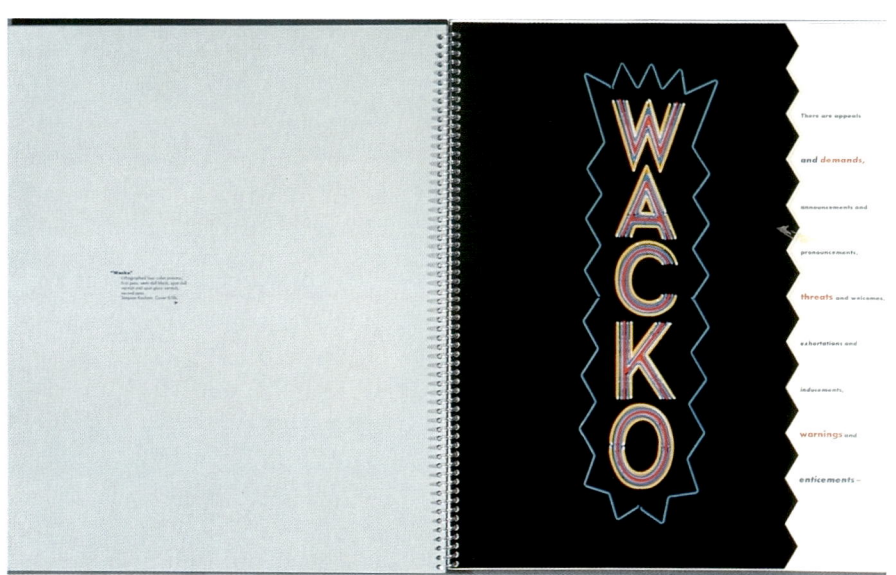

ART DIRECTOR
Ken Cook
DESIGNER
Ken Cook
WRITER
Delphine Hirasuna
PHOTOGRAPHER
Henrik Kam
ILLUSTRATORS
Steve Lyons/Sheldon
Greenburg
CLIENT
Simpson Paper
Company
AGENCY/STUDIO
Cross Associates

▲

BROCHURE, FOLDER

ART DIRECTOR
John Cleveland
DESIGNER
John Cleveland
WRITER
Rose Deneve
PHOTOGRAPHER
Peter Darley Miller
CLIENT
S. D. Warren Company
AGENCY/STUDIO
Bright & Associates
*PRODUCTION
COMPANY*
Bright & Associates

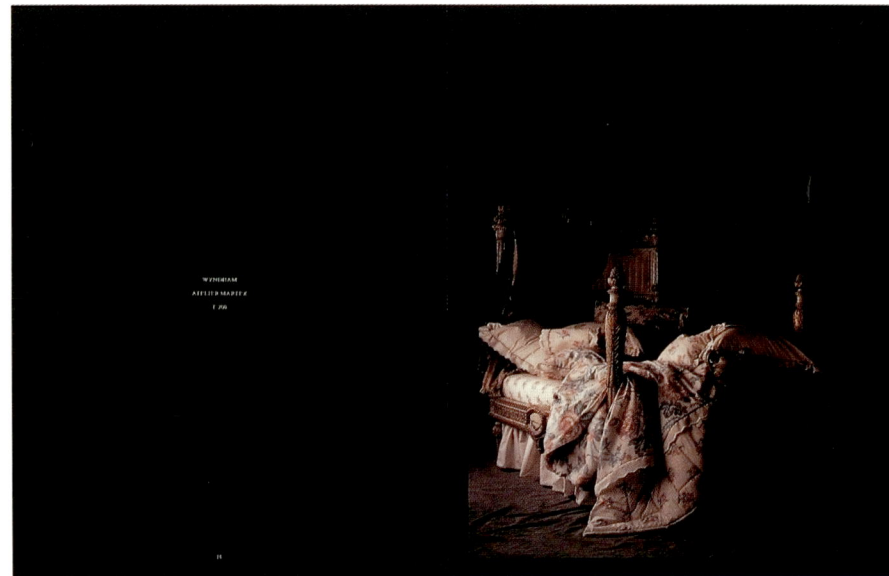

ART DIRECTOR
James Sebastian
DESIGNERS
James Sebastian/
Junko Mayumi
PHOTOGRAPHER
Bruce Wolf
INTERIOR DESIGNER
William Walter
CLIENT
Martex/West Point
 Pepperell
AGENCY/STUDIO
Designframe Inc. — NYC

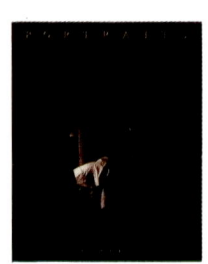

ART DIRECTOR
James Sebastian
DESIGNERS
James Sebastian/
Junko Mayumi
PHOTOGRAPHER
Bruce Wolf
INTERIOR DESIGNER
William Walter
CLIENT
Martex/West Point
Pepperell
AGENCY/STUDIO
Designframe Inc. — NYC

BROCHURE, FOLDER
CLIENT
Consolidated Paper
AGENCY/STUDIO
Wardrop Murtaugh Temple
Advertising

CLIENT
Consolidated Paper
AGENCY/STUDIO
Wardrop Murtaugh Temple
Advertising

ART DIRECTORS
Ron Kovach/
Kerry Grady
DESIGNERS
Ron Kovach/
Kerry Grady
WRITER
Wardrop Murtaugh
Temple, Inc.
PHOTOGRAPHER
Various
ILLUSTRATOR
Various
CLIENT
Consolidated Papers,
Company
AGENCY/STUDIO
Mobium Corporation
for Design and
Communication
*PRODUCTION
COMPANY*
The Hennegan
Company

BROCHURE, FOLDER
ART DIRECTOR
William Wondriska
DESIGNER
William Wondriska
WRITER
William Wondriska
PHOTOGRAPHER
Marc Sitkin
CLIENT
Cambridge Associates
AGENCY/STUDIO
Wondriska Associates, Inc.

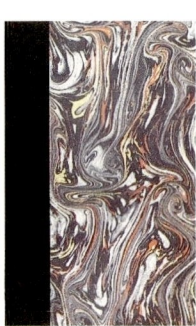

ART DIRECTOR
Jennifer Morla
DESIGNER
Jeanette Schraeder
WRITER
George Crys
PHOTOGRAPHER
Michael Lamotte
ILLUSTRATOR
John Mattos
CLIENT
Simpson Paper Co.
AGENCY/STUDIO
Morla Design

ART DIRECTOR
Jamie Davison
DESIGNERS
Jamie Davison, Rita Damore
WRITER
Lindsay Beaman
PHOTOGRAPHER
Henrik Kam
CLIENT
Triton Container International
Ltd.
AGENCY/STUDIO
Jamie Davison Design, Inc.

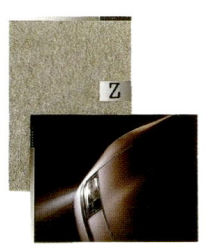

BROCHURE, FOLDER
ART DIRECTORS
Lynne Court/Paul
Ison/Lisa Langhoff
DESIGNER
Lynne Court
PRODUCTION
MANAGER
Christine Ferguson
WRITER
Tony Assenza
PHOTOGRAPHER
Bob Grigg
ILLUSTRATOR
Kevin Hulsey
CLIENT
Nissan Motor
Corporation in U.S.A.
AGENCY/STUDIO
The Designory, Inc.
PRINTER
Anderson Litho Co.

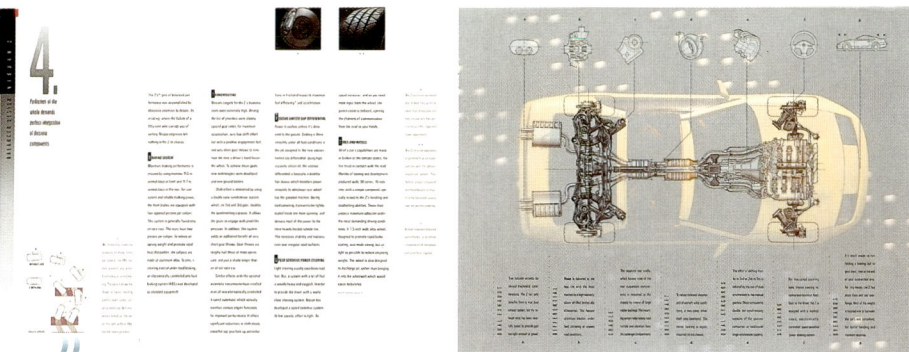

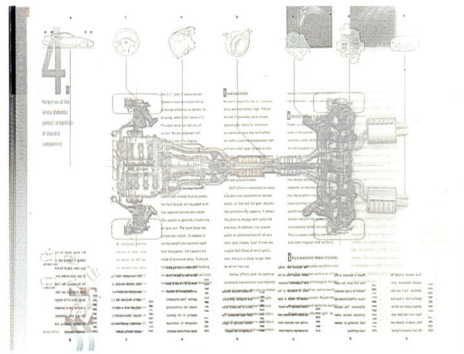

BROCHURE, FOLDER
ART DIRECTORS
David Edelstein/Lanny
French/Rick Jost/ Carol
Davidson
DESIGNERS
David Edelstein, Lanny
French/Rick Jost
WRITERS
David N. Meyer II/
Kathy Cain
PHOTOGRAPHER
Nick Vaccaro
CLIENT
Generra
AGENCY/STUDIO
Edelstein Associates
Advertising Inc.

ART DIRECTORS
David Edelstein/Lanny
French/Rick Jost/Carol
Davidson/Eric Haggard
DESIGNERS
David Edelstein/Lanny
French/Rick Jost/Carol
Davidson/Eric Haggard
WRITER
David N. Meyer II
PHOTOGRAPHERS
Veronica Simm/Barbara
Penoyar/Dan Langley
CLIENT
Generra
AGENCY/STUDIO
Edelstein Associates
Advertising Inc.
▲

BROCHURE, FOLDER
ART DIRECTORS
David Edelstein/Lanny
French/Rick Jost/Carol
Davidson/Eric Haggard
DESIGNERS
David Edelstein/Lanny
French/Rick Jost/Carol
Davidson/Eric Haggard
WRITER
David N. Meyer II
PHOTOGRAPHERS
Veronica Simm/Barbara
Penoyar/Dan Langley
CLIENT
Generra
AGENCY/STUDIO
Edelstein Associates
Advertising Inc.
▲

AMERICANA

COOL MIX

BROCHURE, FOLDER

ART DIRECTORS
David Edelstein/Nancy
Edelstein/Lanny French/
Rick Jost/Carol Davidson
DESIGNERS
David Edelstein/Lanny
French/Rick Jost/Carol
Davidson
PRODUCER
D. Thom Bissett
WRITER
Kathy Cain
PHOTOGRAPHER
Anthony Gordon
CLIENT
Generra
AGENCY/STUDIO
Edelstein Associates
Advertising

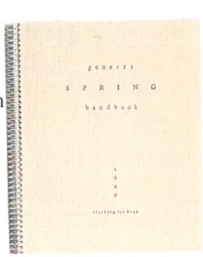

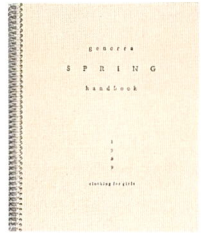

BROCHURE, FOLDER
ART DIRECTORS
David Edelstein/Nancy
Edelstein/Lanny French/
Rick Jost/Carol Davidson
DESIGNERS
David Edelstein/Lanny
French/Rick Jost/Carol
Davidson
PRODUCER
D. Thom Bissett
WRITER
Kathy Cain
PHOTOGRAPHER
Anthony Gordon
CLIENT
Generra
AGENCY/STUDIO
Edelstein Associates
Advertising

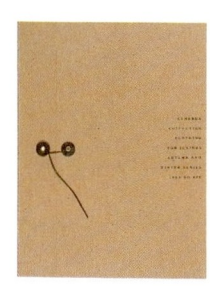

ART DIRECTORS
David Edelstein/Lanny
French/Rick Jost/Carol
Davidson
DESIGNERS
David Edelstein/Lanny
French/Rick Jost/
Carol Davidson
WRITERS
David N. Meyer II/
Kathy Cain
PHOTOGRAPHER
Nick Vaccaro
CLIENT
Generra
AGENCY/STUDIO
Edelstein Associates
Advertising Inc.
▲

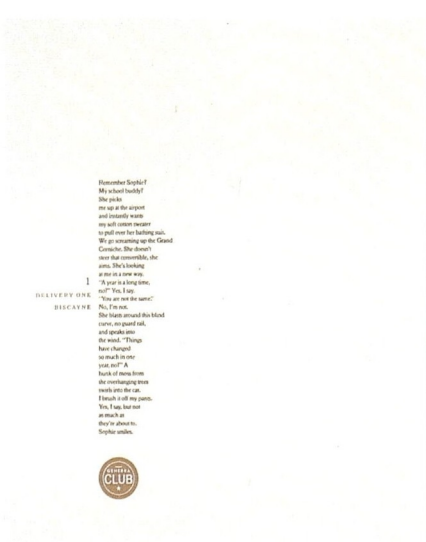

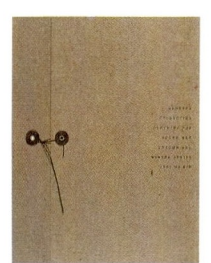

BROCHURE, FOLDER

ART DIRECTORS
David Edelstein/Lanny
French/Rick Jost/Carol
Davidson
DESIGNERS
David Edelstein/Lanny
French/Rick Jost/
Carol Davidson
WRITERS
David N. Meyer II/
Kathy Cain
PHOTOGRAPHER
Nick Vaccaro
CLIENT
Generra
AGENCY/STUDIO
Edelstein Associates
Advertising Inc.
▲

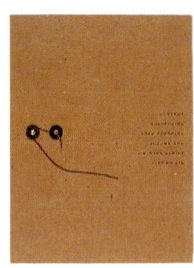

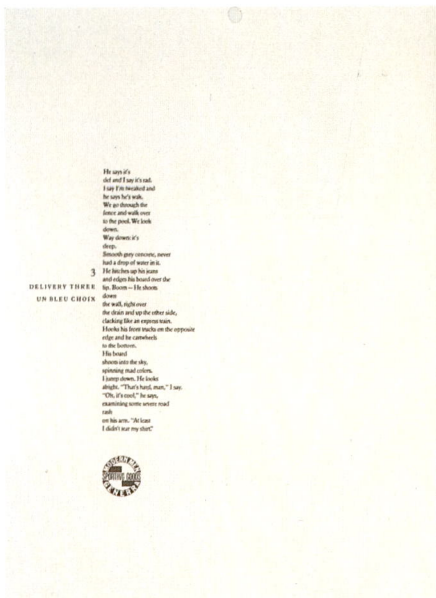

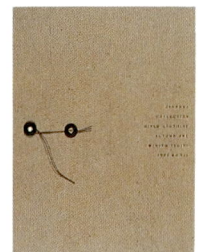

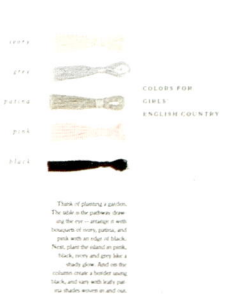

ART DIRECTOR
Douglas Oliver
DESIGNER
Douglas Oliver
WRITER
Margaret Burchett
PHOTOGRAPHER
Bill Varie
CLIENT
W. M. Keck Foundation
AGENCY/STUDIO
Morava & Oliver
Design Office

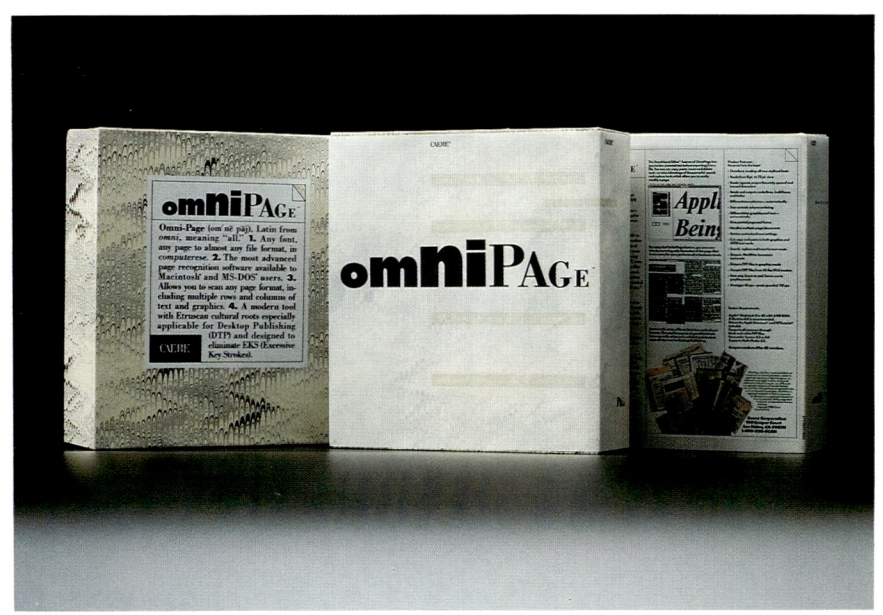

3-D PACKAGING

ART DIRECTOR
Clement Mok
DESIGNER
Charles Routhier
WRITER
Bill Cleary
CLIENT
Caere Corporation
AGENCY/STUDIO
Clement Mok Designs

ART DIRECTOR
Henry Vizcarra
DESIGNERS
Henry Vizcarra/
William Heusttis
CLIENT
Gorky's Cafe & Russian
Brewery
AGENCY/STUDIO
30Sixty Advertising &
Design, Los Angeles

ART DIRECTOR
Michael Brock
DESIGNER
Michael Brock/Gaylen Braun
WRITER
Robert Peak
CLIENT
Duggan's Ingrediants
AGENCY/STUDIO
Michael Brock Design

3-D PACKAGING
ART DIRECTOR
Maureen Erbe
DESIGNERS
Maureen Erbe/Holly
Caporale
CLIENT
Bentley Mills, Inc.
AGENCY/STUDIO
Maureen Erbe Design

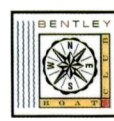

ART DIRECTOR
John Farrell
DESIGNER
Amy Racina
ILLUSTRATOR
John Farrell
CLIENT
Heublein Fine Wines
AGENCY/STUDIO
Colonna, Farrell:
Design Associates
PRODUCTION
COMPANY
F P Label (Printer)

ART DIRECTOR
Jack Anderson
DESIGNERS
Jack Anderson/
Mary Hermes
WRITER
Margy Tylczak
ILLUSTRATOR
Scott McDougall
CLIENT
Broadmoor Baker/
Paul Suzman
AGENCY/STUDIO
Hornall Anderson
Design Works

3-D PACKAGING

ART DIRECTOR
Mike Hicks
DESIGNER
Mike Hicks
WRITER
Mike Hicks
ILLUSTRATOR
Duana Gill
CLIENT
Mangia Pizza
AGENCY/STUDiO
HIXO, Inc.

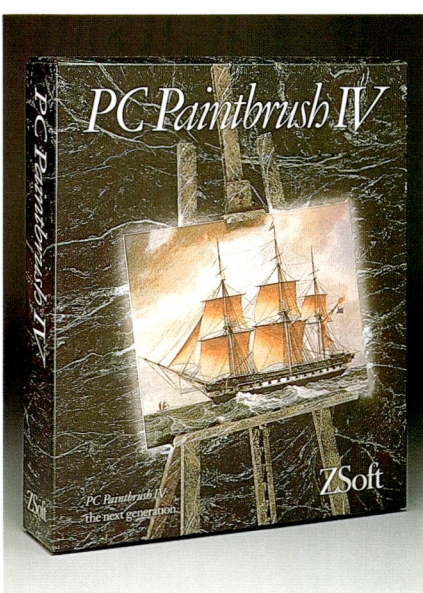

ART DIRECTOR
Paul Curtin
DESIGNERS
Paul Curtin/Ignatius
Tanzil/Peter Locke
ILLUSTRATORS
Ignatius Tanzil/
Paul Curtin
CLIENT
Cocolat
AGENCY/STUDIO
Paul Curtin Design

ART DIRECTOR
Marty Neumeier
DESIGNERS
Marty Neumeier/
Christopher Chu
CREATIVE DIRECTOR
Bob Schonfisch
WRITER
ZSoft/Mediagenic
PHOTOGRAPHER
Jack Gilderoy
CLIENT
ZSoft/Mediagenic
AGENCY/STUDIO
Neumeier Design Team

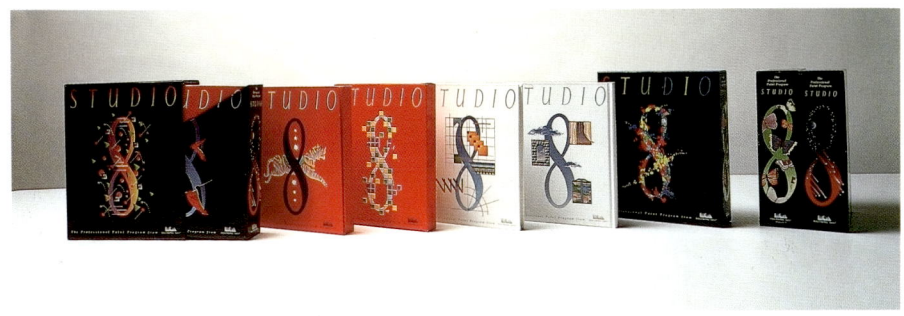

ART DIRECTOR
Michael Cronan
DESIGNER
Michael Cronan
ILLUSTRATORS
Michael Cronan/
Robert Schwarzbach
CLIENT
Electronic Arts
AGENCY/STUDIO
Cronan Design

3-D PACKAGING

ART DIRECTOR
Elizabeth Henry Shubert
DESIGNER
Elizabeth Henry Shubert
CLIENT
A Small, Small World
AGENCY/STUDIO
Shubert/Henry Design Studio

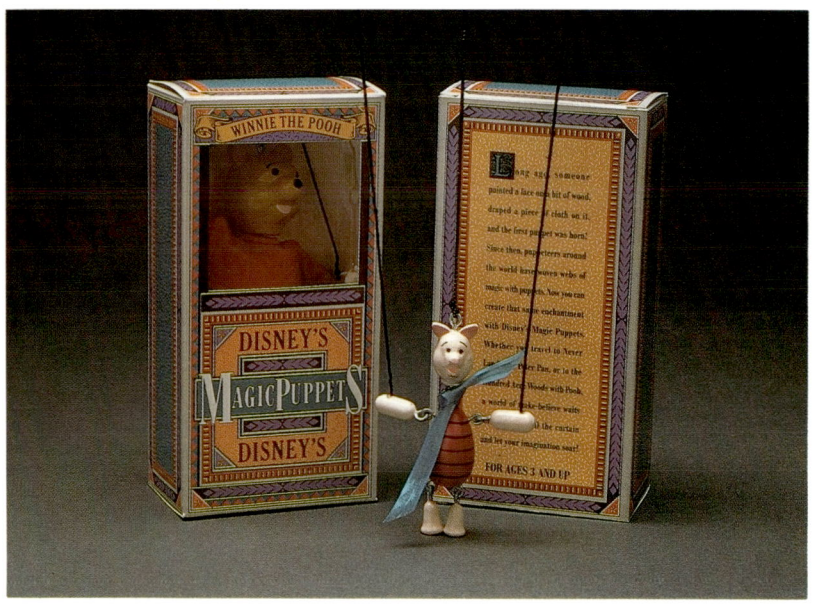

ART DIRECTOR
John Hornall
DESIGNERS
John Hornall/Jani Drewfs/
Mary Hermes
PHOTOGRAPHER
Kevin Latona/Sylvia South
CLIENT
Chateau Ste. Michelle
AGENCY/STUDIO
Hornall Anderson Design
Works

3-D PACKAGING

ART DIRECTOR
Kathleen Forsythe
DESIGNERS
Kathleen Forsythe/Cindy
Ryan/Greg Galvan
CLIENT
Bitstream, Inc.
AGENCY/STUDIO
Forsythe Design

ART DIRECTOR
Jack Anderson
DESIGNERS
Jack Anderson/Cliff
Chung/David Bates
WRITER
Dory Toft
ILLUSTRATORS
Bruce Hale/
David Bates
CLIENT
Northwest Building
Corporation
AGENCY/STUDIO
Hornall Anderson
Design Works

POINT OF PURCHASE, DISPLAY

ART DIRECTORS
Shelly Beck, Jann Church
DESIGNERS
Shelly Beck, Jann Church
PHOTOGRAPHER
Clifford Lester
CLIENT
Mount Palomar Winery
AGENCY/STUDIO
Jann Church Partners
Advertising & Graphic
Design

ART DIRECTOR
John Swieter
DESIGNER
John Swieter/
Jim Vogel
ENGINEERS
Dave Bodderman/
Tony Petrelli
CLIENT
Supre, Inc.
AGENCY/STUDIO
Swieter Design
PRODUCTION
COMPANY
Packaging Corporation
of America

ART DIRECTOR
Glenn Peltz
DESIGNER
Tim Bogardus
ILLUSTRATOR
Lisa Henderling
CLIENT
Mark Irby, Publix Super
Markets, Inc.
AGENCY/STUDIO
Impact Design

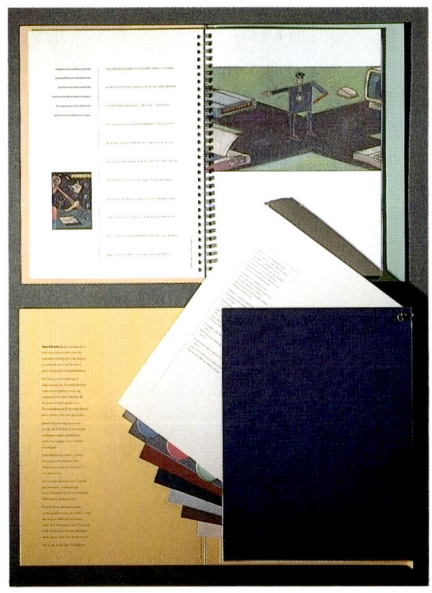

SALES KIT, PRESS KIT

ART DIRECTOR
Rex Peteet
DESIGNERS
Rex Peteet/Judy Dolim
WRITERS
Mary Keck/Rex Peteet
PHOTOGRAPHERS
Stuart Cohen/Dan
Nelken/Richard Reens/
Elle Schuster/Ron Scott
ILLUSTRATORS
Stephen Alcorn/David
Beck/John Craig/
Andrzej Dudzinski/Brad
Holland/James McMullan/
Rex Peteet
CLIENT
James River Corporation
AGENCY/STUDIO
Sibley/Peteet Design
PRODUCTION
COMPANY
Heritage Press/Dallas

ART DIRECTOR
Robert Cipriani
DESIGNER
Robert Cipriani
WRITER
Jim Bailey
PHOTOGRAPHERS
Clint Clemens/John
Goodman/Al Fisher
CLIENT
Thinking Machines
Corporation
AGENCY/STUDIO
Cipriani Kremer
Design Group
PRODUCTION
COMPANY
Acme Printing
Company

ART DIRECTORS
James Sebastian/
John Plunkett
DESIGNERS
James Sebastian/John
Plunkett/Frank Nichols
WRITER
Author- Ralph Stanziola
Copywriter- Francis Piderit
CLIENT
Colorcurve Systems, Inc.
AGENCY/STUDIO
Designframe Inc. – NYC

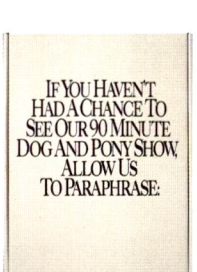

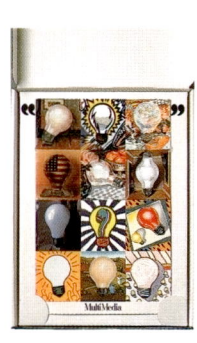

ART DIRECTOR
Jean Robaire
DESIGNER
Jean Robaire
WRITER
John Stein
PHOTOGRAPHER
Paul Gersten
ILLUSTRATORS
David McMaken/Ken Perkins
CLIENT
MultiMedia Group, Inc.,
Los Angeles
AGENCY/STUDIO
Stein Robaire Helm

HOUSE ORGAN,
NEWSLETTER

ART DIRECTOR
Kit Hinrichs
DESIGNERS
Kit Hinrichs/Terri
Driscoll/Lenore Bartz
WRITERS
Stuart Frolick/Karen
Jacobson/Kathy
Cochran/Jean K. Parry
PHOTOGRAPHERS
Jim Miho/Noritoyo
Nakamoto/Steven Heller/
Jim Blakeley/Richard
Eskite/Henrik Kam
ILLUSTRATORS
John Hersey/Nina
Novins/John Cuneo
CLIENT
Art Center College of
Design
AGENCY/STUDIO
Pentagram
▲

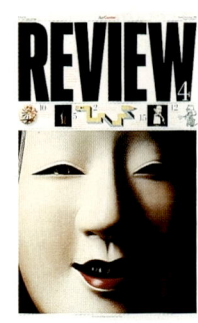

ART DIRECTOR
Kit Hinrichs
DESIGNERS
Kit Hinrichs/
Terri Driscoll
PHOTO
ILLUSTRATION
Dennis Potokar
WRITERS
Jean Keefe Parry/
Karen Jacobson/
Stephen Nowlin
PHOTOGRAPHER
Steven A. Heller
Cover & Principal
ILLUSTRATORS
Ron Impas/John
Mattos/Nicholas
Wilton
CLIENT
Art Center College
of Design
AGENCY/STUDIO
Pentagram
▲

ART DIRECTOR
Kent Hunter
DESIGNERS
Kent Hunter/Kin Yuen
WRITER
MCI Communications
PHOTOGRAPHERS
Mark Jenkinson/
Stuart Watson
ILLUSTRATORS
Phillipe Weisbecker/Gene
Greif/Jose Ortega
CLIENT
MCI Communications
AGENCY/STUDIO
Frankfurt Gips Balkind

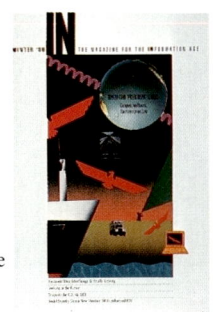

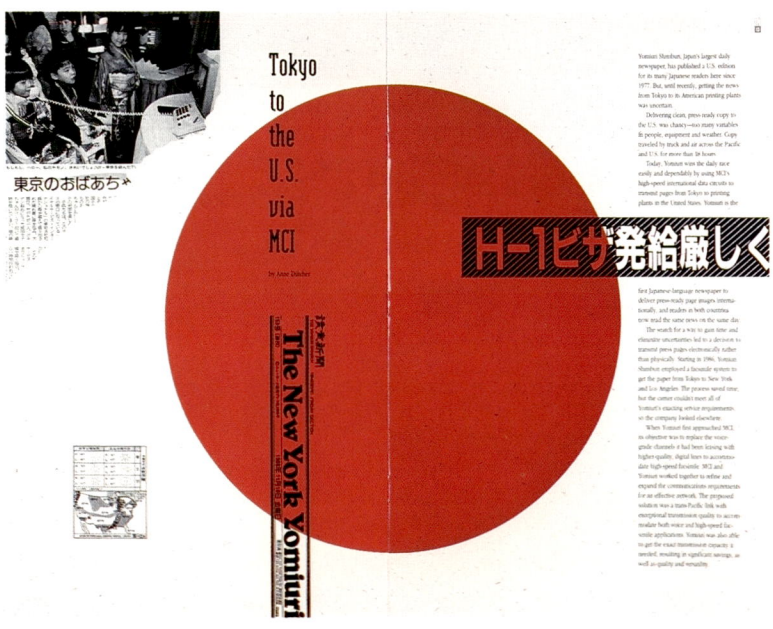

Tall palm trees swaying in warm, tropical breezes. Pink sand beaches blending into crystal clear water. Fragrances of honeysuckle and oleander filling the air. Sound like a typical British colony? The bright and beautiful islands of Bermuda are hardly typical. But, dour chaps, they do, in fact, compose the oldest British colony in the world.

Despite the allure of Bermuda, its first visitors weren't there by choice. The British vessel *Sea Venture* shipwrecked on Bermuda in 1609, and its 150 passengers washed onto an exquisite setting.

Today, Bermuda beckons visitors – sans treacherous landings – to explore its intrigue, romance

Humble Beginnings

The island was uninhabited when the *Sea Venture*'s passengers, led by Sir George Somers, were shipwrecked off what is now St. Catherine's Beach in 1609. After spending nearly a year on Bermuda, the castaways set sail for their original destination of Jamestown, Virginia.

Upon arrival at Jamestown, Sir George arrived to find the inhabitants there sick and starving. He decided to return to Bermuda for more food, and there he died of exhaustion. His nephew, Matthew Somers, buried his heart at Sir George near their original 1609 landing site and carried the corpse back to England.

Swashbuckling stories of "Somers's Island" spread through London like wildfire, and letters of adventure about the alluring island quickly circulated. One fascinated reader – William Shakespeare – even based his play *The Tempest* on the tales.

High Society at Sea Level

The British seized the royal opportunities Bermuda had to offer, including a chance for the well-heeled to settle on the island. In 1883, Princess Louise, daughter of Queen Victoria, came to Bermuda to escape the wintry climate of Canada, where her husband was the governor-general.

Now the Crown Colony had its very own princess. And not coincidentally, the colony soon began its first hotel – the Princess Hotel – in Hamilton. Catering to the rich and famous of the era, the hotel provided the finest amenities and drew many tourists.

Thus began a trend that lasted until World

Governor Sir John Henry Lefroy launched Bermuda tourism in 1872 with the start of steamship service to New York.

BERMUDA

Clipper Ship Surrounded by welcoming blue ocean and sturdy red cedar, and infused with the maritime blood of the British, early Bermudians became acclaimed shipbuilders – and occasional pirates.

and dashing good looks that have been further enhanced through three centuries of British influence.

War II. During the winter, those who could afford it came to Bermuda for "the season," with their maids, steamer trunks and the latest in fashions.

A tropical version of British aristocracy bloomed, replete with horse-drawn carriages, high tea and croquet. Far from the white cliffs of Dover, the blue Caribbean served as a backdrop for Bermuda's winter residents.

Tennis found a loyal following. A century before British court champion Virginia Wade won her Wimbledon title, the island hosted the Western Hemisphere's first tennis tournament.

Other local sports that reflect British traditions include sailing, soccer and cricket. So popular is cricket, in fact, that every year the Cup Match between the island's two cricket teams is deemed an official holiday.

Naturally, the Princess Hotel could not accommodate everyone who flocked to Bermuda. Larger and newer hotels sprang up around the island, and with them, fine tennis courts and golf courses.

Many a good tale starts over the dinner table. In the late 18th century, writer James Boswell reported to his friend Samuel Johnson that he had dined with Captain James Cook upon Cook's return from his second epic voyage. "While I was with the captain," said Boswell, "I catched (sic) the enthusiasm of curiosity and adventure, and felt a strong inclination to go with him on his next voyage."

Ah, Boswell – you are not alone. Today, hundreds of years after Cook, the Pacific explorers who went before and after him are gone, rereading their adventures and first impressions can relive even the most jaded of travelers to look up from the dinner table and think about ships at sea and beautiful Pacific islands.

An Era of Discovery

The year was 1606. In England, Guy Fawkes and his co-conspirators were sentenced to death for their attempts against the throne. William Shakespeare was finishing up his tribute to larger-than-life lovers Antony and Cleopatra; Ben Jonson had just completed his study in human greed, *Volpone*; and the Virginia Company of London sent 120 colonists to Virginia.

Meanwhile, on the other side of the world, while the English explored the mysteries of the human soul, the Spanish and Portuguese were engaging in a more political form of exploration. Pedro Fernandez de Quiros, a Portuguese employed by Spain, was at sail in the South Seas in search of *Terra Australis Incognita*, a fabled Southern continent.

De Quiros's journey took him near the coast of Australia and New Guinea, but he did not land. Later that year, another Portuguese mariner, Luis Vaez de Torres, navigated the strait between New Guinea and Australia. The strait now bears his name, but though de Torres surely sighted Australia, he never approached the shore.

These expeditions, like those led by other explorers – Cook, Bligh, Bougainville, Wallis – were part of a European obsession with "discovery" of lands and navigational routes that would yield gold, spices and other riches.

In the years that followed, many of Europe's most intrepid explorers set out to the Pacific to claim land for the flag they were flying, to chronicle people, flora, fauna, and sadly, sometimes to plunder and murder their way ashore.

When the Parisian boulevardier Louis Antoine de

Bougainville landed in Tahiti in 1768, he was persuaded he had been dropped into the middle of the Garden of Eden. He was a romantic and a classicist as well as a mathematician, this explorer who had already experienced the more sophisticated pleasures of Paris, so he named the island New Cythera in honor of the place Aphrodite had been born.

The English explorer Samuel Wallis had called at Tahiti a year before, and delivered favorable reports. But Bougainville and his men were dumbstruck. He wrote, "The coast rises like an amphitheater, and the mountains are of considerable height. We could hardly believe our eyes when we saw a peak clothed with trees right up to its solitary summit. At a distance it may have been taken for a pyramid of immense height that the hand of an able sculptor had adorned with garlands and foliage. The less elevated lands are interspersed with meadows and little woods, and all along the coast there runs a piece of low, level land covered with plantations. We saw the houses of the islanders amid banana and coconut trees, and our eyes were struck with the sight of a beautiful cascade that came from high in the mountains and poured its foaming waters into the sea."

As if the beauty of landscape weren't enough, Bougainville's crew had further delights in store. The islanders' hospitality extended to food, drink, and the offer of more sensual pleasures from young women.

Together, the Tahitians and Bougainville's crew agreed upon a system of barter – nails, tools and buttons for luscious native fruit. When Bougainville sailed away, he left a legacy of a French country larder-to-be – a garden of oats, rice, corn, barley and onions.

With few exceptions, in fact, the first impressions that the Europeans took away from their South Seas landings were positive – of lush and beautiful scenery, abundant food, open and pleasant natives willing to share with the intruders from the sea.

In The Beginning

The anthropologists suggest that the islands of the South Pacific were probably settled about 1500 years ago by Asians. These earliest explorers, traveling across Micronesia, ventured the South Seas, navigating to and between islands. We don't know what they sought, but guided by

First IMPRESSIONS

European explorers came home from the South Seas with precious cargo – journals rich with their adventures, memories and first impressions.

Only the most abundant tree on Hawaii, can be found as miniatures or dwarf ong-hap(u) tree-ferns in a drier austere, The live goddess Pele supposedly causes seedlings when the tree is luffed blossoms are picked.

HOUSE ORGAN, NEWSLETTER

ART DIRECTOR
Kit Hinrichs
DESIGNERS
Kit Hinrichs/Sandra McHenry
WRITER
Petersen, Skolnick & Dodge
PHOTOGRAPHER
Various Stock
ILLUSTRATORS
Melissa Grimes/Jack Unruh
Calighraphy
Georgia Deaver
CLIENT
Royal Viking Line
AGENCY/STUDIO
Pentagram

ART DIRECTOR
Kit Hinrichs
DESIGNERS
Kit Hinrichs/Sandra McHenry
WRITER
George Cruys
PHOTOGRAPHER
Barry Robinson - Major
Will Mosgrove - Cover
ILLUSTRATORS
Steven Guarnaccia/
Daniel Pelavin
CLIENT
Royal Viking Line
AGENCY/STUDIO
Pentagram

POSTER

DESIGNER
April Greiman
WRITER
Hans Puttnes
CLIENT
Vitra, Int'l
AGENCY/STUDIO
April Greiman, Inc.

▲

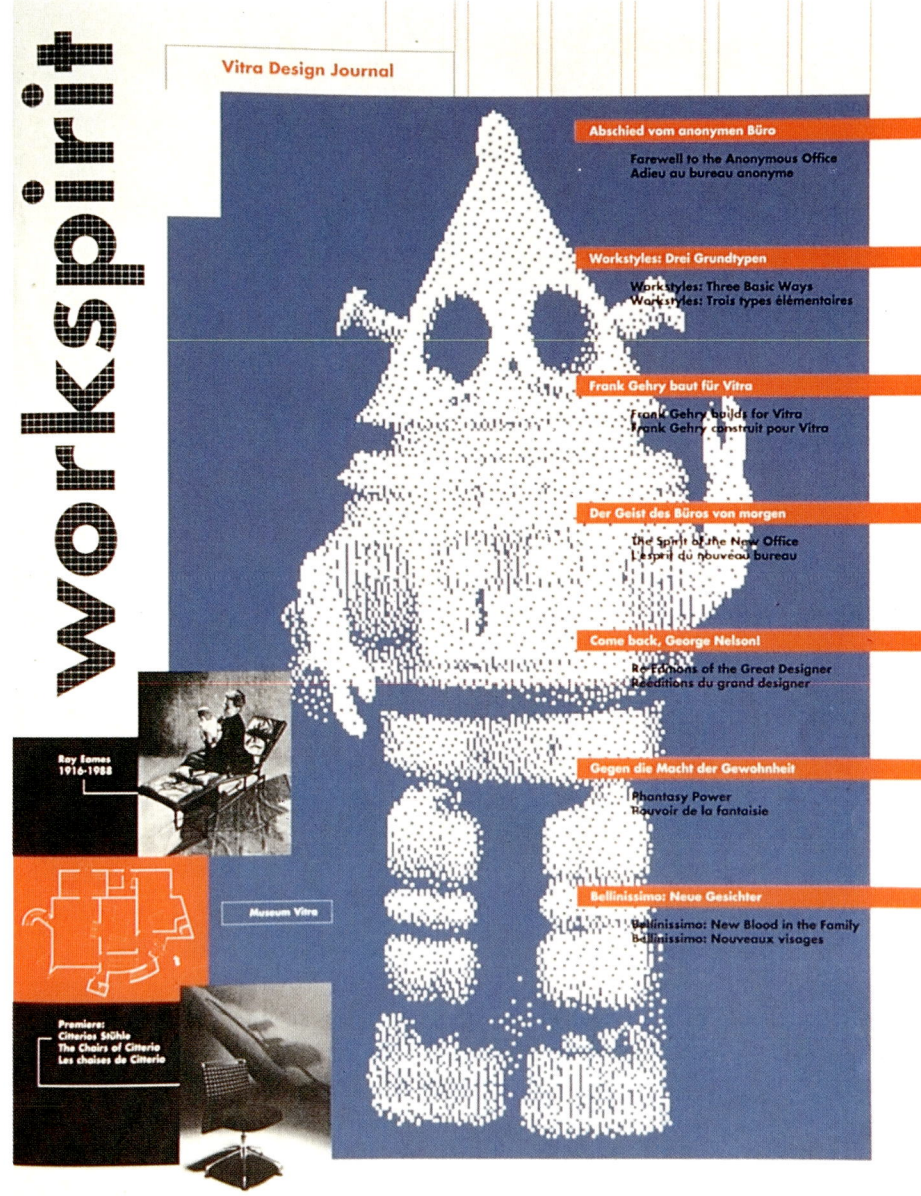

Too much fun isn't always a pretty picture. Party safe.

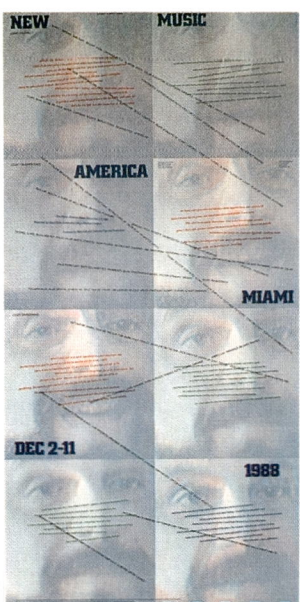

POSTER

ART DIRECTOR
Craig Frazier
DESIGNER
Craig Frazier
WRITER
Craig Frazier
ILLUSTRATOR
Craig Frazier
CLIENT
Friday Night Live/Marin
Public School System
AGENCY/STUDIO
Frazier Design

ART DIRECTOR
Robert Appleton
DESIGNER
Robert Appleton
PRINTER
Bayside Publishing
Corporation
TYPOGRAPHER
Typographic House
WRITERS
Robert Appleton/Robert
Ashley/John Cage/
Russell Frehling/Robert
Irwin/Leroy Jenkins/Joan
LaBarbara/Richard
Landry/Pauline Oliveros
PHOTOGRAPHERS
Phil Niblock and
Robert Appleton
CLIENT
Tigertail Productions/
New Music America
AGENCY/STUDIO
Appleton Design Inc.

ART DIRECTOR
Gerald Reis
DESIGNER
Gerald Reis
ARTIST
John Malmquist
CLIENT
California College of Arts
& Crafts
AGENCY/STUDIO
Gerald Reis & Company

▲

POSTER

ART DIRECTOR
Steve Curry
DESIGNER
Steve Curry
PHOTOGRAPHER
Mark Scott
CLIENT
Graphic Magic
AGENCY/STUDIO
Curry Design

DESIGNER
Ken Eskenazi
ILLUSTRATOR
Tsuruya Kokei
CLIENT
Pacific Asia Museum
AGENCY/STUDIO
Kaiser McEuen Inc.

ART DIRECTOR
Silas Rhodes
DESIGNER
Tony Palladino
ILLUSTRATOR
Tony Palladino
CLIENT
School of Visual Arts

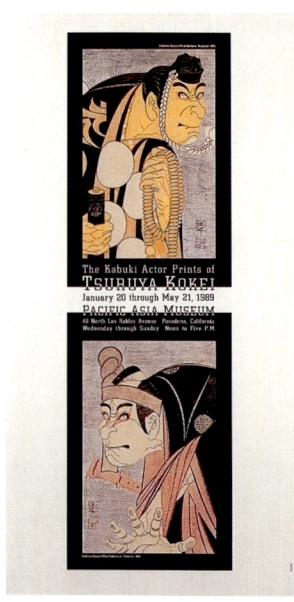

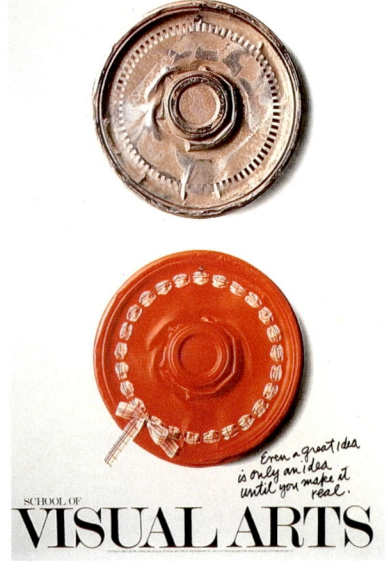

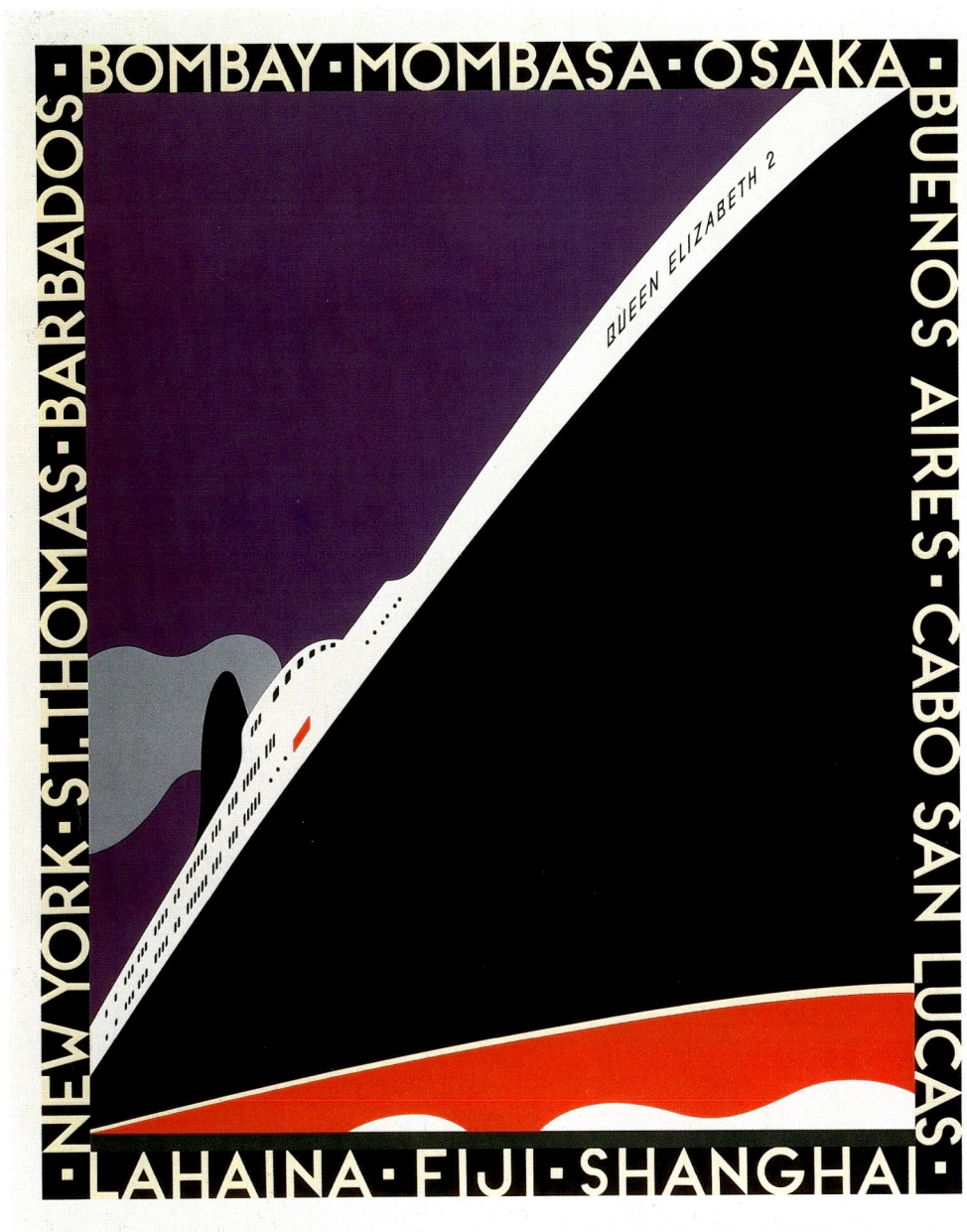

POSTER
ART DIRECTOR
Michael Schwab
DESIGNER
Michael Schwab
PRODUCER
Bella Blue
ILLUSTRATOR
Michael Schwab
CLIENT
QE2
AGENCY/STUDIO
Michael Schwab Design

ART DIRECTOR
InJu Sturgeon
DESIGNER
Woody Pirtle/
Pentagram Design
CLIENT
University of California
at Los Angeles
AGENCY/STUDIO
UCLA Extension

ART DIRECTOR
Karen Boone
DESIGNER
Kit Hinrichs
PHOTOGRAPHER
Terry Heffernan
CLIENT
Square One Restaurant
AGENCY/STUDIO
Pentagram

POSTER

ART DIRECTOR
Neil Shakery
DESIGNER
Neil Shakery
CLIENT
Pentagram
AGENCY/STUDIO
Pentagram

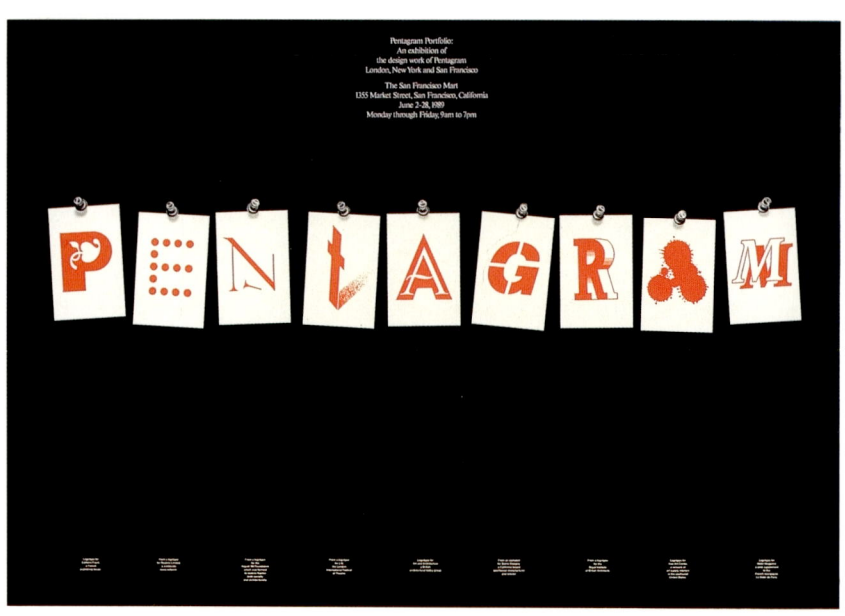

ART DIRECTOR
Jennifer Morla
DESIGNERS
Jennifer Morla/
Marianne Mitten
ILLUSTRATORS
Jennifer Morla/
Marianne Mitten
CLIENT
Stanford Alumni Association
AGENCY/STUDIO
Morla Design

MENU, CALENDAR,
ANNOUNCEMENT
ART DIRECTORS
Dawson Zaug / Lisa Levin
DESIGNER
Lisa Levin
WRITER
Delphine Hirasuna
PHOTOGRAPHER
Various
CLIENT
George Rice & Sons
AGENCY/STUDIO
Cross Associates/Siegel & Gale

ART DIRECTOR
Doug Wolfe
DESIGNER
Buck Smith
WRITER
Buck Smith
CLIENT
Hawthorne/Wolfe, Inc.
AGENCY/STUDIO
Hawthorne/Wolfe, Inc.

to a larger space.

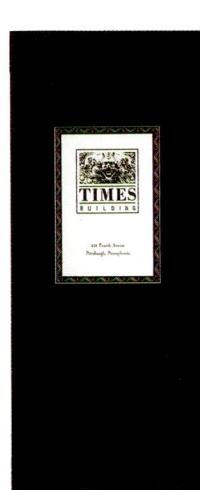

ART DIRECTOR
William Kolano
DESIGNER
William Kolano
WRITER
William Kolano
CLIENT
The Magee Group
AGENCY/STUDIO
Irene Pasinski Associates

DESIGN

*MENU, CALENDAR,
ANNOUNCEMENT*

ART DIRECTORS
David Carter/Lori
B.Wilson
DESIGNER
Lori B.Wilson
WRITER
Lori B.Wilson/
Kathy Lane
ILLUSTRATORS
David Carter/Gary
Lobue Jr./Wai-Tak
Lai/Lori B.Wilson/
Cynthia Waldman/
Randall Hill/Allen
Wearer/Dee Thomas
CLIENT
David Carter Design
AGENCY/STUDIO
David Carter Design

ART DIRECTOR
Kit Hinrichs
DESIGNERS
Kit Hinrichs/Karen
Boone
ILLUSTRATORS
Joe Duffy/Seymour
Chwast/Carol Wald/
Kit Hinrichs/Jack
Unruh/Ivan
Chermayeff/ Philippe
Weisbecker/Woody
Pirtle/Doug Johnson
/James McMullan/
John Craig
CLIENT
New York Art
Directors Club
AGENCY/STUDIO
Pentagram

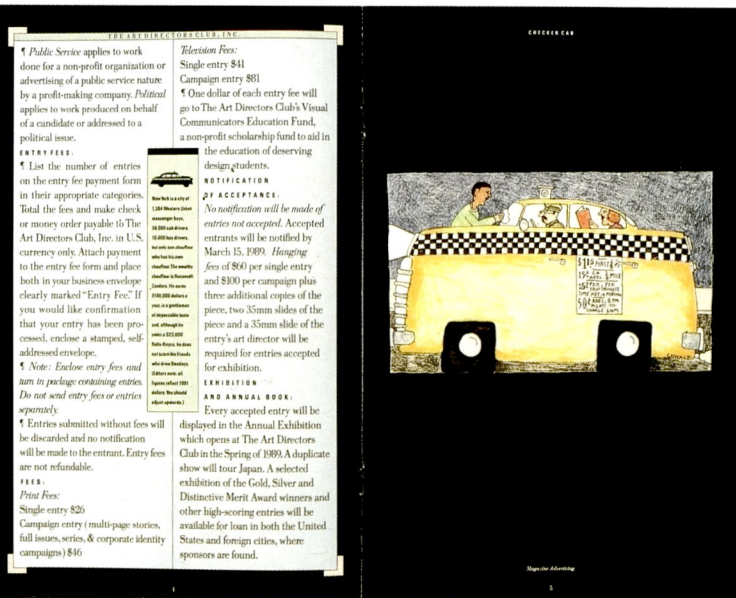

ART DIRECTOR
Robert Kastigar
DESIGNER
Paul Morales
WRITER
Stewart Alsop II
ILLUSTRATOR
Anthony Russo
CLIENT
P.C. Letter
AGENCY/STUDIO
Halleck Design Group

MENU, CALENDAR,
ANNOUNCEMENT
ART DIRECTOR
Ken Eskenazi
DESIGNER
Jeff Burne
ILLUSTRATORS
Jeff Burne/Su Wilson
CLIENT
Princess Cruises
AGENCY/STUDIO
Kaiser McEuen Inc.

ART DIRECTOR
Jim Marrin
DESIGNER
Jim Marrin
PHOTOGRAPHERS
Peter Darley Miller/
Bradford Fowler/
Scott Morgan
CLIENT
Noland Paper Company
AGENCY/STUDIO
Bright & Associates
*PRODUCTION
COMPANY*
Bright & Associates

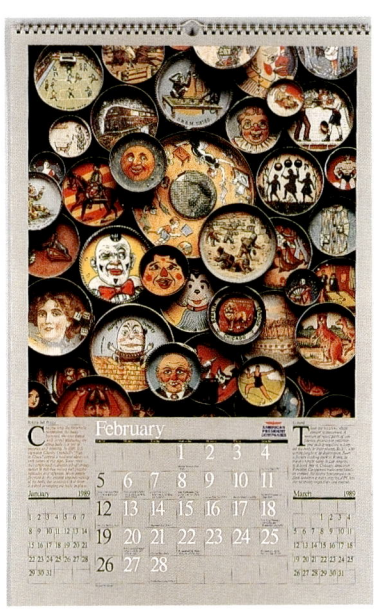

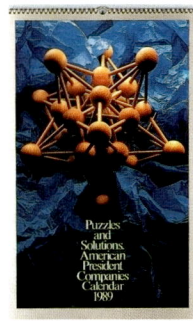

ART DIRECTOR
Kit Hinrichs
DESIGNERS
Kit Hinrichs & Sandra
McHenry
WRITER
Peterson & Dodge
PHOTOGRAPHER
Terry Heffernan
CLIENT
American President
Companies
AGENCY/STUDIO
Pentagram

*MENU, CALENDAR,
ANNOUNCEMENT*
ART DIRECTOR
John Coy
DESIGNERS
John Coy, Anne Burdick
CLIENT
Graduate School of
Architecture & Urban
Planning, U.C.L.A.
AGENCY/STUDIO
COY, Los Angeles
▲

ART DIRECTOR
John Coy
DESIGNER
Laurie Handler
CLIENT
Robata
AGENCY/STUDIO
COY, Los Angeles
▲

ART DIRECTOR
Michael Brock
DESIGNERS
Michael Brock/
Gaylen Braun
PHOTOGRAPHER
Various
CLIENT
L.A. Style
AGENCY/STUDIO
Michael Brock Design

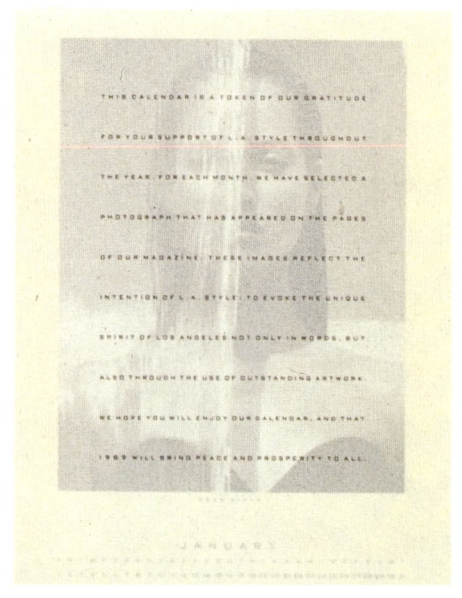

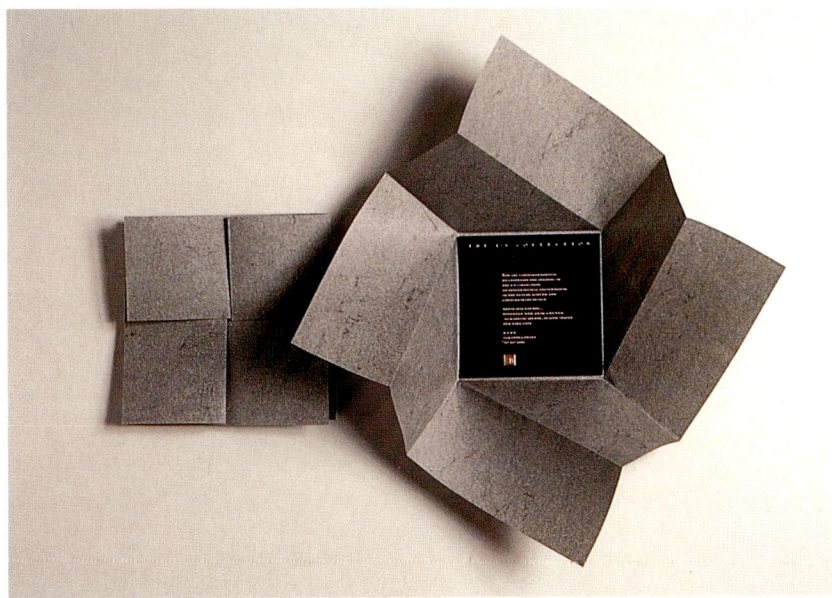

*MENU, CALENDAR,
ANNOUNCEMENT*

ART DIRECTORS
James Sebastian/
John Plunkett
DESIGNERS
James Sebastian/
David Reiss/
Junko Mayumi
CLIENT
The L S Collection
AGENCY/STUDIO
Designframe Inc.,
NYC

ART DIRECTOR
Wai-Tak Lai
DESIGNER
Wai-Tak Lai
ILLUSTRATOR
Jacinda Lai
CLIENT
The Robert D. Zimmer
Group
AGENCY/STUDIO
David Carter Design

MENU, CALENDAR,
ANNOUNCEMENT

ART DIRECTOR
Dan Lennon
DESIGNER
Dan Lennon
WRITER
Linda Lennon
PHOTOGRAPHERS
William Nettles/Luis
Delgado/Steve Burns/
Orlando Cabanban/
Beau Parker/Thomas
Heinser/William
Taylor/Luca Vignelli/
Glen Wexler/Stone
& Steccati
CLIENT
Lackawanna Leather
Company
AGENCY/STUDIO
Lennon & Associates

DESIGNER
David Poe
ILLUSTRATOR
David Poe
CLIENT
Greens Restaurant,
San Francisco
AGENCY/STUDIO
Design Office Of Emery/Poe

ART DIRECTOR
John Sayles
DESIGNER
John Sayles
WRITER
Victor Boutrous
ILLUSTRATOR
John Sayles
CLIENT
Drake University
AGENCY/STUDIO
Sayles Graphic Design, Inc.

MENU, CALENDAR,
ANNOUNCEMENT
ART DIRECTOR
Paul Curtin
DESIGNER
Peter Locke
CLIENT
Catharine Keena and
Paul Curtin
AGENCY/STUDIO
Paul Curtin Design
LETTER PRESS
Julie Holcomb Printers

ART DIRECTOR
Richard C. Runyon
DESIGNER
Richard C. Runyon
CLIENT
Madine Pulaski/Museum
of Flying

MENU, CALENDAR,
ANNOUNCEMENT

ART DIRECTORS
Kurt Meinecke/Barbara Lynk
DESIGNER
Barbara Lynk
WRITERS
Anne McCarthy/Sara Lee
Corporation
ILLUSTRATOR
Barbara Lynk
CLIENT
Sara Lee Corporation
AGENCY/STUDIO
Group/Chicago Inc.
PRINTER
Bruce Offset Company

ART DIRECTOR
Gordon Hochhalter
DESIGNER
Dan Larocca
WRITER
Gordon Hochhalter
CLIENT
R. R. Donnelley & Sons
 Company
AGENCY/STUDIO
R. R. Donnelley

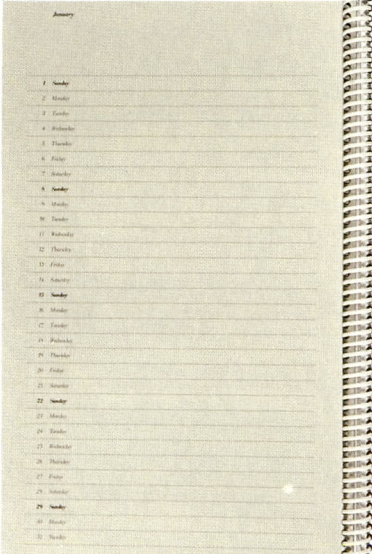

SELF-PROMOTION
ART DIRECTOR
Michael Hall
DESIGNER
Michael Hall
ILLUSTRATOR
Michael Hall
CLIENT
Hall Kelley
AGENCY/STUDIO
Hall Kelley, Inc.

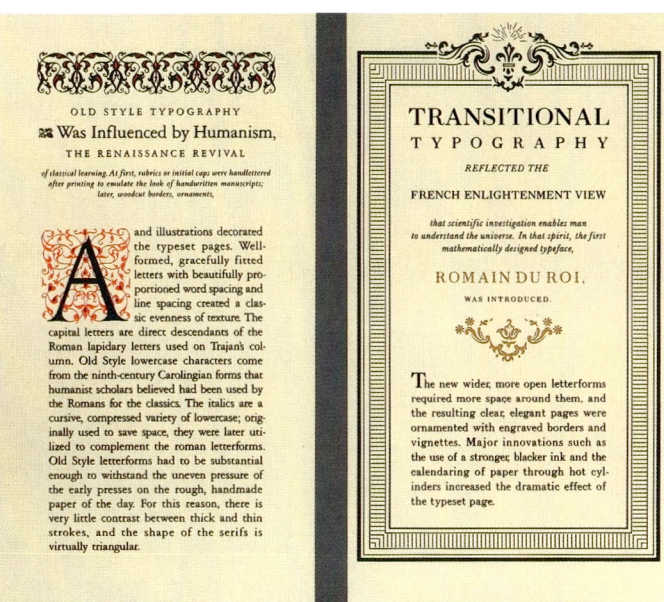

OLD STYLE TYPOGRAPHY
Was Influenced by Humanism,
THE RENAISSANCE REVIVAL

of classical learning. At first, rubrics or initial caps were handlettered after printing to emulate the look of handwritten manuscripts; later, woodcut borders, ornaments,

A nd illustrations decorated the typeset pages. Well-formed, gracefully fitted letters with beautifully pro-portioned word spacing and line spacing created a clas-sic evenness of texture. The capital letters are direct descendants of the Roman lapidary letters used on Trajan's col-umn. Old Style lowercase characters come from the ninth-century Carolingian forms that humanist scholars believed had been used by the Romans for the classics. The italics are a cursive, compressed variety of lowercase; orig-inally used to save space, they were later uti-lized to complement the roman letterforms. Old Style letterforms had to be substantial enough to withstand the uneven pressure of the early presses on the rough, handmade paper of the day. For this reason, there is very little contrast between thick and thin strokes, and the shape of the serifs is virtually triangular.

TRANSITIONAL
TYPOGRAPHY
REFLECTED THE
FRENCH ENLIGHTENMENT VIEW

that scientific investigation enables man to understand the universe. In that spirit, the first mathematically designed typeface,

ROMAIN DU ROI,

WAS INTRODUCED.

The new wider, more open letterforms required more space around them, and the resulting clear, elegant pages were ornamented with engraved borders and vignettes. Major innovations such as the use of a stronger, blacker ink and the calendaring of paper through hot cyl-inders increased the dramatic effect of the typeset page.

ART DIRECTOR
Leah Toby Hoffmitz
DESIGNER
Terry Irwin/Leah Toby Hoffmitz
WRITER
Leah Toby Hoffmitz/ Shawn Woodyard
LETTERER
Leah Toby Hoffmitz
CLIENT
Characters & Color
AGENCY/STUDIO
Letterform Design

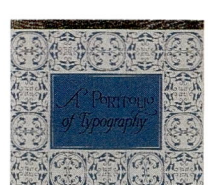

ART DIRECTOR
John Van Dyke
DESIGNER
John Van Dyke
CALLIGRAPHY
Georgia Deaver
WRITER
Jon Bell
PHOTOGRAPHER
Terry Heffernan
CLIENT
Mead
AGENCY/STUDIO
Van Dyke Design Company
Seattle

SELF-PROMOTION
ART DIRECTOR
Craig Frazier
DESIGNERS
Craig Frazier/
Deborah Hagemann/
Grant Peterson
WRITER
Craig Frazier
CLIENT
Frazier Design
AGENCY/STUDIO
Frazier Design

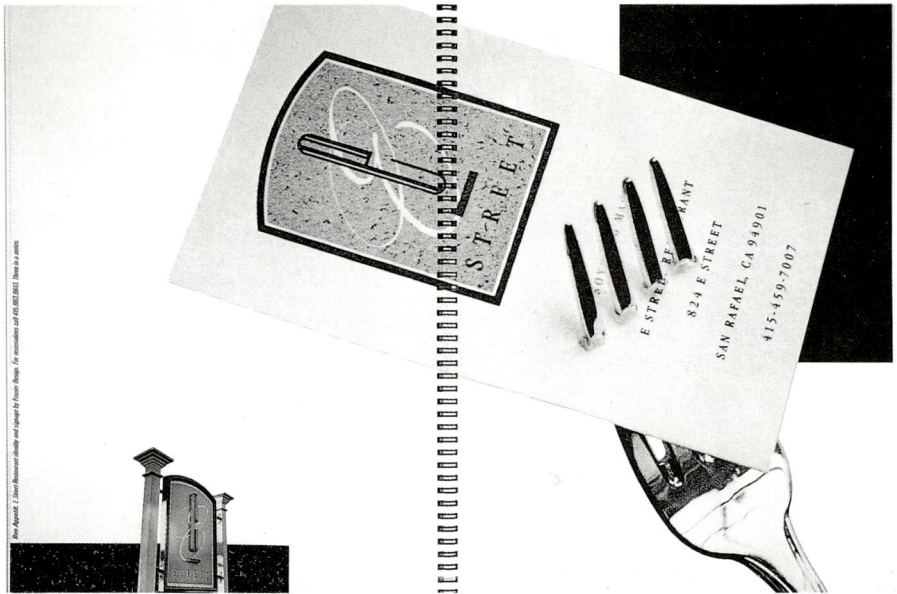

ART DIRECTOR
Craig Frazier
DESIGNERS
Craig Frazier/Deborah
Hagemann
WRITER
John Frazier
CLIENT
John Frazier
AGENCY/STUDIO
Frazier Design

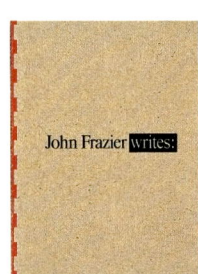

John Frazier writes:

On humor in advertising: Consumers are bombarded by too many lousy ads to waste time being cute and clever. Which is not to say humor doesn't have its place in advertising; I just want to make sure they're laughing with me.

ART DIRECTOR
Craig Frazier
DESIGNERS
Craig Frazier/Darrel
Kolosta
WRITER
Greg Karraker
PHOTOGRAPHER
Rudi Legname
ILLUSTRATORS
Craig Frazier/Darrel
Kolosta
CLIENT
Fong & Fong
AGENCY/STUDIO
Frazier Design

SELF-PROMOTION

ART DIRECTOR
Kimberly Baer
WRITER
Candace Pearson
PHOTOGRAPHER
Jeff Corwin
CLIENT
Jeff Corwin
AGENCY/STUDIO
Kimberly Baer Design
Associates

SMURFS · *Channeling* · VIDEO GAMES · *Saturday Night Live* · THE DUST BUSTER

ART DIRTECTORS
Craig Bernhardt/Janice Fudyma
DESIGNER
Iris Brown
CONTRIBUTING DESIGNERS
Frank Baseman/Carol Melloni/
Jane Sobczak
WRITER
Barry Bohrer
PHOTOGRAPHER
Various
ILLUSTRATOR
Various
CLIENT
Bernhardt Fudyma Design
Group
AGENCY/STUDIO
Bernhardt Fudyma Design
Group
▲

Ohio as a distant land. Where once I had bicycled, I now drove through Grantham, where Newton had set out the plague.

ART DIRECTOR
Doug Wolfe
DESIGNER
Doug Wolfe
WRITER
Louis Bencze
PHOTOGRAPHER
Louis Bencze
CLIENT
Louis Bencze
AGENCY/STUDIO
Hawthorne/Wolfe, Inc.

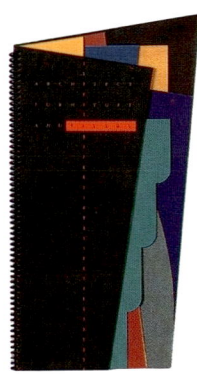

ART DIRECTORS
Ken Cook, Jim Cross
DESIGNER
Ken Cook
WRITER
Delphine Hirasuna
PHOTOGRAPHER
Henrik Kam
ILLUSTRATOR
Steve Lyons
CLIENT
Simpson Paper Company
AGENCY/STUDIO
Cross Associates,
San Francisco
PRODUCTION COMPANY
Graphic Center, Sacramento

SELF-PROMOTION

DESIGNER
Tom Bonauro
PHOTOGRAPHER
Michele Clement
CLIENT
Michele Clement Studio
AGENCY/STUDIO
Michele Clement Studio
▲

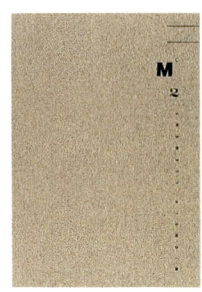
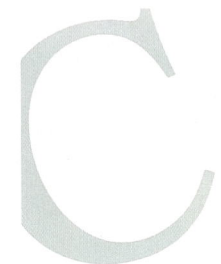

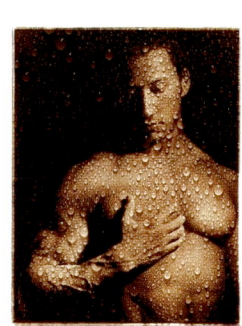

ART DIRECTOR
Michael Osborne
DESIGNERS
Michael Osborne/
Elizabeth Burrill/
Ted Jacobs
WRITER
Elizabeth Burrill
CLIENT
Michael Osborne
Design, Inc.
AGENCY/STUDIO
Michael Osborne
Design, Inc.

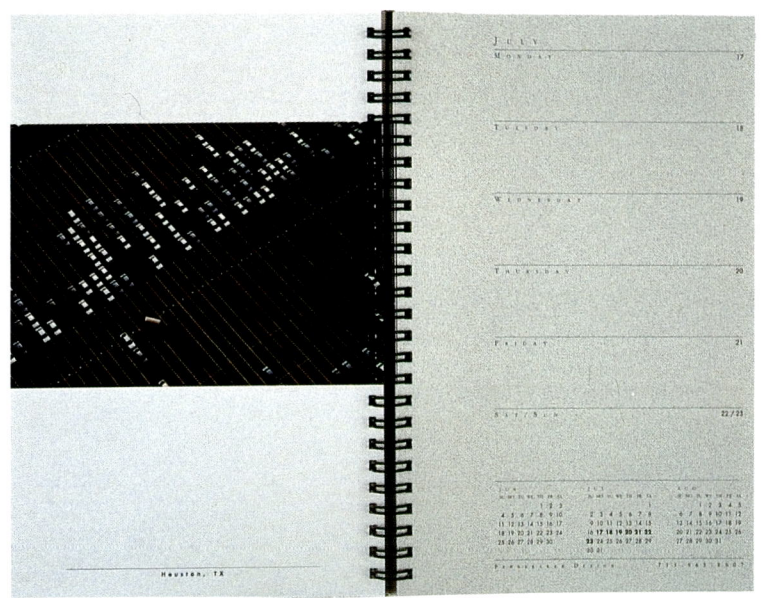

SELF-PROMOTION

ART DIRECTOR
Ward Pennebaker
DESIGNERS
Ward Pennebaker/
Robert Grayson
WRITER
Ward Pennebaker
PHOTOGRAPHER
Cameron Davidson
CLIENT
Pennebaker Design
AGENCY/STUDIO
Pennebaker Design

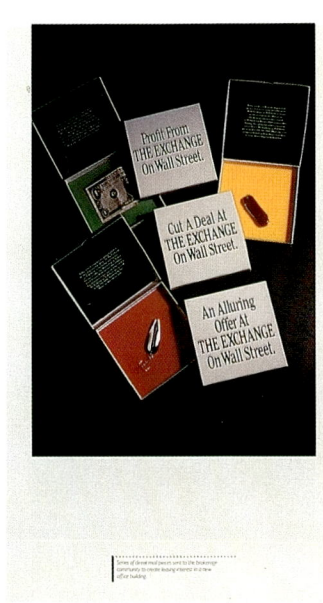

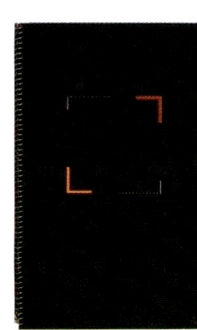

ART DIRECTOR
Tom Poth
DESIGNER
Tom Poth
WRITER
Mike Hicks
PHOTOGRAPHER
Richard Krall
CLIENT
Hixo, Inc.
AGENCY/STUDIO
Hixo, Inc.

SELF-PROMOTION
ART DIRECTORS
Keith Bright/Randall Hensley
DESIGNER
Randall Hensley
WRITER
John Salvati
ILLUSTRATOR
Randall Hensley
CLIENT
Bright & Associates
AGENCY/STUDIO
Bright & Associates
PRODUCTION COMPANY
Bright & Associates

S. CLAUS ENTERPRISES

CORPORATE IDENTITY STANDARDS

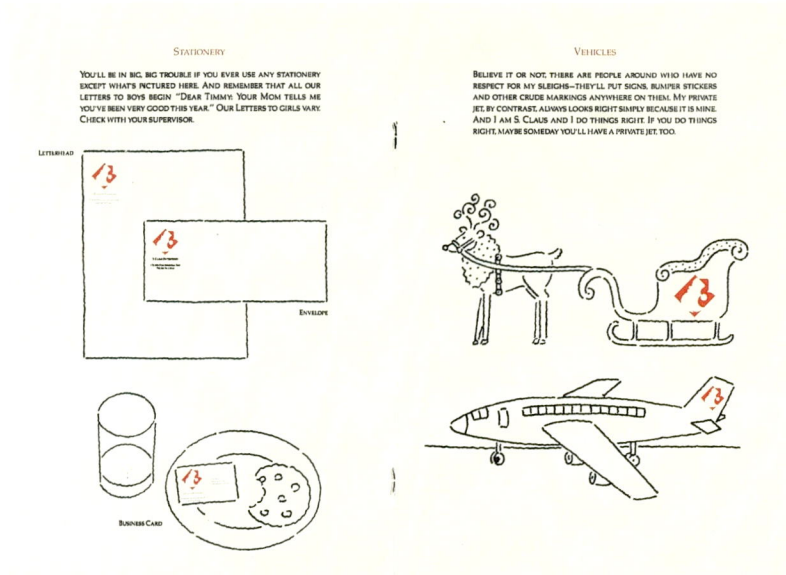

STATIONERY

YOU'LL BE IN BIG, BIG TROUBLE IF YOU EVER USE ANY STATIONERY EXCEPT WHAT'S PICTURED HERE. AND REMEMBER THAT ALL OUR LETTERS TO BOYS BEGIN "DEAR TIMMY: YOUR MOM TELLS ME YOU'VE BEEN VERY GOOD THIS YEAR." OUR LETTERS TO GIRLS VARY. CHECK WITH YOUR SUPERVISOR.

VEHICLES

BELIEVE IT OR NOT, THERE ARE PEOPLE AROUND WHO HAVE NO RESPECT FOR MY SLEIGHS—THEY'LL PUT SIGNS, BUMPER STICKERS AND OTHER CRUDE MARKINGS ANYWHERE ON THEM. MY PRIVATE JET, BY CONTRAST, ALWAYS LOOKS RIGHT SIMPLY BECAUSE IT IS MINE. AND I AM S. CLAUS AND I DO THINGS RIGHT. IF YOU DO THINGS RIGHT, MAYBE SOMEDAY YOU'LL HAVE A PRIVATE JET, TOO.

ART DIRECTORS
Barbara Vick/Amy Knapp
DESIGNERS
Amy Knapp/Barbara Vick
WRITER
Alex Cichy
PHOTOGRAPHER
Steve Calarco
CLIENT
Self Promotion
AGENCY/STUDIO
SBG Partners

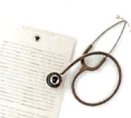

VAN HAYES DESIGN Fast and friendly service, pleasing prices.

SELF-PROMOTION

ART DIRECTOR
Van Hayes
DESIGNER
Van Hayes
ILLUSTRATOR
Van Hayes
CLIENT
Van Hayes Design
AGENCY/STUDIO
Van Hayes Design

ART DIRECTORS
Stanley Church/Robert
Wallace
DESIGNER
Stanley Church
CLIENT
Wallace Church Associates,
Inc.
AGENCY/STUDIO
Wallace Church Associates,
Inc.

SELF-PROMOTION

  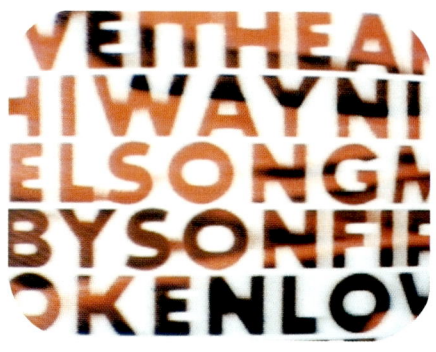

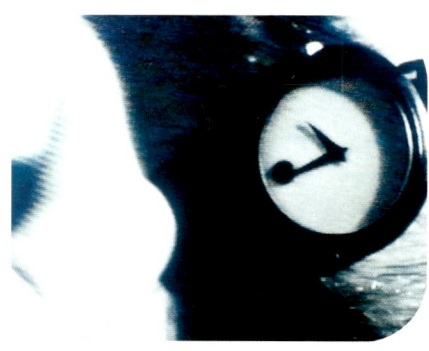  

ART DIRECTORS
Jeffrey Bacon/John
O'Brien
EDITOR
Keith Salmon
PRODUCER
Cynthia Schneider
DIRECTOR
Jim Edwards
*DIRECTOR OF
PHOTOGRAPHY*
Bob Graham
CLIENT
Bacon/O'Brien
AGENCY/STUDIO
Cimarron/Bacon/O'Brien
*PRODUCTION
COMPANY*
Ace and Edie 2

"BITS AND PIECES"

Video: Live action footage with a selection of personal photos, sketches, and finished graphic design.

Audio: "We don't want to do it if we can't do it better than anyone else."

COLE·HAAN

MEN'S FOOTWEAR · SPRING 1989

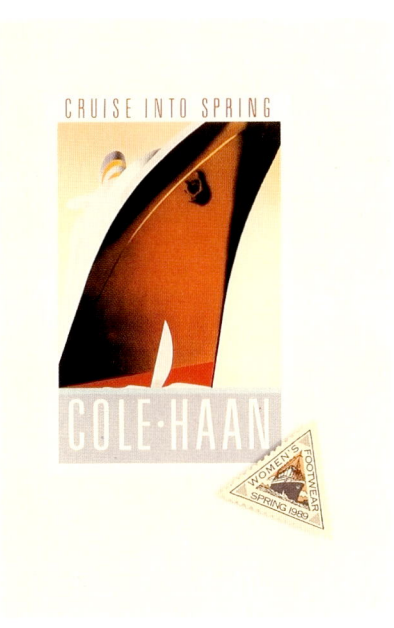

CATALOG
ART DIRECTOR
Robert Cipriani
DESIGNER
Rosemary Conroy
WRITER
Brian Flood
PHOTOGRAPHER
Jack Richmond
Photography
CLIENT
Cole-Haan
AGENCY/STUDIO
Cipriani Kremer Design
Group
*PRODUCTION
COMPANY*
Acme Printing Company

ART DIRECTOR
Rosemary Conroy
DESIGNER
Rosemary Conroy
WRITER
Brian Flood
PHOTOGRAPHER
John Holt Studio
ILLUSTRATOR
Calderwood & Preg
CLIENT
Cole-Haan
AGENCY/STUDIO
Cipriani Kremer Design
Group

ART DIRECTOR
Rosemary Conroy
DESIGNER
Rosemary Conroy
WRITER
Brian Flood
PHOTOGRAPHER
Jack Richmond
Photography
ILLUSTRATOR
Cheryl Roberts
CLIENT
Cole-Haan
AGENCY/STUDIO
Cipriani Kremer Design
Group
*PRODUCTION
COMPANY*
Acme Printing Company

DESIGN

CATALOG
ART DIRECTORS
John Doyle/Ann Dakis/
Margaret McGovern/
Amy Watt
DESIGNERS
John Doyle/Ann Dakis/
Margaret McGovern/
Amy Watt
WRITERS
Peter Pappas/
Paul Silverman
PHOTOGRAPHERS
John Holt, Eric Meola
CLIENT
Timberland
AGENCY/STUDIO
Mullen

ART DIRECTOR
Jack Anderson
DESIGNERS
Jack Anderson/Juliet
Shen/Mary Hermes
WRITER
Steve Sandoz
PHOTOGRAPHER
Mark Burnside
ILLUSTRATORS
John & Leilani
Fortune
CLIENT
Diadora USA
AGENCY/STUDIO
Hornall Anderson
Design Works

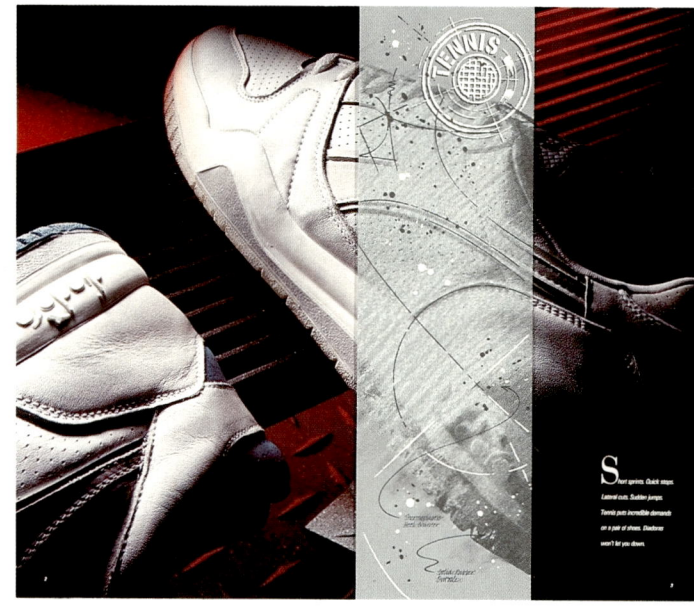

ART DIRECTOR
Pat Samata
DESIGNERS
Pat and Greg Samata
WRITERS
Robert Walker/Dan
Fredricks
PHOTOGRAPHERS
Terry Heffernan/
Dennis Dooley
CLIENT
The Parker Pen
Company
AGENCY/STUDIO
Samata Associates

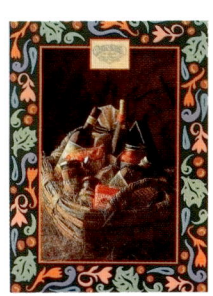

CATALOG

ART DIRECTOR
David Poe
DESIGNER
David Poe/Jonathan Mulcare
PHOTOGRAPHER
Alan Krosnick
CLIENT
Piedmont Grocery
AGENCY/STUDIO
Design Office of Emery/Poe

ART DIRECTOR
Tony Rostron
DESIGNER
Tony Rostron
WRITER
Gerry Kane
PHOTOGRAPHER
Henrik Kam
ILLUSTRATOR
Craig Austin
CLIENT
Agilis Corporation
AGENCY/STUDIO
Matrix Graphic Design

VISUAL IDENTITY

ART DIRECTOR
Ken Hegstrom
DESIGNER
Ken Hegstrom
ILLUSTRATOR
Ken Hegstrom
CLIENT
Danken Creative
AGENCY/STUDIO
Hegstrom Design

ART DIRECTORS
Keith Bright/Ray
Wood
DESIGNERS
Il Chung/Ray Wood
CLIENT
Eyecare Center of
America
AGENCY/STUDIO
Bright & Associates
*PRODUCTION
COMPANY*
Bright & Associates

EyeMasters

DESIGNER
Barry Deutsch
CLIENT
Interactive Network, Inc.
AGENCY/STUDIO
SBG Partners

ART DIRECTOR
Courtney Reeser
DESIGNERS
Tom McNulty/Ben
Wheeler
ILLUSTRATOR
Hank Osuna
CLIENT
ADVO
AGENCY/STUDIO
SBG Partners

INTERACTIVE NETWORK

ADVO

ART DIRECTOR
Gregory Thomas
DESIGNER
Gregory Thomas
ILLUSTRATOR
Barry Zauss
CLIENT
Barry Zauss &
Associates
AGENCY/STUDIO
Gregory Thomas
& Associates

ART DIRECTOR
Craig Butler
DESIGNER
Amy Dakos
ILLUSTRATOR
Amy Dakos
CLIENT
Stockland-Martel
AGENCY/STUDIO
Butler Kosh Brooks

VISUAL IDENTITY

ART DIRECTOR
Don Faia
DESIGNER
Don Faia
ILLUSTRATOR
Don Faia
CLIENT
Evelyn Peairs
AGENCY/STUDIO
Don Faia Design

ART DIRECTOR
John Coy
DESIGNERS
Sean Alatorre/Tom Bouman
CLIENT
Riordan Foundation
AGENCY/STUDIO
COY, Los Angeles

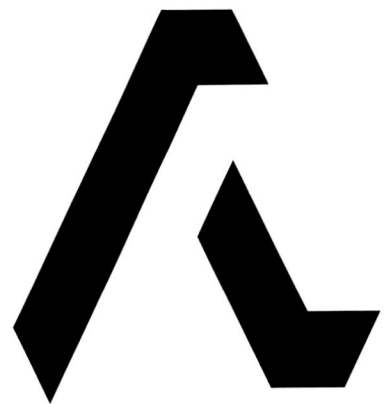

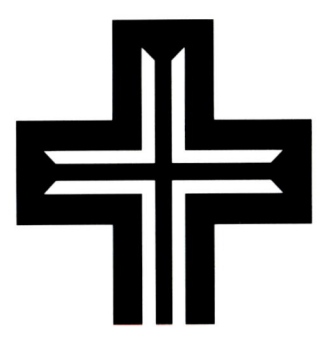

ART DIRECTOR
Roslyn Eskind
DESIGNER
Malcolm Waddell
CLIENT
Alias Inc.
AGENCY/STUDIO
Eskind Waddell

ART DIRECTOR
Keith Puccinelli
DESIGNER
Keith Puccinelli
ILLUSTRATOR
Keith Puccinelli
CLIENT
Marian Medical Center
AGENCY/STUDIO
Puccinelli Design

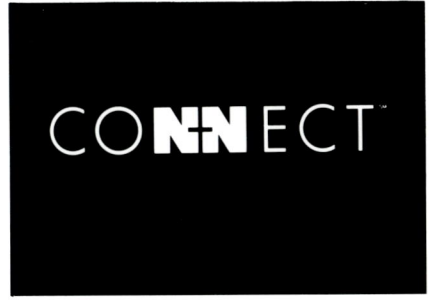

ART DIRECTOR
Clement Mok
DESIGNER
Clement Mok
CLIENT
Connect Incorporated
AGENCY/STUDIO
Clement Mok Designs

ART DIRECTOR
John Benelli
DESIGNER
John Benelli
ILLUSTRATOR
John Benelli
CLIENT
Peter Benelli Surfboards
AGENCY/STUDIO
Benelli Design
PRODUCTION ARTIST
Karen Abrams

VISUAL IDENTITY
ART DIRECTOR
Bennett Peji
DESIGNER
Bennett Peji
CLIENT
Judy Mills
AGENCY/STUDIO
Bennett Peji Design

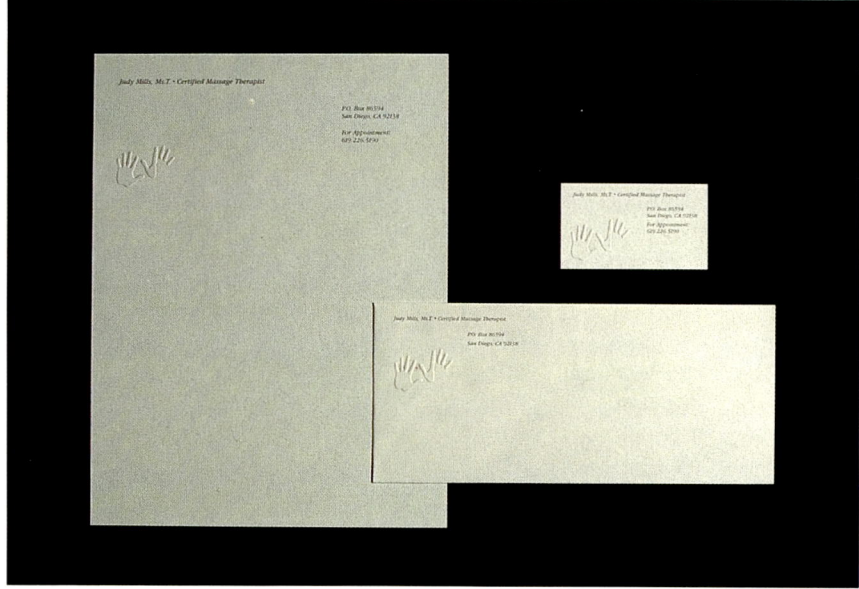

ART DIRECTOR
Lisa Levin
DESIGNER
Lisa Levin
CLIENT
Roger Paperno Photography
AGENCY/STUDIO
Lisa Levin Design

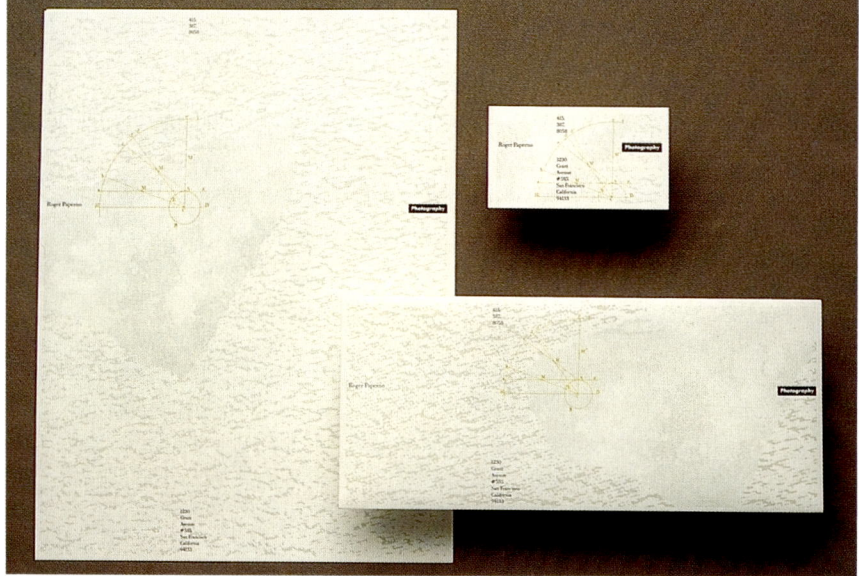

ART DIRECTOR
Christopher Hadden
DESIGNER
Christopher Hadden
ILLUSTRATOR
Judy Labrasca
CLIENT
Woolies Handknits
AGENCY/STUDIO
Christopher Hadden
Design

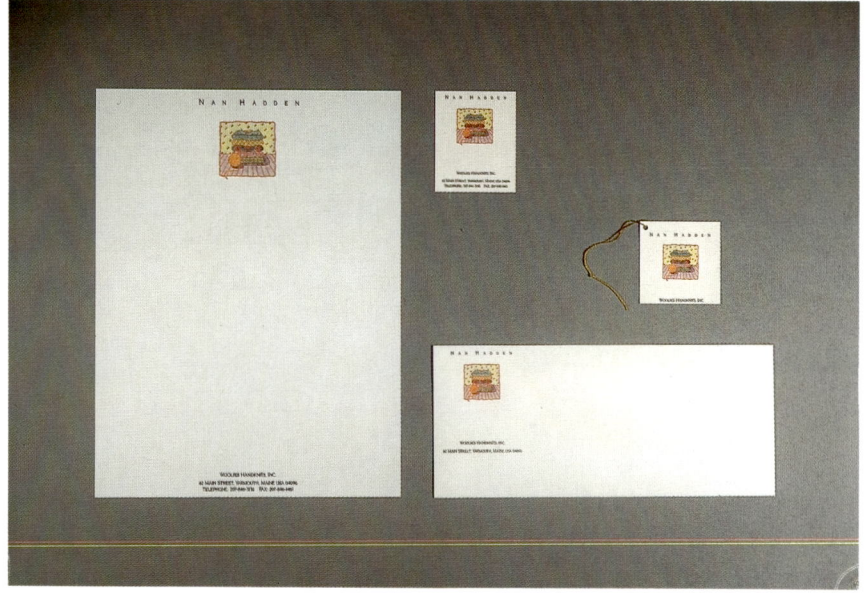

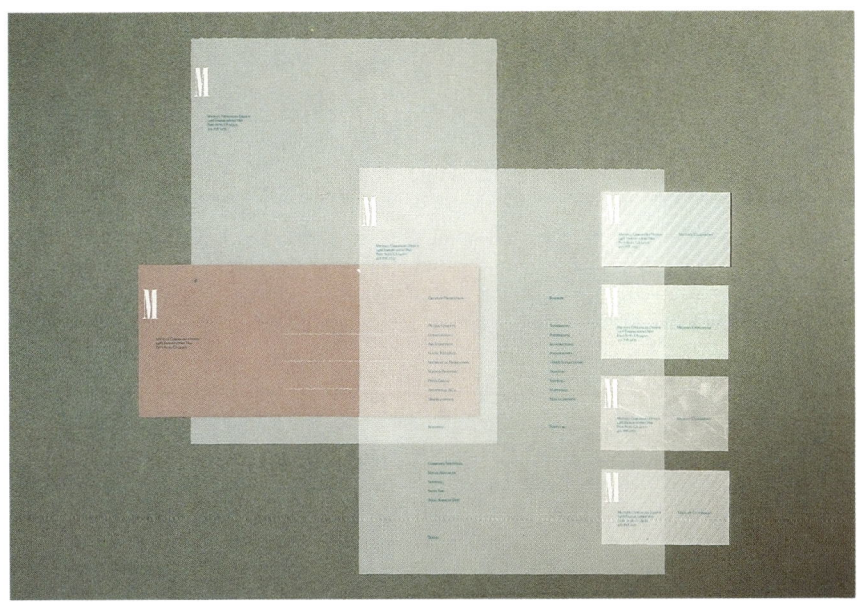

VISUAL IDENTITY

ART DIRECTOR
Michael Chikamura
DESIGNER
Randy Lim
CLIENT
Michael Chikamura Design
AGENCY/STUDIO
Michael Chikamura Design
▲

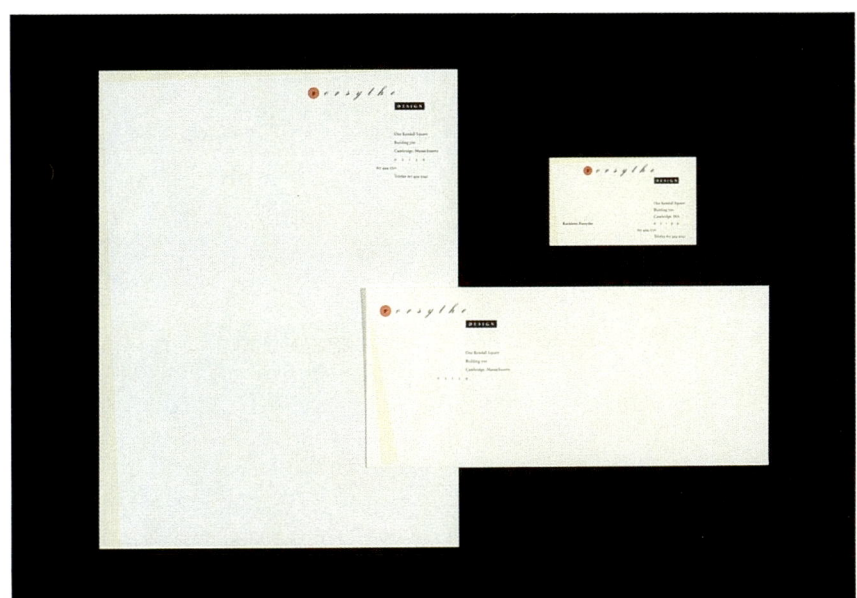

ART DIRECTOR
Kathleen Forsythe
*DESIGNER*S
Kathleen Forsythe/
Julie Steinhilber
CLIENT
Forsythe Design
AGENCY/STUDIO
Forsythe Design

ART DIRECTOR
Ken Cook/C. Randall
Sherman
DESIGNER
C. Randall Sherman/
Ken Cook
CLIENT
Van Yahres Tree
Company
AGENCY/STUDIO
Cipriani Kremer
Design Group
*PRODUCTION
COMPANY*
Worth Higgins, Inc.

VISUAL IDENTITY
ART DIRECTOR
Thom Smith
*DESIGNER*S
Thom Smith/Gregg
Frederickson
CLIENT
Robert Lightman
& Associates
AGENCY/STUDIO
Smith Group

ART DIRECTOR
Mike Hicks
DESIGNER
Mike Hicks
ILLUSTRATOR
Harrison Saunders
CLIENT
HIXO, Inc.
AGENCY/STUDIO
HIXO, Inc.

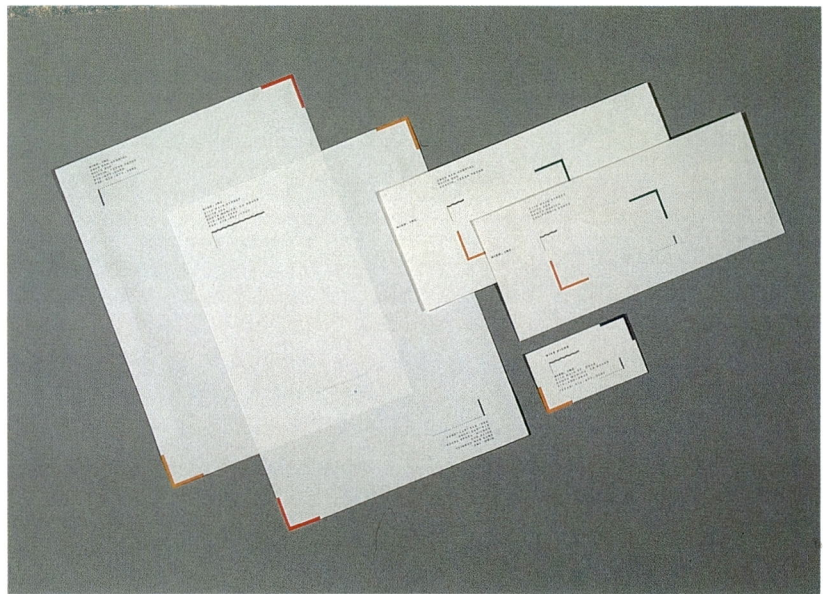

ART DIRECTOR
John Sayles
DESIGNER
John Sayles
ILLUSTRATOR
John Sayles
CLIENT
Chicago Dog and
Deli
AGENCY/STUDIO
Sayles Graphic
Design, Inc.

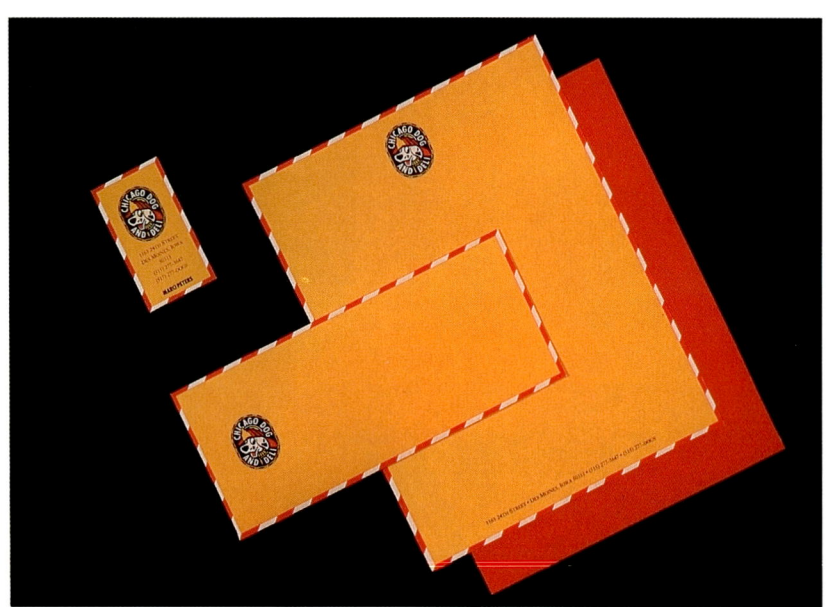

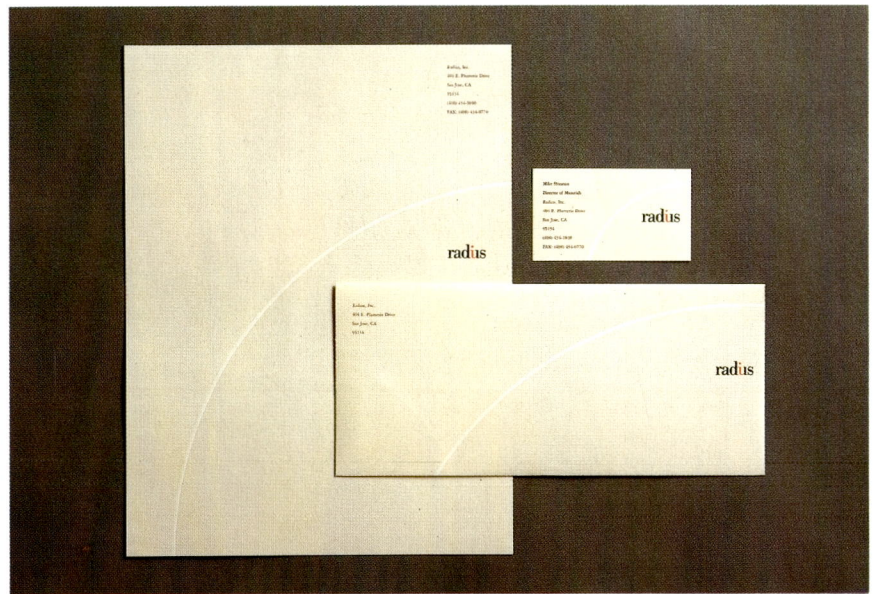

VISUAL IDENTITY

ART DIRECTOR
Gordon Mortensen
DESIGNER
Gordon Mortensen
CLIENT
Radius, Inc.
AGENCY/STUDIO
Mortensen Design/
Palo Alto

DESIGNER
Mitchell Mauk
CLIENT
Robert Duncan
AGENCY/STUDIO
Mauk Design

▲

ART DIRECTOR
William Wondriska
DESIGNER
Christopher Passehl
PHOTOGRAPHER
Provided by client
CLIENT
Mary Duffy Morris
AGENCY/STUDIO
Wondriska Associates,
Inc.

VISUAL IDENTITY
ART DIRECTOR
Darren Hanshaw
DESIGNER
Darren Hanshaw
CLIENT
Editel
AGENCY/STUDIO
Darren Hanshaw Design

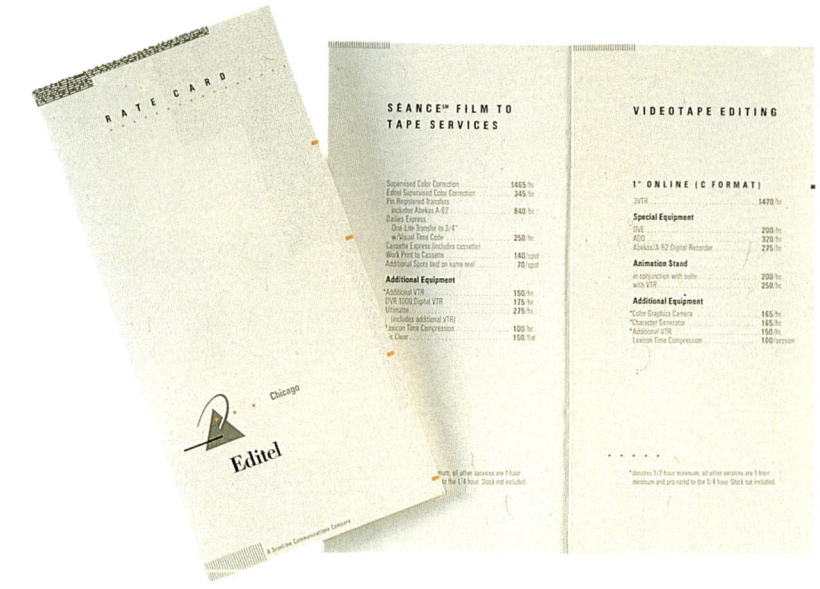

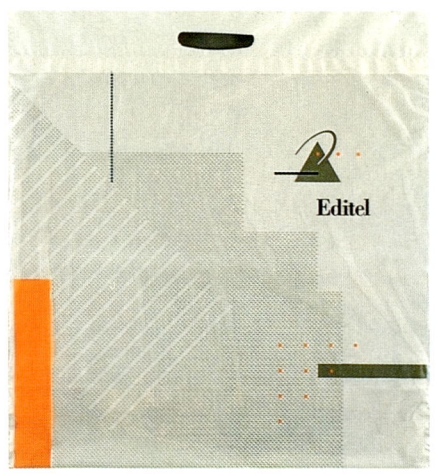

VISUAL IDENTITY
ART DIRECTOR
Keith Bright/Ray
Wood
DESIGNER
Wilson Ong
CLIENT
Los Angeles Sports
Council
AGENCY/STUDIO
Bright & Associates
*PRODUCTION
COMPANY*
Bright & Associates

ART DIRECTOR
Gordon Mortensen
DESIGNER
Gordon Mortensen
WRITER
Barbara Gibson
CLIENT
Radius, Inc.
AGENCY/STUDIO
Mortensen Design

ENVIRONMENTAL GRAPHICS

ART DIRECTOR
Mike Hicks
DESIGNERS
Mike Hicks/Melinda
Currier
CLIENT
Aspect Ratio
AGENCY/STUDIO
Hixo

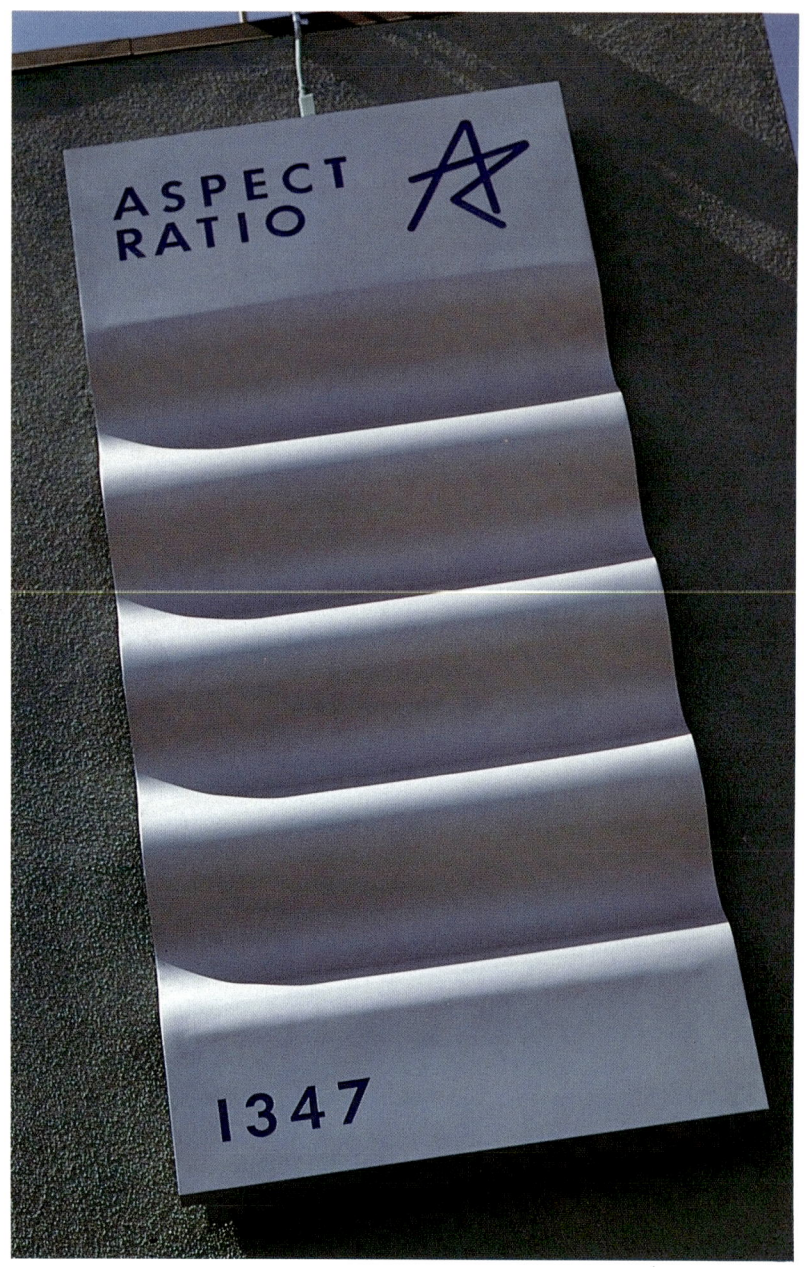

ENVIRONMENTAL GRAPHICS

ART DIRECTOR
Michael Schwab
DESIGNERS
Michael Schwab/
Kenneth Gilliam
ILLUSTRATOR
Michael Schwab
CLIENT
Sun Micro Systems
AGENCY/STUDIO
Michael Schwab Design,
Kenneth Gilliam & Assoc.

ENVIRONMENTAL GRAPHICS

ART DIRECTOR
Gerry Rosentswieg
DESIGNER
Gerry Rosentswieg
WRITER
David Alderman
PHOTOGRAPHER
Ferguson/Kirchner
ILLUSTRATOR
Jim Goss
CLIENT
Monster Burger, Inc.
AGENCY/STUDIO
The Graphics Studio
*PRODUCTION
COMPANY*
Solberg & Lowe,
A.I.A.

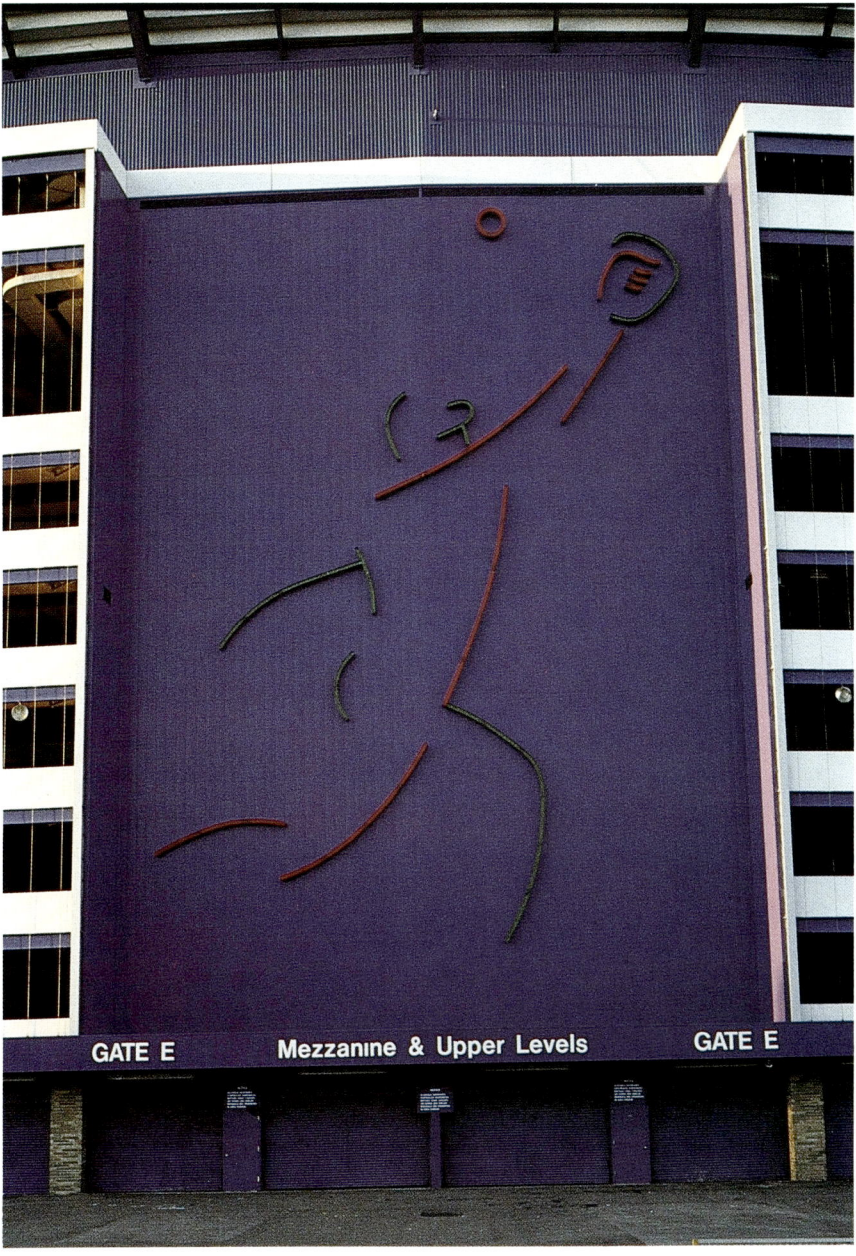

ENVIRONMENTAL GRAPHICS
ART DIRECTOR
Rudolph de Harak
DESIGNER
Richard Poulin
CLIENT
Sterling Equities, Inc.
AGENCY/STUDIO
de Harak & Poulin Associates, Inc.
FABRICATOR
Universal Unlimited, Inc.

ENVIRONMENTAL GRAPHICS

ART DIRECTOR
Takenobu Igarashi
DESIGNERS
Takenobu Igarashi/
Kazuhiro Hayase
DIRECTORS
Wolfgang Heuwinkel/
Zanders Feinpapiere
AG
PHOTOGRAPHER
Nacasa & Partners
CLIENT
Zanders Feinpapiere
AG
AGENCY/STUDIO
Igarashi Studio
PRODUCTION
COMPANY
Ad Point, Co. Ltd.

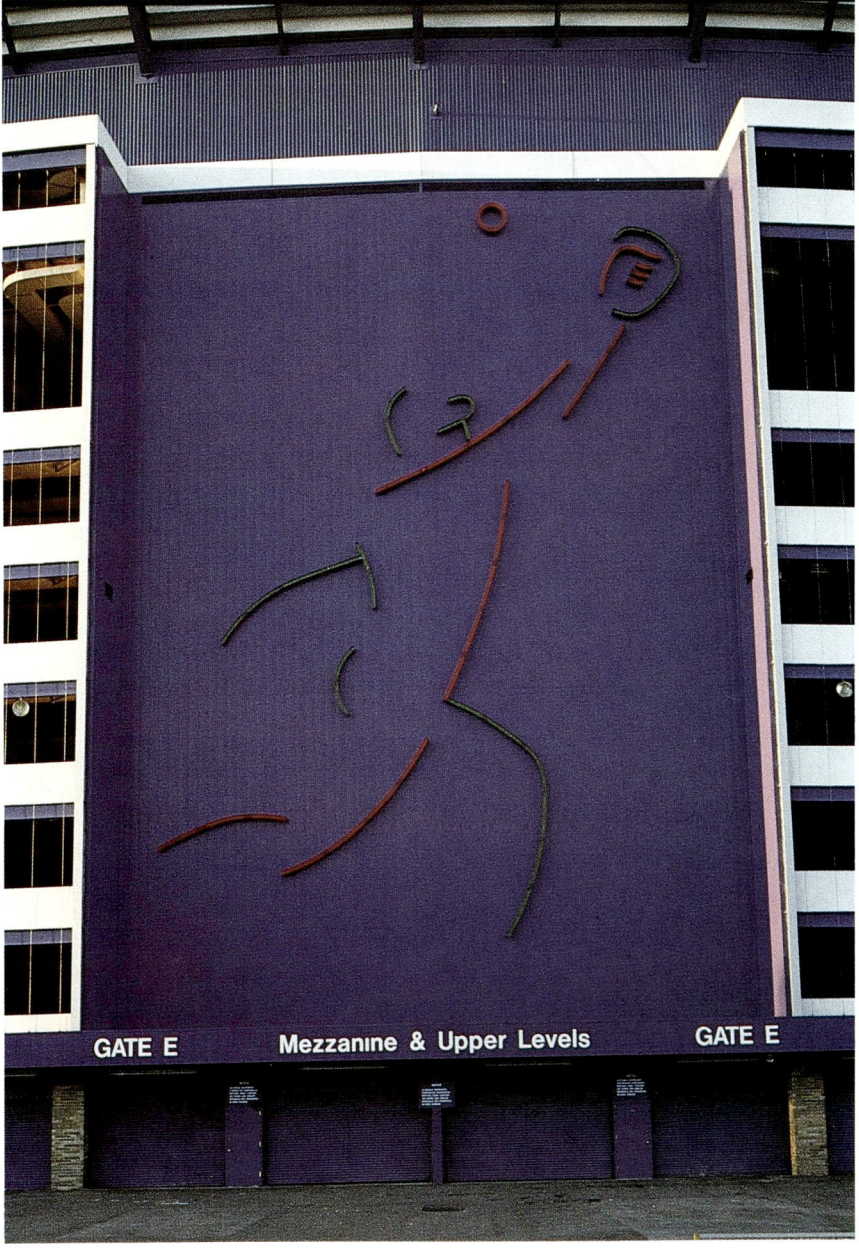

ENVIRONMENTAL GRAPHICS
ART DIRECTOR
Rudolph de Harak
DESIGNER
Richard Poulin
CLIENT
Sterling Equities, Inc.
AGENCY/STUDIO
de Harak & Poulin Associates,
Inc.
FABRICATOR
Universal Unlimited, Inc.

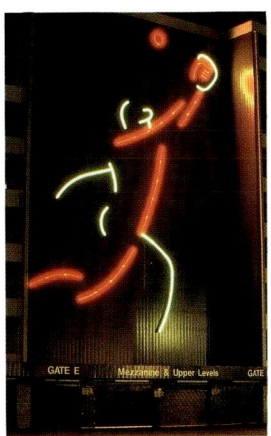

DESIGN

ENVIRONMENTAL GRAPHICS

ART DIRECTOR
Takenobu Igarashi
DESIGNERS
Takenobu Igarashi/
Kazuhiro Hayase
DIRECTORS
Wolfgang Heuwinkel/
Zanders Feinpapiere
AG
PHOTOGRAPHER
Nacasa & Partners
CLIENT
Zanders Feinpapiere
AG
AGENCY/STUDIO
Igarashi Studio
*PRODUCTION
COMPANY*
Ad Point, Co. Ltd.

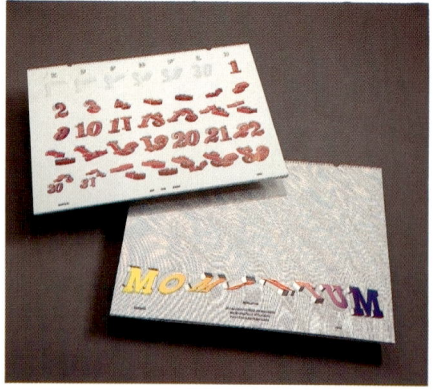

ENVIRONMENTAL GRAPHICS

ART DIRECTOR
Darren Hanshaw
DESIGNER
Richard Scheve
CLIENT
Editel
AGENCY/STUDIO
Darren Hanshaw Design

editorial

EDITORIAL

BOOK DESIGN
ART DIRECTOR
Susan Mitchell
DESIGNERS
Keith Sheridan/
Craig Warner
PHOTOGRAPHER
Raymond Meier
CLIENT
Random House, Inc.
AGENCY/STUDIO
Keith Sheridan
Associates, Inc.

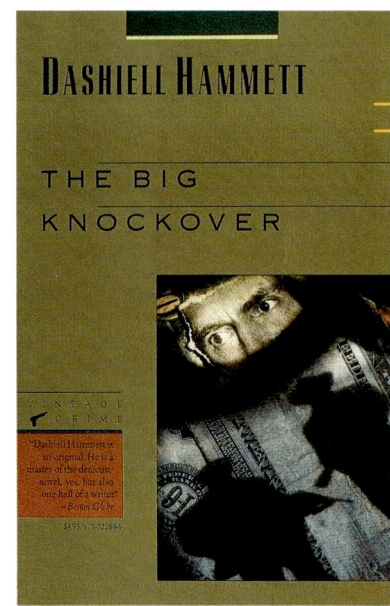

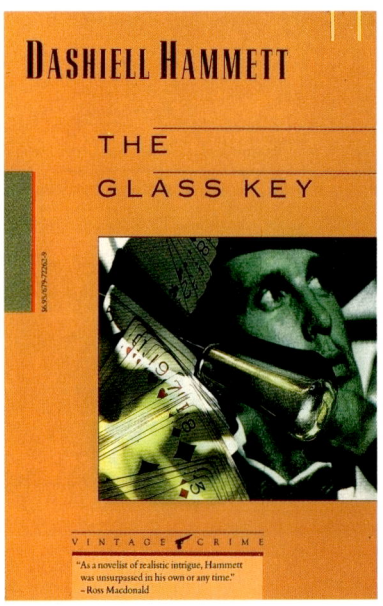

ART DIRECTOR
Bruce Hall
ILLUSTRATOR
Peter Caras
CLIENT
Pocket Books

ART DIRECTOR
Robbin Schiff
DESIGNER
Keith Sheridan
ILLUSTRATOR
Earl Schuler
CLIENT
Atlantic Monthly Press
AGENCY/STUDIO
Keith Sheridan Associates,
Inc.
▲

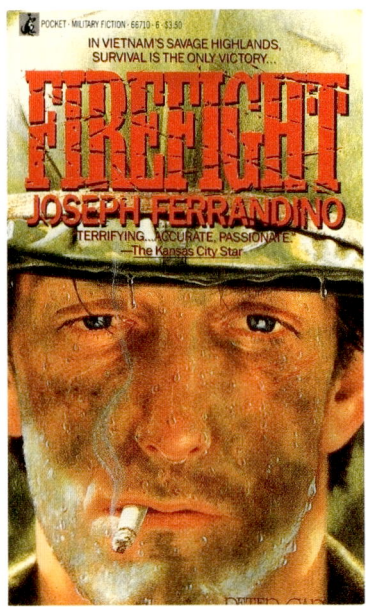

BOOK DESIGN

ART DIRECTOR
Jacqueline Jones
DESIGNER
Jacqueline Jones
PRODUCER
Amy Nathan
WRITER
Jo Mancuso
PHOTOGRAPHER
Kathryn Kleinman
FOOD STYLIST
Amy Nathan
CLIENT
Chronicle Books
AGENCY/STUDIO
Jacqueline Jones Design

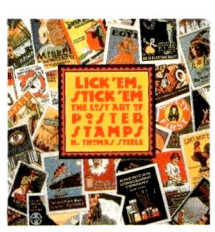

ART DIRECTOR
Tommy Steele
DESIGNER
Tommy Steele
WRITER
Tommy Steele
PHOTOGRAPHER
Tommy Steele
CLIENT
Abbeville Press, Inc.
AGENCY/STUDIO
Steeleworks Design

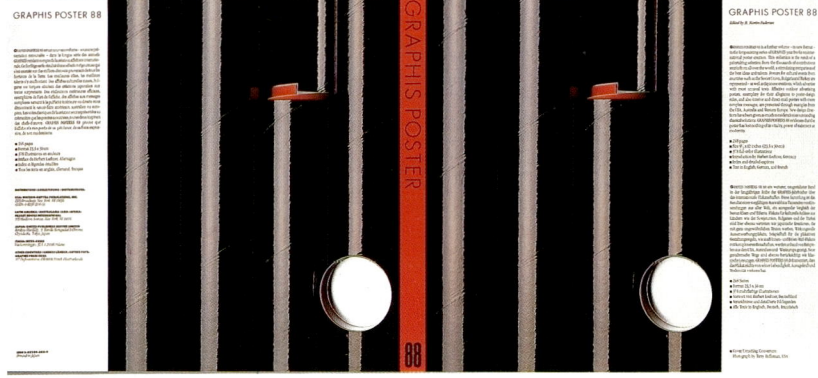

ART DIRECTOR
Martin Pedersen
DESIGNER
Martin Pedersen
PHOTOGRAPHER
Terry Heffernan
CLIENT
Graphis
AGENCY/STUDIO
Graphis - New York

EDITORIAL

BOOK DESIGN
ART DIRECTOR
Lloyd Ziff
DESIGNERS
Lloyd Ziff/Giovanni
C. Russo
WRITER
Alan Olshan
PHOTOGRAPHER
Current -
Annie Leibovitz
Past -
Various
CLIENT
American Ballet
Theatre
AGENCY/STUDIO
Lloyd Ziff Design
Group
PRINTER
Rapoport Printing
Corporation

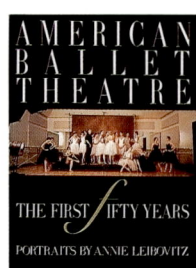

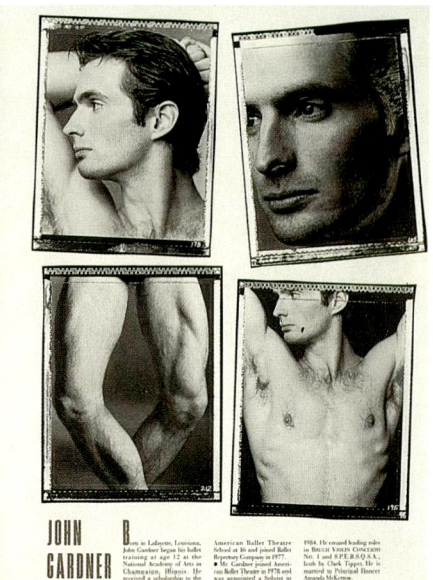

ART DIRECTOR
Gerry Rosentswieg
DESIGNER
Gerry Rosentswieg
WRITER
Julie Prendiville
PHOTOGRAPHER
Various Photographers
ILLUSTRATOR
Various Photographers
CLIENT
Madison Square Press
AGENCY/STUDIO
The Graphics Studio

ART DIRECTORS
Bob Rome/David
Tanimoto
DESIGNER
David Tanimoto
*PRODUCTION
MANAGER*
Christine Ferguson
WRITER
Ron Wakefield
PHOTOGRAPHERS
Jeff Zwart/Vic Huber
ILLUSTRATORS
Kevin Hulsey/Dennis
Atkinson
CLIENT
Lexus Division: Toyota
Motor Sales, U.S.A., Inc.
AGENCY/STUDIO
The Designory, Inc.
*PRODUCTION
COMPANY*
George Rice & Sons

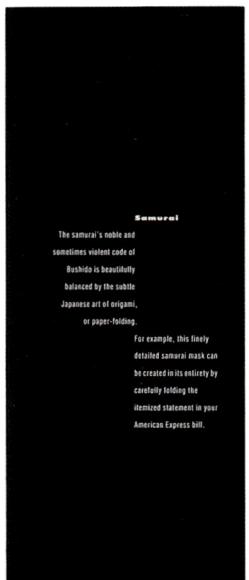

Samurai

The samurai's noble and
sometimes violent code of
Bushido is beautifully
balanced by the subtle
Japanese art of origami,
or paper-folding.

For example, this finely
detailed samurai mask can
be created in its entirety by
carefully folding the
itemized statement in your
American Express bill.

BOOK DESIGN

ART DIRECTOR
Greg Samata
DESIGNER
Pat & Greg Samata
WRITER
Steve Higgins
ILLUSTRATOR
Paul Thompson
CLIENT
Samata Associates
AGENCY/STUDIO
Samata Associates

ART DIRECTOR
Butler Kosh Brooks
DESIGNER
Kosh, Larry Brooks
ILLUSTRATOR
Brian Cronin
CLIENT
The WORKBOOK,
Scott & Daughters
Publishing
AGENCY/STUDIO
Butler Kosh Brooks

MAGAZINE COVER
ART DIRECTOR
Susan Silton
DESIGNER
Susan Silton
PHOTOGRAPHER
Susan Silton
CLIENT
Fotofolio
AGENCY/STUDIO
S o S : Susan Silton

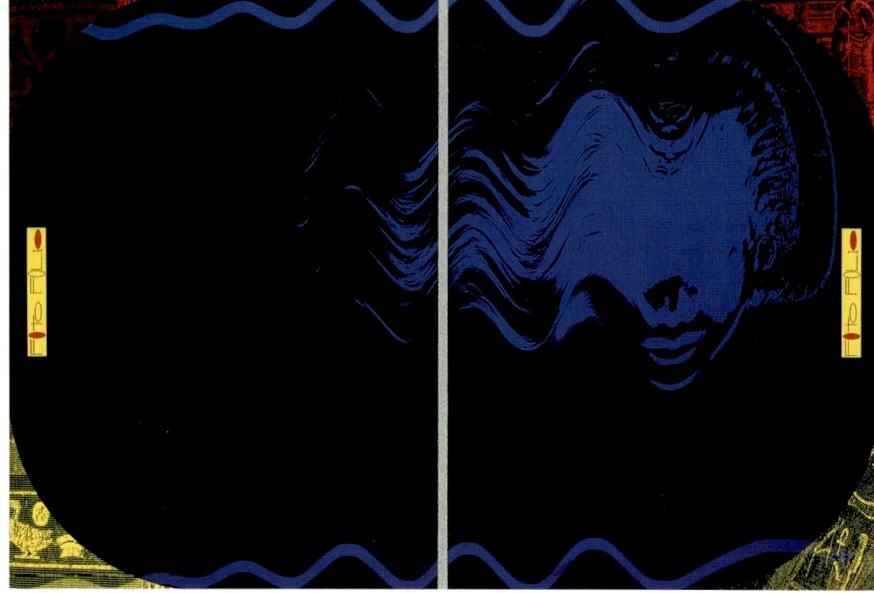

ART DIRECTOR
Marilyn Babcock
DESIGNERS
Michael Brock/
Marilyn Babcock
DESIGN DIRECTOR
Michael Brock
PHOTOGRAPHER
Herb Ritts
CLIENT
L.A. Style
AGENCY/STUDIO
Michael Brock Design

ART DIRECTORS
Mark McGeoch /
Dennis Gagarin
DESIGNER
Mark McGeoch/
Dennis Gagarin
WRITER
Marilyn Kochman
PHOTOGRAPHER
Jeanne Carley/Carter Dow
& Various
ILLUSTRATOR
Various
CLIENT
Consolidated Freightways
AGENCY/STUDIO
Gagarin McGeoch
Advertising & Design
PRODUCTION COMPANY
Southern California
Lithographics

ART DIRECTOR
Miles Abernethy
DESIGNER
Miles Abernethy
PHOTOGRAPHER
Brian Hill
CLIENT
Audi of America, Inc.
AGENCY/STUDIO
SHR Design
Communications

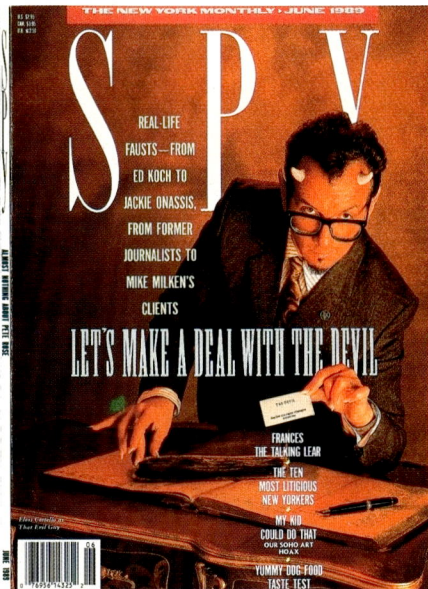

ART DIRECTOR
Matthew Drace
DESIGNER
Matthew Drace
PHOTOGRAPHER
Stefano Massei
AGENCY/STUDIO
San Francisco Focus
Magazine

MAGAZINE COVER

ART DIRECTOR
B. W. Honeycutt
PHOTOGRAPHER
Tom Zimberoff
CLIENT
SPY Magazine

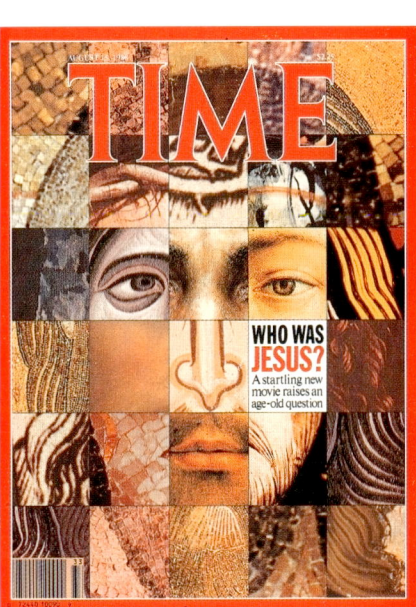

ART DIRECTOR
Rudy Hoglund
DESIGNER
Mirko Ilíc
PHOTOGRAPHER
Roberto Brosan
CLIENT
Time Magazine
AGENCY/STUDIO
Time Magazine

ART DIRECTOR
Rudy Hoglund
DESIGNER
Tom Bentkowski
CLIENT
Time Magazine

MAGAZINE COVER

ART DIRECTOR	*ART DIRECTOR*
Ken Cook	Ken Cook
DESIGNER	*DESIGNER*
Ken Cook	Ken Cook
WRITERS	*WRITERS*
Delphine Hirasuna/	Delphine Hirasuna/
Mary Lou Edmondson/	Kathleen Harper/
Kathleen Harper	Ellen Newman
PHOTOGRAPHER	*PHOTOGRAPHER*
Steve Underwood/	Steve Underwood
Scotty Morris	*ILLUSTRATORS*
ILLUSTRATORS	Byron Gin/Daniel
Byron Gin/	Pelavin/Max Seabaugh
Daniel Pelavin	*CLIENT*
CLIENT	San Francisco
San Francisco	Zoological Society
Zoological Society	*AGENCY/STUDIO*
AGENCY/STUDIO	Cross Associates,
Cross Associates,	San Francisco
San Francisco	

MAGAZINE COVER

ART DIRECTOR
Matthew Drace
DESIGNERS
Matthew Drace/
Mark Ulriksen
PHOTOGRAPHERS
Leslie Flores/Jock
McDonald
ILLUSTRATOR
Alan Cober
AGENCY/STUDIO
San Francisco Focus
Magazine

THE INTERVIEW

H Ed Moose

BY KEN KELLEY

The name is Moose. Not Moose. Just Moose in the singular. He is the onetime social worker turned restaurateur. Not the former close associate of Ronald Reagan. Restaurateur? Well, bar 'n' grill man. Proprietor of the city's premier celebrity joint. Schmoozer. Raconteur. Wheeler-dealer. King of North Beach. Baseball fan. Politician without portfolio. Philosopher. Remember—it's Moose, not Moose. Think antlers.

He first hit San Francisco in 1961, a refugee from his home turf of St. Louis, a child of the Depression who'd just received his degree in psychiatric social work. When he saw the explosive, diverse energy of North Beach in those days, it was love at first sight. Since then, he's gotten to be an old pro in the worlds of business, politics, the lively arts, and baseball. A key player in the attempt to keep the Giants in San Francisco, he was the chairman of the Proposition W Committee to build the downtown stadium—it lost—and he was a primary force in convincing former mayor Dianne Feinstein to stop being phlegmatic and get pragmatic about the issue.

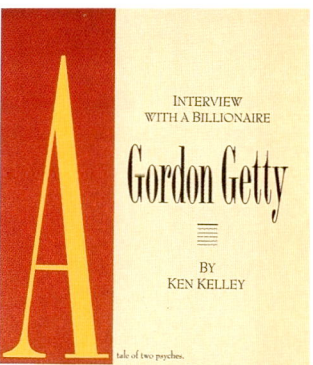

INTERVIEW WITH A BILLIONAIRE

A Gordon Getty

BY KEN KELLEY

He's the richest man in America, but his favorite car is a Buick. He triggered the largest corporate takeover in history, yet he calls himself a poor businessman. A self-taught composer, he wants to be remembered with Beethoven. His wife is San Francisco's leading socialite—but he hates parties. He's an idiosyncratic intellectual who happens to be a billionaire. Meet Gordon Peter Getty.

A tale of two psyches.

He is certainly the richest man in San Francisco—and perhaps the country. Fame is thy name when you're a Getty. Gordon Getty's father, Jean Paul Getty, was the only billionaire to rival John D. Rockefeller for the distinction of being the richest man in the twentieth century. Fame has its own price tag, too—the Getty family's scandals were played out in the world press before Gordon Getty was a gleam in his father's eye. Jean Paul Getty's extramarital trysts were the stuff gossip columnists jumped on with glee. And since Daddy Dearest never talked to reporters, items had to be gleaned from the kiss-and-tellers.

Gordon Getty's parents separated in 1945, and his mom moved to San Francisco. Both tried to shield their progeny from the controversy, fame, and tragedy that seemed to be attached to the family

THE INTERVIEW

T Randy Shilts

BY KEN KELLEY

A man and his dog. The man, Randy Shilts, follows in the grand old tradition of muckrakers and whistle blowers. A fighter. Persistent. And now a celebrity. The dog, Dash. His steadfast friend through it all.

Ten years ago Randy Shilts hit bottom. He lost one job in journalism, and nobody would give him another because he was gay. Today the thirty-seven-year-old author of *And the Band Played On: Politics, People and the AIDS Epidemic* is one of the most celebrated journalists in the country.

Shilts' first brush with San Francisco media came in 1975. Nearing graduation from the University of Oregon, he came here to compete in a national writing championship sponsored by the Hearst Foundation. He placed second, only to have the award snatched away when the Hearst folks discovered he was gay. Instead of returning to the closet, he knocked on new doors—and

MAGAZINE DESIGN
ART DIRECTOR
Bryan L. Peterson
DESIGNER
Bryan L. Peterson
PHOTOGRAPHER
Tom Ryan
CLIENT
Northern Telecom
AGENCY/STUDIO
Peterson & Company

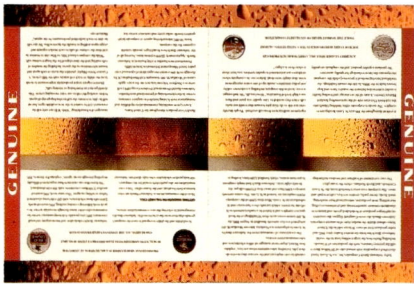

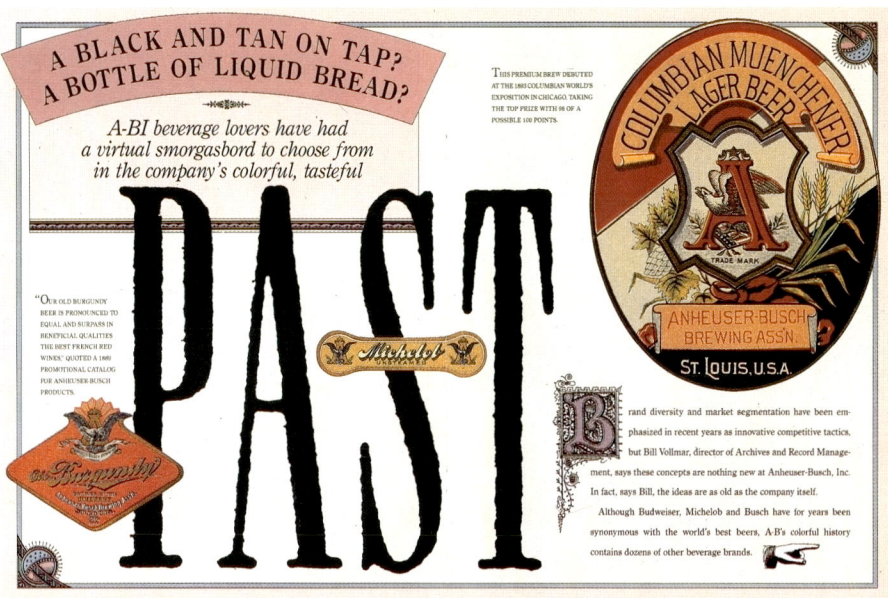

A BLACK AND TAN ON TAP?
A BOTTLE OF LIQUID BREAD?

A-BI beverage lovers have had a virtual smorgasbord to choose from in the company's colorful, tasteful

PAST

"OUR OLD BURGUNDY BEER IS PRONOUNCED TO EQUAL AND SURPASS IN BENEFICIAL QUALITIES THE BEST FRENCH RED WINES," QUOTED A 1889 PROMOTIONAL CATALOG FOR ANHEUSER-BUSCH PRODUCTS.

THIS PREMIUM BREW DEBUTED AT THE 1893 COLUMBIAN WORLD'S EXPOSITION IN CHICAGO TAKING THE TOP PRIZE WITH 96 OF A POSSIBLE 100 POINTS.

Brand diversity and market segmentation have been emphasized in recent years as innovative competitive tactics, but Bill Vollmar, director of Archives and Record Management, says these concepts are nothing new at Anheuser-Busch, Inc. In fact, says Bill, the ideas are as old as the company itself.

Although Budweiser, Michelob and Busch have for years been synonymous with the world's best beers, A-B's colorful history contains dozens of other beverage brands.

A JAPANESE CAR COMPANY SHIFTS ITS VOICE AND DATA SYSTEM INTO FOUR-WHEEL DRIVE.

The building is a blocky, bold monolith of angles, edges and rectangles. If the soul of an automobile has colors, they're all here, on the exterior and throughout the carpets, walls and fixtures of the new office complex. Slate gray like cast aluminum. A charcoal hue befitting an engine block. Black as flat as anodized body trim. The gleaming mirror-metal of chrome. Glassy expanses like great windshields. ○ Inside, an atrium pierces the heart of the modern seven-story building—a huge, cylindrical elevator tower tying the levels together. As you peer up from the lobby, it makes the office complex look eerily as though it's a luxurious gantry for a rocket awaiting countdown. ○ Actually it's the new headquarters of Subaru of America, in Cherry Hill, New Jersey. Subaru is the U.S. importer of some unusual Japanese cars—a company that has carved out a tidy niche for itself in a crowded automotive market by dealing in distinctive small cars that some still think "odd and somewhat quirky," in the words of Subaru Director of Public Relations Fred Heiler. ○ Others, however, increasingly regard Subaru as the progenitor of one of the hotter new automotive markets: on-road passenger cars with four-wheel drive (4WD). Off-road four-wheeling has been around for decades—Jeeps, fat-tired pickups and the like—but only in the last half-dozen years has everybody from Porsche to Ford begun offering the option of powering all four corners of pure highway machinery.

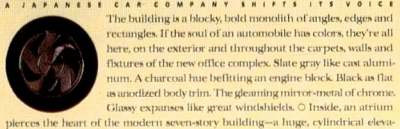

IN SEARCH OF
LEADERS

BY DONNA BOSS & MITCHELL SCHECHTER

Never before have bright, innovative hospitality management school graduates been in greater demand. And never before have they been wooed as persistently by recruiters who are offering eye-opening starting salaries, benefits and career opportunities. As a result, these managers-to-be can afford to be highly selective when choosing the types of employers and employment that best suit their ambitions and dreams.

Directors and dietitians are well aware that they must compete aggressively for these graduates by offering career opportunities commensurate with the competition's. They must also market their jobs not only to these potential managers but, also, to those who provide educational guidance.

With this in mind, *Food Management* organized a conference which included representatives from eight hospitality management schools and five major foodservice associations. During the two-day "In Search of Leaders" conference,

ILLUSTRATIONS BY JOHN HOWARD

MAGAZINE DESIGN

ART DIRECTOR
Buck Smith
DESIGNER
Buck Smith
WRITER
Vic Svec
CLIENT
Anheuser-Bush, Inc.
AGENCY/STUDIO
Hawthorne/Wolfe, Inc.

ART DIRECTOR
Bryan L. Peterson
DESIGNER
Bryan L. Peterson
PHOTOGRAPHER
Tom Ryan
CLIENT
Northern Telecom
AGENCY/STUDIO
Peterson & Company

ART DIRECTOR
Rod Gonzalez
DESIGNER
Rod Gonzalez
WRITERS
Donna Boss/
Mitchell Schechter
ILLUSTRATOR
John Howard
CLIENT
Food Management
Magazine

MAGAZINE COVER
ART DIRECTOR
Deborah Hardison
DESIGNER
Jonathan Tuttle
DESIGN DIRECTOR
Bett McLean
WRITER
Robert Sharoff
PHOTOGRAPHER
Hans Neleman
CLIENT
Whittle Communications
AGENCY/STUDIO
Whittle Communications

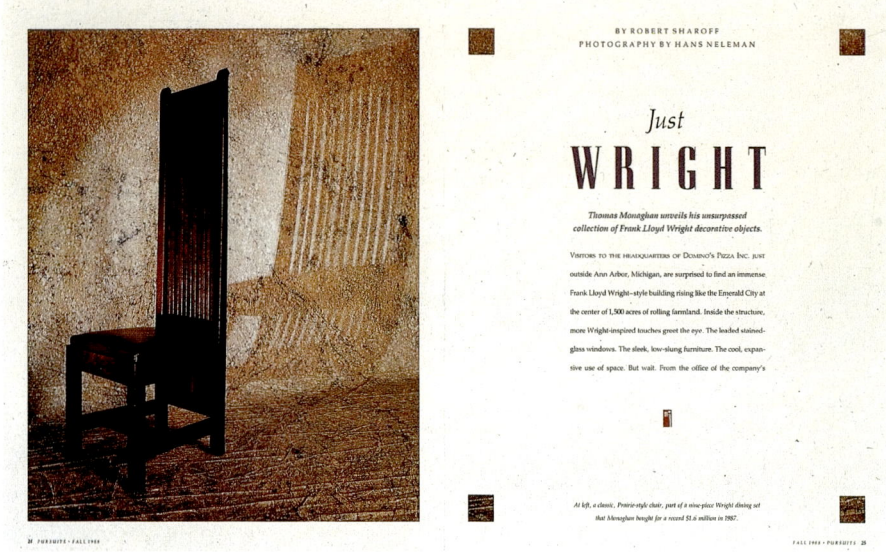

ART DIRECTOR
Matthew Drace
DESIGNER
Mark Ulriksen
PHOTOGRAPHER
Leslie Flores
AGENCY/STUDIO
San Francisco Focus
Magazine

MAGAZINE DESIGN

ART DIRECTOR
Deborah Hardison
DESIGNER
Deborah Hardison
DESIGN DIRECTOR
Bett McLean
WRITER
Margaret Morrow Leske
PHOTOGRAPHER
Michele Clement
CLIENT
Whittle Communications
AGENCY/STUDIO
Whittle Communications

Stepping Out

A musician beats out the rhythm over and over again: da-ta-da-da-da-la. The dancers—she in a circa-1940s dress, he in sailor's blue and white—glide through a sequence of movements: Step, turn, step-step-step, dip. Step, turn, step-step-step, dip. Twelve, 13, 14 times they repeat the motions without a break until they hit the steps just right. This exhausting routine hardly seems like fun, but rehearsing dance suites— whether the rapid footwork, dips, and twirls of American swing (right) or the slow, ritualized movements of traditional Shaker worship dances—is obviously pure joy for members of the Westwind International Folk Ensemble.

The San Francisco group, which this year celebrates its 30th anniversary, consists of 22 amateur hoofers, including a zoologist, an antiques dealer, an engineer, two advertising executives, and even an acupuncturist. This spring the troupe will practice at least 20 grueling hours a month, perfecting dances it will perform during August at international folk festivals in Holland, Belgium, and Italy.

*The Westwind
Dancers Move
To the Rhythms
Of the World.*

PHOTOGRAPHY BY
Michele Clement
TEXT BY Margaret
Morrow Leske

*Eric Bennion and
Hillery Roberts (front)
and David Reyna
and Lori Koch (rear)
dance the swing to
couples did 40 years
ago in USO canteens.
Koch, with Bennion,
kicks up her heels
(opposite page).*

---

*The ensemble turns
out for a rollicking
performance of the
Texas Knockdown
Balsa, an interpretation of dances popularized by prairie
settlers in the
mid-19th century.*

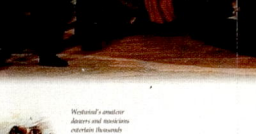

*Westwind's amateur
dancers and musicians
entertain thousands
of folk-dance enthusiasts each year at
concerts, fairs, and
festivals.*

Many folk-dance companies, including professional troupes, compete each year for the chance to represent the United States at these festivals, but Westwind has twice been chosen for the coveted honor because it achieves a rare authenticity in staging, costuming, and musical accompaniment in addition to dance.

*The artist composite
of a Shaker ceremony
is accidentally broken
to one dancer and
then another whirls
and cries out in
spiritual ecstasy.*

ART DIRECTOR
Matthew Drace
DESIGNER
Hazel Boissiere
ILLUSTRATOR
Bart de Haas
AGENCY/STUDIO
San Francisco Focus
Magazine

GUNG HO
ON
AMERICA

SURE, ALL THOSE GLOOMY PREDICTIONS ABOUT AMERICA'S FUTURE IN THE PACIFIC CENTURY HAVE YOU DEPRESSED. EVERY DAY YOU HEAR MORE ABOUT HOW THE ASIAN INVASION SPELLS DOOM FOR THE US ECONOMY. NO WONDER YOU CAN BARELY LEAVE THE HOUSE. THE DECLINE-OF-AMERICA THESIS NOW SEEMS TO BE THE LEADING SCHOOL OF ECONOMIC THOUGHT; IN THIS COUNTRY, ECONOMIC ANGST HAS BECOME A VIRTUAL COTTAGE INDUSTRY. WE'VE ALL HEARD THE LITANY—AMERICA CAN'T COMPETE WITH ASIA BECAUSE WE HAVEN'T

BY MARK K. POWELSON

SEND US YOUR HIGHLY EDUCATED, YOUR YOUNG AND ENERGETIC, YOUR SOLVENT MASSES YEARNING TO INVEST . . .

two hundred thirteen

MAGAZINE DESIGN
ART DIRECTOR
David Carson
DESIGNER
David Carson
PHOTOGRAPHER
Jeff Katz
CLIENT
Musician Magazine
AGENCY/STUDIO
Carson Design

ART DIRECTOR
Michael Brock
DESIGNER
Michael Brock
DESIGN DIRECTOR
Michael Brock
PHOTOGRAPHER
Ron Leighton
CLIENT
L.A. Style
AGENCY/STUDIO
Michael Brock Design

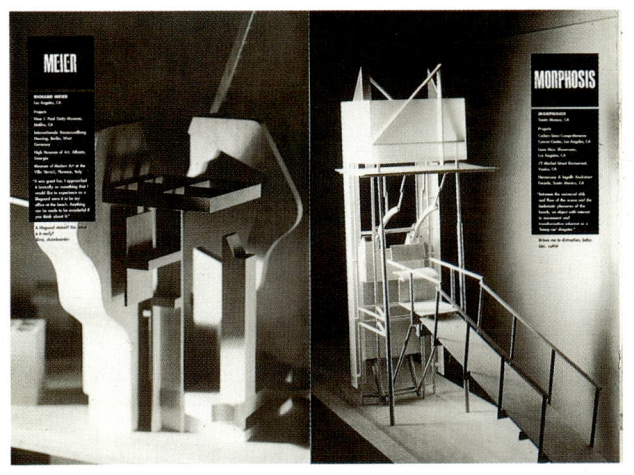

MAGAZINE DESIGN

ART DIRECTOR
Amy Dakos/Craig Butler
DESIGNER
Craig Butler
WRITERS
Terry Bissel/Dotti Bradley
PHOTOGRAPHER
Melissa Rodwell
CLIENT
Tom Sewell/Publisher
AGENCY/STUDIO
Butler Kosh Brooks

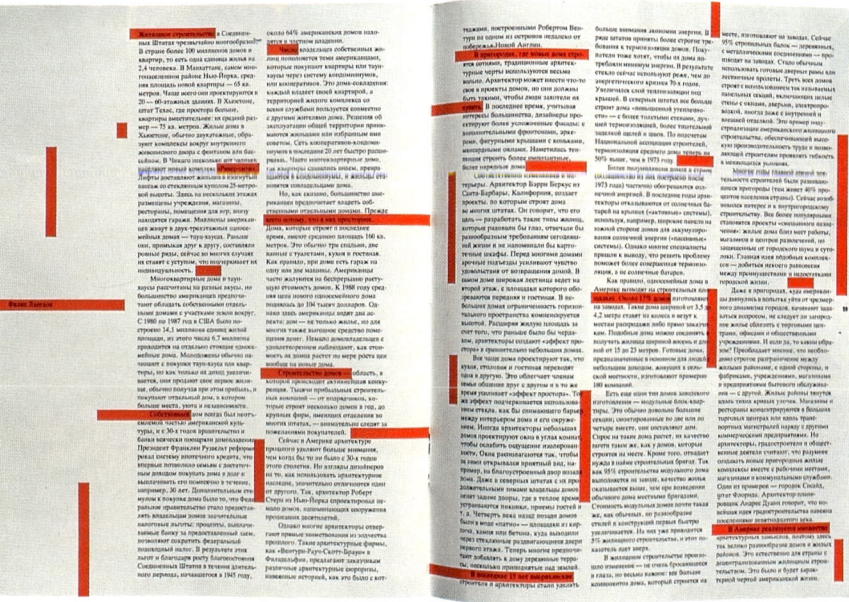

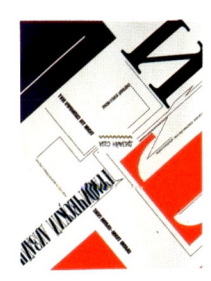

ART DIRECTOR
Nan Dearborn
DESIGNER
Miho
PROJECT DIRECTOR
Ron Underwood
WRITERS
Brian Horrigan/Ilya
Suslov/Ralph Caplan/
Jeffrey Meikle/Stephan
MacDonald/Ann de
Forest/Philip Meggs/
Robert Campbell/Philip
Langdon/Michael Crosby
PHOTOGRAPHERS
Steven Heller, U.S.I.A./
Ford/ Wurman/April
Greiman/ etc.
CLIENT
U.S.Information Agency,
Washington D.C.
AGENCY/STUDIO
Miho

THREE LINES OF AURORA
HEADLINE COME FOR THE

E THIS IS NINE POINT CAPS ON 17 CENTER
This is 11 on seventeen cent. expand. After trying vainly dummy sell it for three
years, Chicago's Schine family, heirs dummy a theater and hotel empire, have decided dummy put the landmark on the
auction block. A first round of non-
binding bids is due on June 1.
After that, the highest
bidders deemed dummy
have enough financial
backing will be asked for final
offers. Local realdummyrs value it at a
relatively modest $75 million.After trying vainly
dummy sell it for three years, Chi naked for final
offers. Local After trying vainly dummy sell it
for three years, Chicago's Schine family, heirs
dummy a theater and hotel empire, have decided
dum Local After trying vainly dummy. This is
twelve on eighteen cent. exp. After trying vainly
dummy sell it for three years, Chicago's Schine
family, heirs dummy a theater and hotel empire,
have decided dummy put the landmark on the
auction block. A first round of non-binding bids

MANAGING INNOVATION

ART DIRECTOR
Jay Petrow
ILLUSTRATORS
Cover - Roy Wiemann,
Inside spread - Terry Allen
CLIENT
Business Week
PRODUCTION COMPANY
McGraw Hill

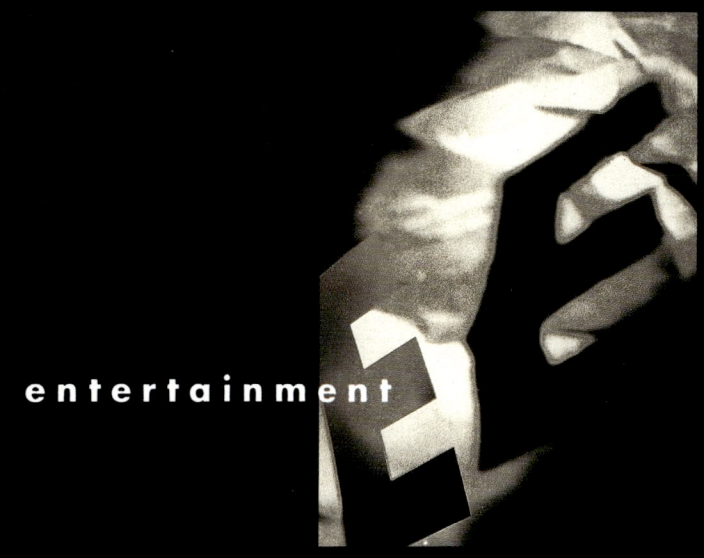

entertainment

MOTION PICTURE PRINT
ART DIRECTOR
Mike Rose
DESIGNERS
John Armistead/Mike Rose
WRITER
Susan Nicholas
PHOTOGRAPHER
Dick Kaiser
CLIENT
NBC
AGENCY/STUDIO
DMB&B

ART DIRECTOR
Peter Bemis
DESIGNER
Patrick Casciato
ILLUSTRATOR
John Hamagami
CLIENT
Twentieth Century Fox
Film Corp.
AGENCY/STUDIO
Frankfurt Gips Balkind

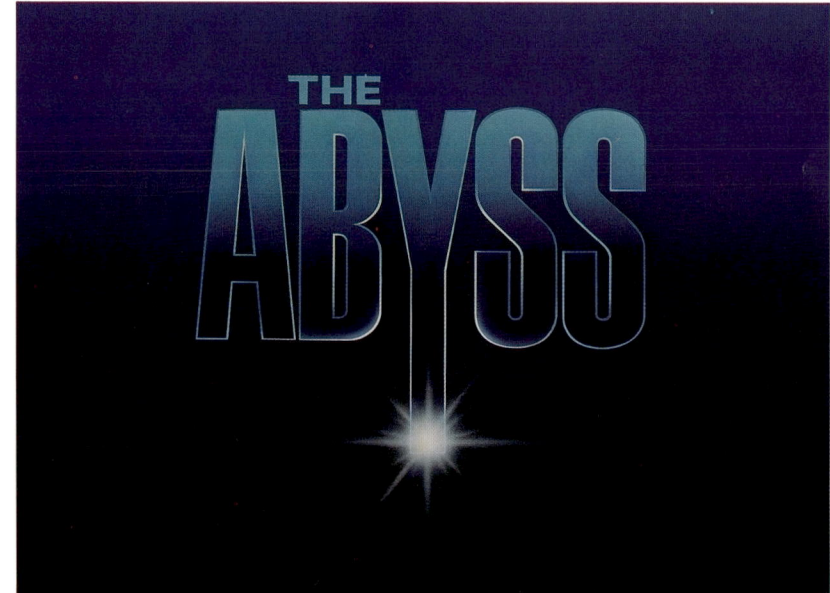

ART DIRECTOR
David Kaiser
DESIGNER
Dan McLean
ILLUSTRATOR
Bryan Haynes
CLIENT
The American
Film Market
AGENCY/STUDIO
Kaiser
Communications, Inc.
PRODUCTION
COMPANY
Kaiser
Communications, Inc.

ART DIRECTOR
Anthony Sella
DESIGNER
Anthony Sella
CREATIVE
DIRECTOR
Robert Jahn
WRITER
Toby Muller
ILLUSTRATOR
Nancy Stahl - painter
CLIENT
Buena Vista Pictures
Marketing
AGENCY/STUDIO
Touchstone Pictures
PRODUCTION
COMPANY
George Rice &
Sons Printers

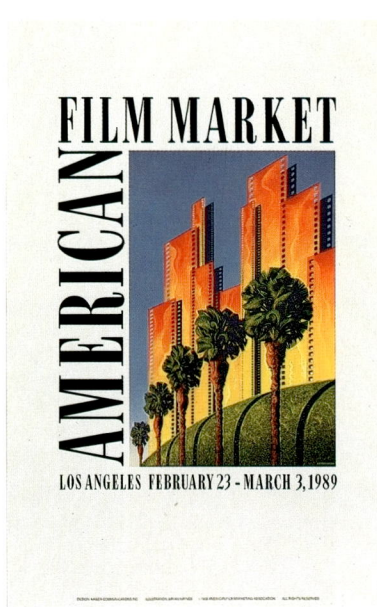

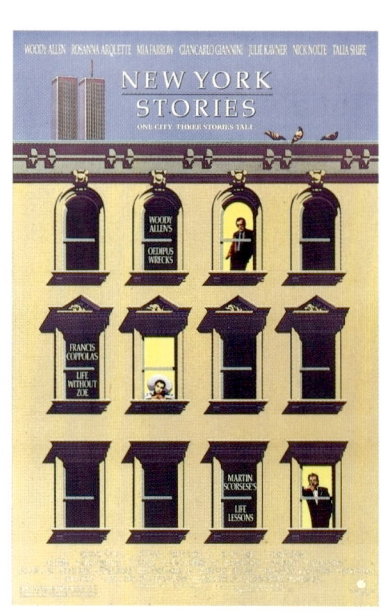

MOTION PICTURE PRINT

ART DIRECTORS
Tom Martin/Michael
C. Gross
DESIGNER
Tom Martin
CREATIVE
DIRECTOR
David Sameth
WRITERS
Tom Martin/David
Sameth
PHOTOGRAPHER
Annie Leibovitz
CLIENT
MCA Universal
Pictures
AGENCY/STUDIO
MCA Universal
Pictures
PRODUCTION
COMPANY
A&L Graphico

ART DIRECTOR
Tom Martin/
Michael C. Gross
DESIGNER
Tom Martin
CREATIVE DIRECTOR
David Sameth
WRITER
Tom Martin/David Sameth
PHOTOGRAPHER
Annie Leibovitz
CLIENT
MCA Universal Pictures
AGENCY/STUDIO
MCA Universal Pictures

ART DIRECTOR
Tom Martin
DESIGNER
Tom Martin
CREATIVE DIRECTOR
David Sameth
WRITER
Tom Martin
PHOTOGRAPHER
Annie Leibovitz
CLIENT
MCA Universal Pictures
AGENCY/STUDIO
MCA Universal Pictures

ART DIRECTOR
Tom Martin
DESIGNER
Tom Martin
CREATIVE DIRECTOR
David Sameth
WRITER
Tom Martin
PHOTOGRAPHER
Annie Leibovitz
CLIENT
MCA Universal Pictures
AGENCY/STUDIO
MCA Universal Pictures

MOTION PICTURE PRINT

ART DIRECTOR
Scott A. Mednick
DESIGNERS
Scott A. Mednick/
Jamie Graupner
PHOTOGRAPHER
John Shaefer
CLIENT
Vestron Pictures
AGENCY/STUDIO
Scott Mednick &
Associates

ART DIRECTOR
David Kaiser
DESIGNERS
David Kaiser/
Peter Wilson
ILLUSTRATOR
H. R. Gieger
CLIENT
American Cinema
Marketing
*PRODUCTION
COMPANY*
Kaiser
Communications, Inc.

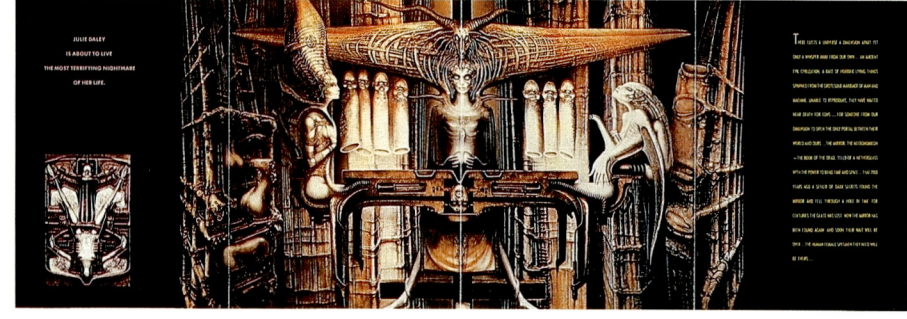

TELEVISION PRINT

ART DIRECTOR
Billy Pittard
DESIGNER
Jacques Dupuy
DIRECTORS
Bob Bibb/Lew Goldstein
ILLUSTRATOR
Jacques Dupuy
CLIENT
Fox Broadcasting On-
Air Promotion
AGENCY/STUDIO
Pittard/Sullivan Design

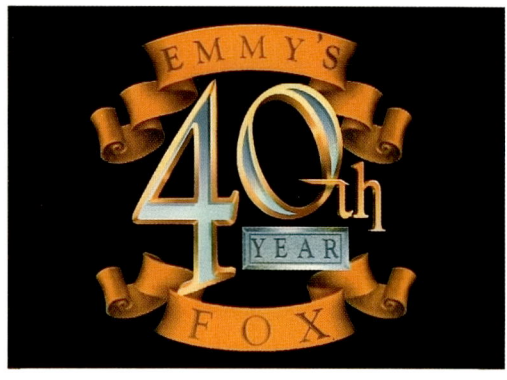

ART DIRECTOR
Ed Sullivan
DESIGNER
Jacques Dupuy
PRODUCER
Billy Pittard
DIRECTOR
Stu Weiss
ILLUSTRATOR
Jacques Dupuy
CLIENT
NBC On-Air Promotion
AGENCY/STUDIO
Pittard/Sullivan Design

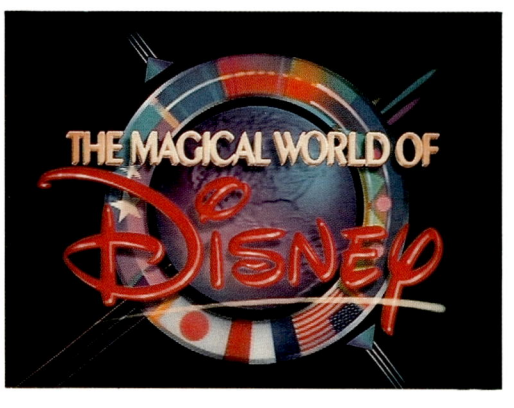

TELEVISION PRINT

ART DIRECTORS
Randy Hipke/Brad Jansen
DESIGNER
Brad Jansen
ILLUSTRATOR
Justin Carroll
CLIENT
Orion Television
Entertainment
AGENCY/STUDIO
Hipke, Inc.
PRINTER
Anderson Printing

Based on the true, triumphant story of the rescue that united a Texas town—and all of America.

EVERYBODY'S BABY:
THE RESCUE OF JESSICA McCLURE

Starring
Beau Bridges Patty Duke
ABC Sunday Night Movie
9:00 PM

ART DIRECTOR
Bill Spewak
DESIGNER
Bill Spewak
WRITERS
Bill Spewak/John Barker
PHOTOGRAPHER
ABC Television Network
CLIENT
ABC Television Network
AGENCY/STUDIO
Grey Entertainment &
Media

ART DIRECTORS
Randy Hipke/
Brad Jansen
DESIGNERS
Randy Hipke/
Brad Jansen
CLIENT
Paramount Domestic
Television
*PRODUCTION
COMPANY*
Hipke, Inc./Joseph
Smith Studios/
Anderson Printing

TELEVISION VIDEO

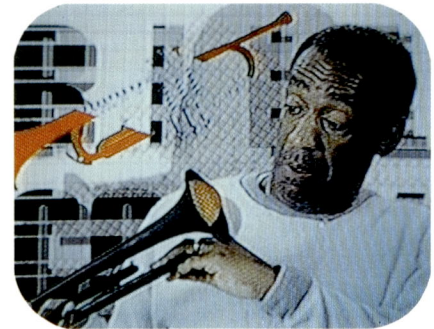  

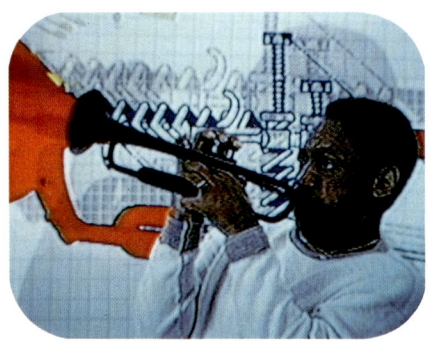  

  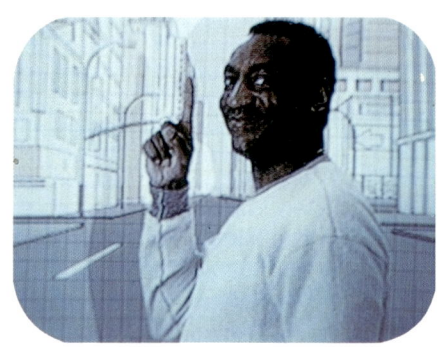

ART DIRECTORS
Chuck Stepner/
Chris Carlisle
DESIGNERS
Chuck Stepner/
Chris Carlisle/
Steve Lowe/Martin
Brierly
PRODUCERS
Chuck Stepner/
Chris Carlisle
DIRECTORS
Steve Lowe/Martin
Brierly
WRITERS
Chuck Stepner/
Chris Carlisle
PHOTOGRAPHER
Marc Reshovsky
CLIENT
NBC Advertising
& Promotion
AGENCY/STUDIO
NBC Advertising
& Promotion
*PRODUCTION
COMPANY*
Propaganda Films

THURSDAY NIGHT PROMO "IKO IKO"

See the people on the screen
Thursday on my TV
Funniest things you ever seen
Only on *N-B-C*

Talkin' 'bout
Thursday *(Thursday)*
Thursday *(Thursday)*
Thursday on my TV
Funniest things you ever seen
Only on *N-B-C*
Only on *N-B-C*

"DISNEY FEVER COVERS
THE GLOBE"

"Disney Fever Sunday night
When you wish upon a star
Disney Fever there you are."
*CATCH THE FEVER! THE MAGICAL
WORLD OF DISNEY PREMIERES
SUNDAY, OCTOBER NINTH
ON N-B-C*

ANIMATORS
Kurt Friedmann/
Brad Gensurowsky/
Christina Hills
PRODUCER
Eric Jacobson
CLIENT
NBC Advertising
& Promotion
AGENCY/STUDIO
NBC Advertising
& Promotion
*PRODUCTION
COMPANY*
NBC Magic Room

TELEVISION VIDEO

ART DIRECTORS
Shelton Scott/Steven Grasse
PRODUCER
Janet Mason
DIRECTOR
Bill Randall
WRITER
Steven Grasse/Shelton Scott
CLIENT
WCIX/Channel 6
AGENCY/STUDIO
Beber Silverstein, Miami
PRODUCTION COMPANY
AFI, Miami

"DALLAS"

ANNCR: Dallas is now on Channel 6.
The plot's just as rich.
The characters are experiencing just as many ups and downs.
And J.R.'s just as low down and dirty...
...maybe even more so.

VO: Dallas. Friday nights at 9 on CBS, the new Channel 6.

ANNCR: How much for the butter creams.

"FREDDY"

ANNCR: Freddy's Nightmares are still on Channel 6.
(NERVOUS STUTTER) SSsoo, S...S...
Saturday Late Nights will be just as s...s...scary.
J...just as frightening.
And just as all together e...e...eerie as ever before.

SFX: ALARM CLOCK RINGING

ANNCR: (EVEN MORE FRIGHTENED)
Maybe even more so.

VO: Freddy's Nightmares, Saturday nights at 11:30 on CBS, the new Channel 6.

"KNOTS LANDING"

ANNCR: Knot's Landing is now on Channel 6.
It's just as steamy.
And Abbey is just as...shall we say...fun loving... and eager to please.
(HA, HA) Maybe even more so.

VO: Knot's Landing. Thursday nights at 10 on CBS, the new Channel 6.

  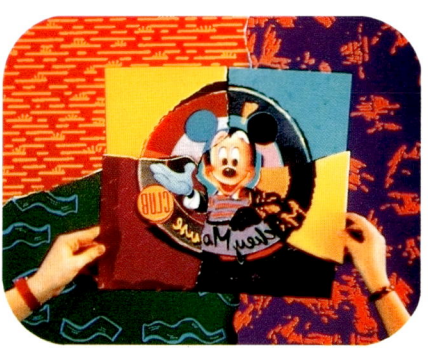

"MICKEY MOUSE CLUB OPEN"

"Who's the leader of the band
that's made for you & me…"

"M-I-C-K-E-Y M-O-U-S-E!"

"Hey there, Hi there, Ho there
You're as welcome as can be…"

"M-I-C-K-E-Y M-O-U-S-E!"

"Mickey Mouse! Mickey Mouse!
Forever let us hold our banner high!…"

"Come along and sing a song
and join the jamboree!…"

"M-I-C-K-E-Y M-O-U-S-E!"

CREATIVE DIRECTOR
Mike Nichols
DESIGNER
Lydia Pryzluska
PRODUCER
Chris Whitney
CREATIVE DIRECTOR
Mike Nichols
*ANIMATION
DIRECTOR*
Carl Willat
HARRY OPERATOR
Jonathan Keeton
CLIENT
The Disney Channel
*PRODUCTION
COMPANY*
Colossal Pictures

TELEVISION VIDEO

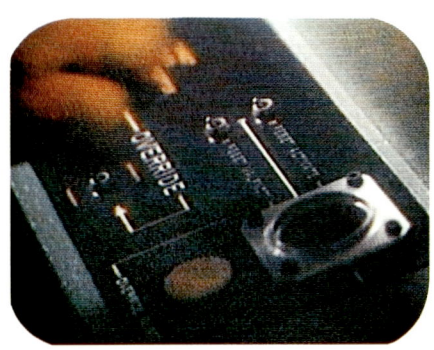  

PRODUCTION DESIGN
Ted Haworth
EXECUTIVE PRODUCER
Joe Salvaggio
PRODUCER
Paul Fuentes
DIRECTOR
Paul Fuentes
WRITER
Paul Fuentes/Joe Salvaggio
PHOTOGRAPHER
(D.P.) Timothy Galfas
CLIENT
Home Box Office
AGENCY/STUDIO
Home Box Office Broadcast
Advertising & Promotion
PRODUCTION COMPANY
Varitel

"HAWAII '89 OPEN"

MULL: This, class is perhaps the greatest archealogical discovery of our time. A dwelling, known as the split level ranch!...MARVELOUS!"

STUDENT 1: What's this, professor?

MULL: CAREFUL! it's very rare! Placed upon the rear end of land vehicles, these indicated one's political preferences, of course, that was before the Quayle dynasty.

STUDENT 2: What is this, professor?

MULL: Fuckin' coke bottle...

STUDENT 3: Who's this, professor?

MULL: Let me see...Ha! This was once the husband of Robin Givens!

STUDENT 4: Not the Robin Givens!

MULL: Yes!

MULL: Elvis Presley wore a buckle very similar to that, many think that's what killed him.

STUDENT 4: Professor!

MULL: Yes...

STUDENT 4: What is it?

MULL: That's odd–too big for a bagel, isn't it? Let's check

STUDENT 4: What is it, professor?

MULL: I have no idea.

ANNOUNCER VOICE OVER: HBO. The best time on TV.

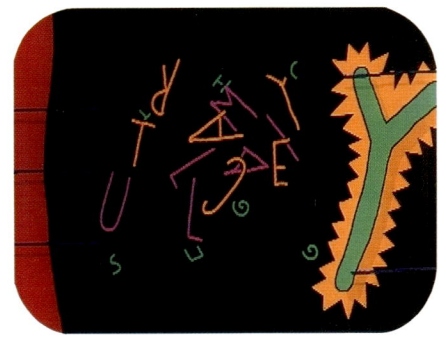  

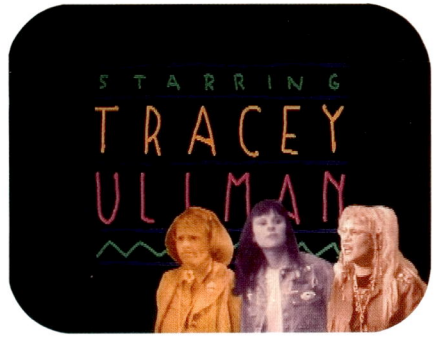  

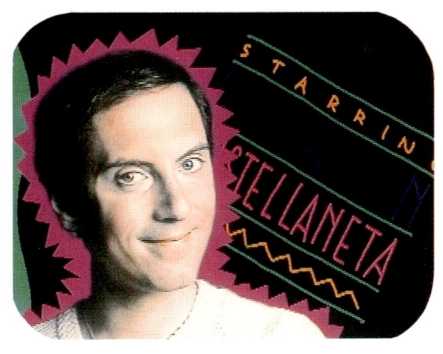  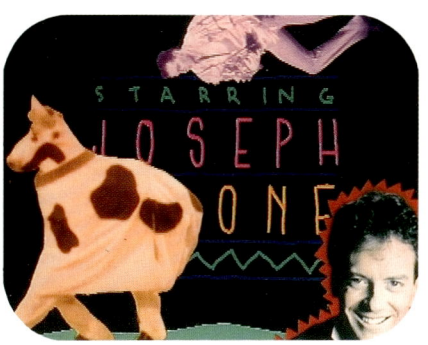

"THE TRACEY ULLMAN SHOW"

Everybody, it's time to go
Stand on guard, getting ready for the show
And if you're thinking that you may or
you might
Then you're thinking right!

ART DIRECTOR
Ed Sullivan
DESIGNER
Jeff Boortz
PRODUCER
Billy Pittard
DIRECTOR
James L. Brooks
ILLUSTRATOR
Jeff Boortz
CLIENT
Gracie Films
AGENCY/STUDIO
Pittard/Sullivan Design
PRODUCTION COMPANY
Pittard/Sullivan Design

TELEVISION VIDEO

 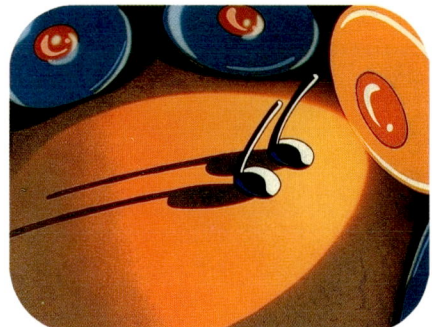 

 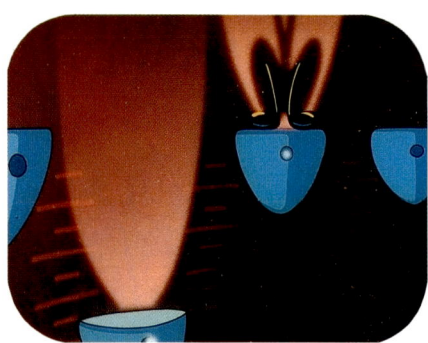 

ART DIRECTOR
Michael Brunsfeld
DESIGNERS
Michael Brunsfeld/
Chuck Eyler/Robin
Steele
PRODUCER
Chris Whitney
DIRECTOR
Michael Brunsfeld
PHOTOGRAPHERS
Melissa Mullin/
Weston Guinta/
Franklin Stevenson
ILLUSTRATOR
Tia Kratter
CLIENT
The Disney Channel
*PRODUCTION
COMPANY*
Colossal Pictures

"DTV"

Music and sound effects only.

  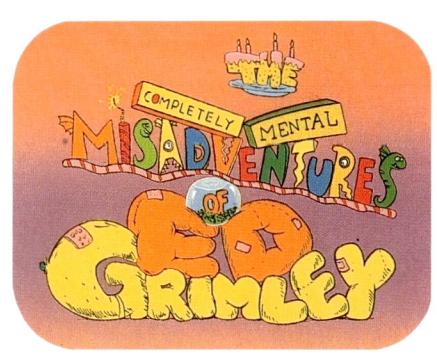

"THE COMPLETELY MENTAL
MISADVENTURES OF ED GRIMLEY"

Music and sound effects only.

ART DIRECTORS
George Evelyn/
John Hays
DESIGNERS
Kent Melton/Don
 Dougherty
PRODUCERS
Scott Shaw/Chris
Whitney/John Hays
DIRECTORS
George Evelyn/
John Hays
PHOTOGRAPHER
Don Smith
ILLUSTRATOR
Japhet Asher
CLIENT
Hanna Barbera
Productions Inc.
PRODUCTION
COMPANY
Colossal Pictures

TELEVISION VIDEO

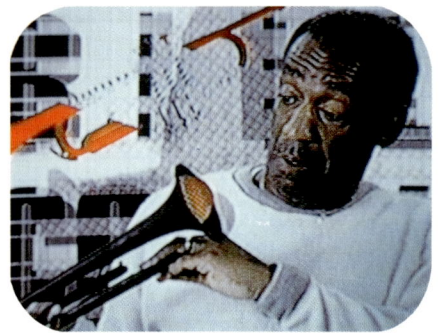  

ART DIRECTOR
Chuck Stepner/
Chris Carlisle
DESIGNERS
Chuck Stepner/Chris
Carlisle/Steve Lowe/
Martin Brierly
PRODUCERS
Chuck Stepner/
Chris Carlisle
DIRECTORS
Steve Lowe/
Martin Brierly
WRITER
Chuck Stepner/
Chris Carlisle
PHOTOGRAPHER
Marc Reshovsky
CLIENT
NBC Advertising
& Promotion
AGENCY/STUDIO
NBC Advertising
& Promotion
PRODUCTION
COMPANY
Propaganda Films

"NBC FALL CAMPAIGN
THEME PIECE"

SINGERS: Our place is your place
Our house is your house
Come celebrate with us at home
this fall
Feel the excitement
Share in the good times
Home is something you can
believe in
Home is somewhere you can get
it all
CHORUS: Only on *NBC, NBC*
Miles above the rest
Only on *NBC, NBC*
Come home to the best

Only on *NBC, NBC*
Join the family
Come home to the best
only on *NBC*

SINGERS: Join in the party
The Celebration
This is an offer you just can't
refuse
The laughter's flowin'
The stars are glowin'
Home is where the colors are
brighter
Home is number one where you
just can't lose

CHORUS: Only on *NBC, NBC*
Miles above the rest
Only on *NBC, NBC*

Only on *NBC, NBC*
It's where you want to be
Come home to the best
Only on *NBC*

BRIDGE: Home, sweet home
where you can call the tune
Where somethin' good is waitin'
for you
Morning, night and noon.

Home, sweet home
Where all your friends await
Some to greet you early
Some to entertain you late

Home, sweet home
with shows that can't be beat
*THE HUXTABLES, THE HOGANS
HUNTER* and *THE HEAT*

BRIDGE: Home, sweet home
You're in a *DIFFERENT WORLD*
with *ALF* and *MATLOCK, L.A. LAW*
and all those *GOLDEN GIRLS*

*Home, sweet home
You've got the best for company
The nest is never empty when
You're home to NBC*

RECORDS
ART DIRECTORS
Tommy Steele/Bill Burks
DESIGNER
Jeffery Fey
AGENCY/STUDIO
Capitol Records Art
Department

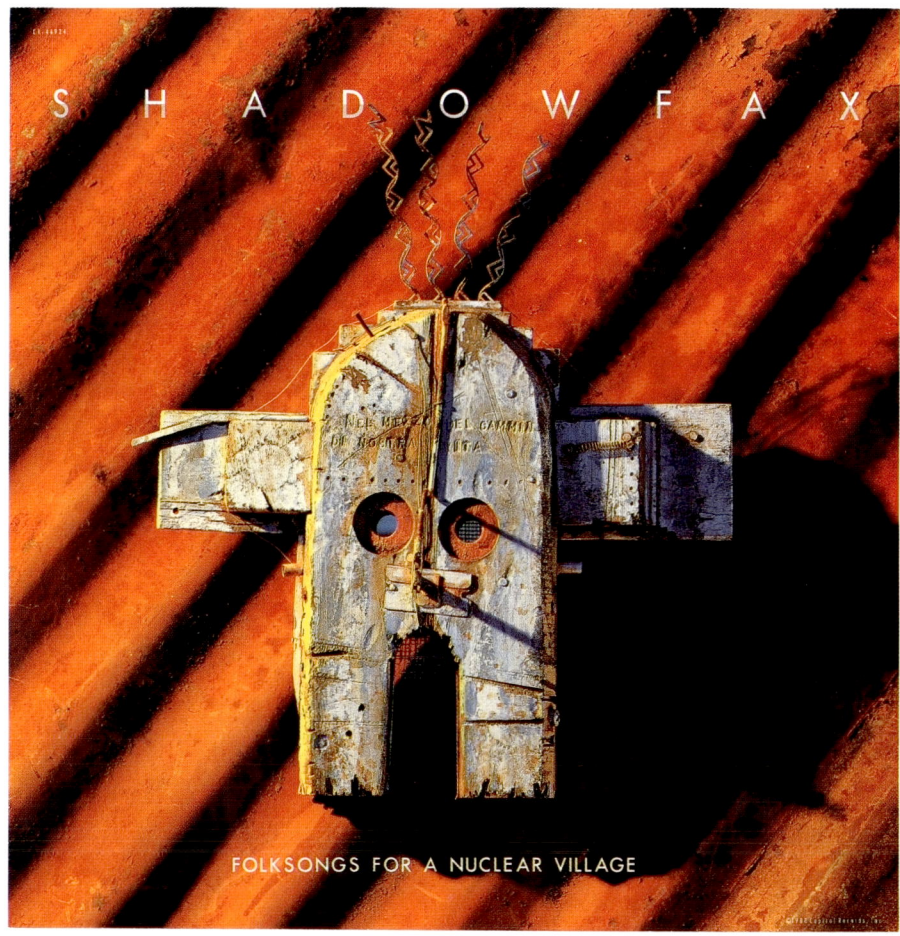

ART DIRECTORS
Tommy Steele/
Roland Young
DESIGN
Shiffman/Young
Design Group
PHOTOGRAPHER
Pete McArthur
SCULPTOR
Michael C. McMillen
AGENCY/STUDIO
Capitol Records
Art Department

RECORDS

ART DIRECTOR
Roger Gorman
DESIGNER
Richard Patrick
PHOTOGRAPHER
Robert Andrew
CLIENT
EMI Manhattan
Records
AGENCY/STUDIO
Reiner Design
Consultants, Inc.

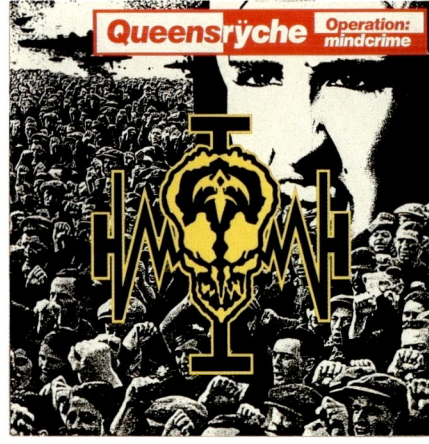

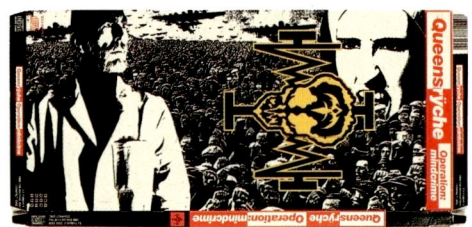

ART DIRECTOR
Tommy Steele
DESIGNERS
Mark Ryden/Peter
Walberg
ILLUSTRATOR
Mark Ryden
AGENCY/STUDIO
Capitol Records
Art Department

ART DIRECTOR
Tommy Steele
DESIGNER
Stephen Gilmore
AGENCY/STUDIO
Capitol Records Art
Department

ART DIRECTOR
Melanie Nissen
DESIGNER
Alan Disparte/
Margo Chase
CLIENT
Virgin Records
AGENCY/STUDIO
Margo Chase Design

ART DIRECTOR
Robert P. deVito
DESIGNER
Eric Read
CLIENT
Memtek Products
AGENCY/STUDIO
Axion Design, Inc.

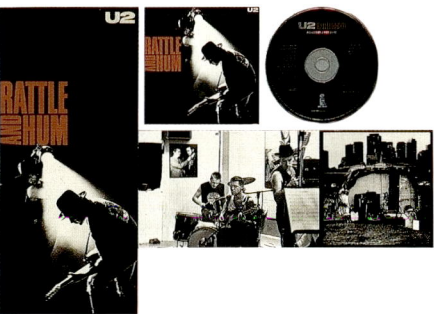

RECORDS

ART DIRECTORS
Norm Ung/Tracy
Weston
DESIGNER
Riea Pendleton-
Owens
DIRECTORS
Bono/The Edge/
Adam Clayton/Larry
Mullen Jr.
PHOTOGRAPHERS
Anton Corbijn/
Thomas Busler/Phil
Joanou/Robert
Brinkman
CLIENT
Island Records
AGENCY/STUDIO
DZN, The Design
Group
*PRODUCTION
COMPANY*
Principle Management

DESIGNER
Tom Bonauro
PHOTOGRAPHER
Michele Clement
CLIENT
EMI/Blue Note Records

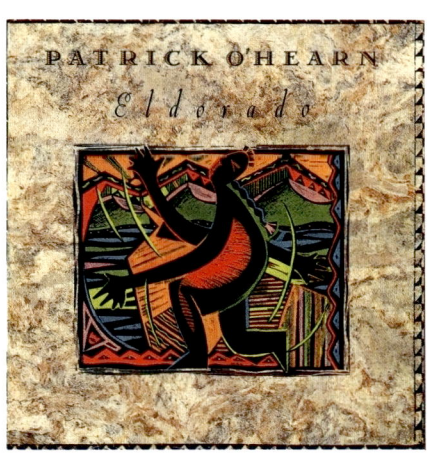

ART DIRECTOR
Norman Moore
DESIGNER
Norman Moore
PHOTOGRAPHER
Robert Torbet
CLIENT
Private Music
AGENCY/STUDIO
Design/Art, Inc.

ART DIRECTOR
Norman Moore
DESIGNER
Norman Moore
ILLUSTRATOR
Nancy Nimoy
CLIENT
Private Music
AGENCY/STUDIO
Design/Art, Inc.

RECORDS

ART DIRECTOR
Tommy Steele
DESIGNER
Mark Ryden
ILLUSTRATOR
Mark Ryden
AGENCY/STUDIO
Capitol Records
Art Department

ART DIRECTORS
Tommy Steele/Jeffery Fey
DESIGNER
Jeffery Fey
PHOTOGRAPHER
Glen Wexler
AGENEY/STUDIO
Capitol Records Art
Department

RECORDS

ART DIRECTOR
Tommy Steele
DESIGNER
Andy Engel
CLIENT
Capitol Records/Blue Note
Records
AGENCY/STUDIO
Andy Engel Design, Inc.

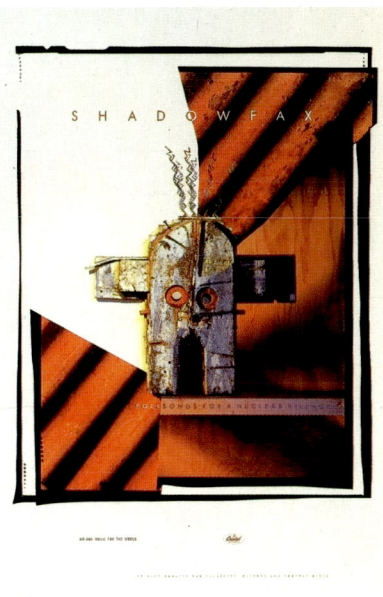

ART DIRECTORS
Tommy Steele/Roland
Young
DESIGNER
Shiffman/Young Design
Group
PHOTOGRAPHER
Pete McArthur
SCULPTOR
Michael C. McMillen
AGENCY/STUDIO
Capitol Records Art
Department

RECORDS
ART DIRECTOR
Lynn Robb
DESIGNER
Lynn Robb
WRITER
David Keeps
PHOTOGRAPHERS
Victoria Pearson-
Cameron/Steven
Meisel/Adrian
Buckmaster
ILLUSTRATOR
Sally Simonetti
CLIENT
Jody Watley
AGENCY/STUDIO
Lynn Robb Design

ART DIRECTOR
Roger Gorman
DESIGNER
Richard Patrick
PHOTOGRAPHER
Jeff Katz
CLIENT
Brockum, Inc./Prince
AGENCY/STUDIO
Reiner Design
Consultants, Inc.

ART DIRECTOR
Lisa Robins
DESIGNER
Lisa Robins
ILLUSTRATOR
Duardo/Evans
CLIENT
Media Home
Entertainment
AGENCY/STUDIO
Media Home
Entertainment

HOME VIDEO
ART DIRECTOR
Lisa Robins
DESIGNER
Lisa Robins
ILLUSTRATOR
Tom McKeith
CLIENT
Media Home Entertainment
AGENCY/STUDIO
Media Home Entertainment

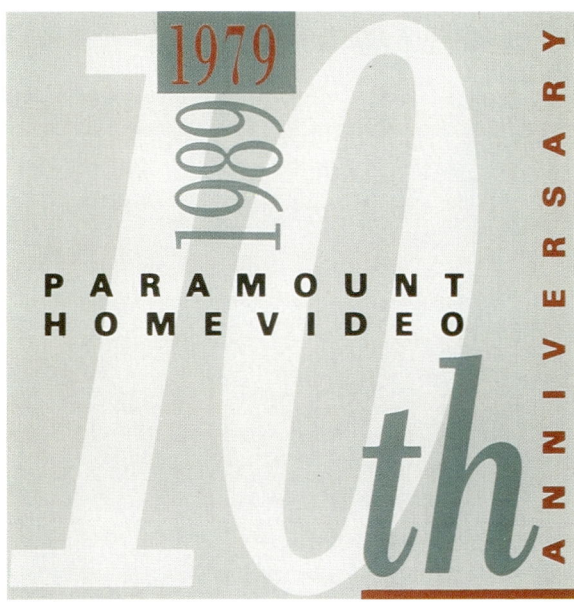

ART DIRECTOR
Henry Vizcarra
DESIGNER
Pam Harnois
CLIENT
Paramount Home
Video
AGENCY/STUDIO
30Sixty Advertising
& Design

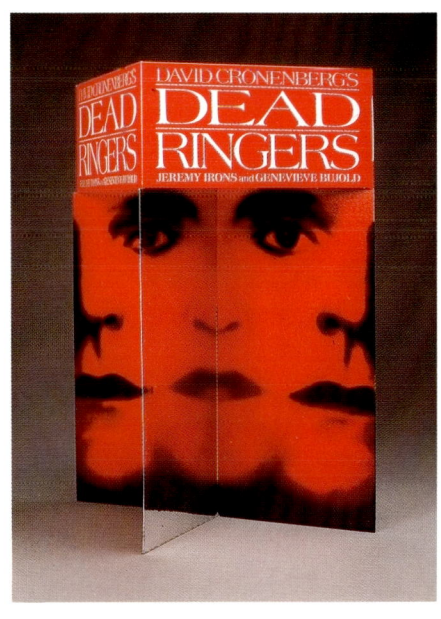

ART DIRECTOR
Cathy Leavy
DESIGNER
Cathy Leavy
THEATRICAL ART
DESIGN
Nathan Trant
CLIENT
Media Home
Entertainment
AGENCY/STUDIO
Media Home
Entertainment

index

If you'd like to talk to a salesman, call our competition.

Our representatives don't have any experience selling cars, encyclopedias or cemetery plots.

In fact, we're happy to say, they don't have any selling experience at all.

Instead, the reps of Jarrin-King used to be dot etchers, etching foremen, strippers, stripping foremen, scanner operators, scanner foremen, color department heads and plant managers.

It's not that we aren't interested in selling anything.

It's just that we feel when it comes to separations, you'd rather deal with somebody who has the eye of a craftsman.

Instead of the mouth of a salesman.

JARRIN-KING
C O L O R   S E P A R A T O R S
5935 Kester Avenue • Van Nuys, CA 91411 • (818) 988-4460
FAX (818) 988-0734